AIRBNB, SHORT-TERM RENTALS AND THE FUTURE OF HOUSING

How do Airbnb and short-term rentals affect housing and communities? Locating the origins and success of Airbnb in the conditions wrought by the 2008 financial crisis, the authors bring together a diverse body of literature and construct case studies of cities in the US, Australia and Germany to examine the struggles of local authorities to protect their housing and neighborhoods from the increasing professionalization and commercialization of Airbnb.

The book argues that the most disruptive impact of Airbnb and short-term rentals has been on housing and neighborhoods in urban centers where housing markets are stressed. Despite its claims, Airbnb has revealed itself as platform capitalism, incentivizing speculation in residential housing. At the heart of this trajectory is its business model and control over access to data. In a first narrative, the authors discuss how Airbnb has institutionalized short-term rentals, consequently removing long-term rentals, contributing to rising rents and changing neighborhood milieus as visitors replace long-term residents. In a second narrative the authors trace the transformation of short-term rentals into a multibillion-dollar hybrid real estate sector promoting a variety of flexible tenure models. While these models provide more options for owners and investors, they have the potential to undermine housing security and exacerbate housing inequality.

While the overall effects have been similar across countries and cities, depending on housing systems, local response has varied from less restrictive in Australia to increasingly restrictive in the United States and most restrictive in Germany. Although Airbnb has made some concessions, it has not given any city the data needed to efficiently enforce regulations, making for costly externalities. Written in a clear and direct style, this volume will appeal to students and scholars in Urban Studies, Urban Planning, Housing and Tourism Studies.

Lily M. Hoffman, Professor Emerita at CCNY and the CUNY Graduate Center, received her PhD in Sociology from Columbia University. Her research interests lie in the social/spatial impact of urban restructuring, including housing, tourism, urban governance and planning policy in comparative perspective. Among other publications, she is author of *The Politics of Knowledge: Activist Movements in Medicine and Planning*; co-editor of *Cities and Visitors: Regulating People, Markets and City Space*, with Susan S. Fainstein and Dennis R. Judd; and co-editor of *Pandemics and Emerging Infectious Diseases: The Sociological Agenda* with Robert Dingwall and Karen Staniland.

Barbara Schmitter Heisler is Professor Emerita, Gettysburg College. She received a PhD in Sociology from the University of Chicago and was the recipient of a German Marshall Fund Fellowship and the Berlin Prize. Her research, which has focused on international migration, racial and ethnic relations and housing, has been published in numerous journals and book chapters. Professor Heisler is co-editor of a special issue of the *Annals of the American Academy of Political and Social Science* and the author of two books, *From German Prisoner of War to American Citizen* and *An Artist as Soldier*.

AIRBNB, SHORT-TERM RENTALS AND THE FUTURE OF HOUSING

*Lily M. Hoffman and
Barbara Schmitter Heisler*

LONDON AND NEW YORK

First published 2021
by Routledge
2 Park Square, Milton Park, Abingdon, Oxon OX14 4RN

and by Routledge
52 Vanderbilt Avenue, New York, NY 10017

Routledge is an imprint of the Taylor & Francis Group, an informa business

© 2021 Lily M. Hoffman and Barbara Schmitter Heisler

The right of Lily M. Hoffman and Barbara Schmitter Heisler to be identified as authors of this work has been asserted by them in accordance with sections 77 and 78 of the Copyright, Designs and Patents Act 1988.

All rights reserved. No part of this book may be reprinted or reproduced or utilised in any form or by any electronic, mechanical, or other means, now known or hereafter invented, including photocopying and recording, or in any information storage or retrieval system, without permission in writing from the publishers.

Trademark notice: Product or corporate names may be trademarks or registered trademarks, and are used only for identification and explanation without intent to infringe.

British Library Cataloguing-in-Publication Data
A catalogue record for this book is available from the British Library

Library of Congress Cataloging-in-Publication Data
A catalog record for this book has been requested

ISBN: 978-0-367-23417-1 (hbk)
ISBN: 978-0-367-23418-8 (pbk)
ISBN: 978-0-429-27976-8 (ebk)

Typeset in Bembo
by Apex CoVantage, LLC

To Joel and Martin for homesharing

CONTENTS

Preface	*viii*
Introduction	1
PART ONE **The American experience**	**7**
1 The sharing economy, Airbnb and the financialization of housing in the United States	9
2 Cities, data and data wars	23
3 The Airbnb effect, challenges to housing and localities	56
PART TWO **Moving beyond the US**	**79**
4 Australia, Airbnb's most penetrated market	81
5 Germany, one of Airbnb's least penetrated markets	104
Conclusion: Repositioning short-term rentals in the housing market	136
Index	*146*

PREFACE

When this project began in the summer of 2017, most studies of Airbnb and short-term rentals were within a tourism framework and only occasionally referred to housing issues or gentrification. At the International Sociological Association meetings in Toronto, July 2018, Lily Hoffman presented a paper on Airbnb, short-term rentals and the financialization of housing, placing the subject within the housing framework. At these meetings, she met with Routledge about the book project. Barbara Schmitter Heisler, a former collaborator, joined as co-author of the book.

It has been a tumultuous few years. Empirical studies of Airbnb's effects have begun to appear, cities have turned to regulating short-term rentals and a billion-dollar sector has emerged. All along Airbnb has been and is still a moving target.

At the time of this writing, the future of Airbnb is uncertain as the Covid-19 pandemic, which has brought travel to a halt, has also revealed underlying problems with the Airbnb business model for its hosts, its guests and for the platform itself. Some suggest that many STRs will return to the residential market and that Airbnb will transform again, finding new niches. Discussing plans for the crisis, CEO Brian Chesky wrote to his employees: "Airbnb was born during a global crisis. It didn't stop us then, and it won't stop us now."

Whatever the future of Airbnb, short-term rentals have become an important part of the housing market and are here to stay.

April 2020

INTRODUCTION

Within a short decade, the homesharing platform Airbnb grew from a small San Francisco start-up to a multibillion-dollar business and a recognized brand name. Offering travelers a more "authentic experience" in homes rather than hotel rooms and offering hosts a revenue stream to help pay the mortgage or rent, Airbnb has been widely recognized as a disruptor in the tourism and hospitality industry. In this book, we will argue that Airbnb's disruptive impact extends beyond the tourism industry and that by incentivizing the use of residential space for visitors, Airbnb and other homesharing platforms have disrupted local housing markets, most notably in large cities where urban tourism intersects with already stressed housing conditions.[1]

While most of the academic literature and media reports have taken a tourism perspective, short-term rentals (STRs) straddle both the tourism and the residential housing markets. Given the critical importance of housing as a component of social and spatial inequality and the current climate of housing crises in most Western societies, we argue that it is important to position STRs within a housing perspective. Because housing is a basic human need for which demand is inelastic, even a small loss of supply can have a relatively large adverse effect. This is particularly the case in popular urban neighborhoods where tight housing markets already exist. By adding visitors to the mix, Airbnb has scrambled markets and populations which, for the most part, were compartmentalized, with visitors staying in commercial accommodations in commercially zoned districts. Now visitors compete for living space with local residents.

This introduces several questions at the heart of this book: How do we understand the rise and exponential growth of Airbnb and STRs as a global phenomenon? What is their impact on housing and neighborhoods and how have cities responded to these challenges? Going forward, what are the implications of a large and growing STR sector for the future of housing?

To answer these questions, we present two narratives: the first describes how Airbnb legitimated and institutionalized STRs as a new revenue stream for owners and renters. Attracting commercial operators along with mom-and-pop hosts, Airbnb and STRs have contributed to rising housing costs, lack of availability, displacement and gentrification. The second narrative is more about transformation than scale. We describe the evolution of the short-term rental sector, repositioning it within real estate where new actors promote a variety of tenure models that have the potential to further undermine housing security.

Setting the stage

Context matters. Airbnb was founded during the 2008 financial crisis when the housing bubble, at the heart of the financial meltdown, exacerbated the lack of affordable housing in major US cities, and the Great Recession – as it was called – gave rise to a generation of college graduates without jobs.

Airbnb's well-known and iconic "origins" story illustrates the fit between the social-economic conditions and the birth and trajectory of the platform. Two college graduates – we can call them millennials – newly arrived in San Francisco in the fall of 2007, placed a few airbeds on their floor to help pay the rent, and by the summer of 2008, they had a functioning website. Born of necessity and conceived and marketed as a solution to the affordable housing crisis in the most expensive city in the US, Airbnb's founders – to use the idiom – "killed two birds with one stone": they helped pay the rent and provided affordable lodgings for visitors.

Airbnb was not the first venture to use the internet to bring potential hosts together with users. However, earlier companies such as VRBO (founded in 1995) operated like digital "classifieds" and focused on vacation rentals in resort destinations. In contrast, Airbnb introduced cutting-edge technology – a fully interactive digital platform that handled all the requisite financial transactions – and, taking advantage of the rise in urban tourism, focused on urban destinations.

Funded by venture capital which aggressively promoted its growth, Airbnb rapidly outpaced its rivals, buying up competitors and expanding services. By 2011, Airbnb had achieved "unicorn status" as a start-up valued at more than $ 1 billion. At its tenth anniversary in 2018, the $ 31 billion company had over five million listings in 81,000 cities in 191 countries and had diversified to include luxury homes, boutique hotels, restaurant reservations, tours and activities as well as branded apartment buildings.

STRs and the financialization of housing

Given the trajectory of this "disruptor" and its impact on housing, we have approached these questions through the lens of financialization. We argue that by incentivizing and institutionalizing the STR, Airbnb has significantly contributed to the financialization of housing. It has encouraged the shift from long-term to short-term tenures and has drawn investors who are increasingly corporate and institutional to the residential real estate market. Moreover, in partnering with real estate owners and operators, Airbnb has opened the door to flexible tenure models that attract additional capital and threaten the security of residential housing.

We do not suggest that Airbnb and similar platforms set out to disrupt the housing market nor that they are the cause of the contemporary housing crisis in cities in the US and abroad. Nor did Airbnb introduce financialization to the housing market; it is well-recognized that financialization preceded and led to the Global Financial Crisis (GFC). However, Airbnb fit these scenarios in several ways. It marketed itself with a savvy generational pitch of lean and green and rode the perfect storm, offering new revenue options to stressed homeowners and renters. At the same time, Airbnb's business model fit the neoliberal *Zeitgeist* by identifying "underutilized" living space as an asset that could easily be turned into revenue, setting in motion a feedback cycle which reinforced both the housing crisis and the need for additional revenue and feeding a growing short-term rental sector propelled by increasing numbers of financialized operators and operations.

Although we draw upon the literature on the financialization of housing, we find that this literature tends to dichotomize short-term and long-term tenures as separate categories, whereas we visualize the boundary as increasingly fluid.[2]

Questions and answers

While the disruptive effects of Airbnb and STRs have received considerable media attention, their overall impact on housing and local communities remains poorly understood and strongly contested. Attempts to assess impact have been hampered by Airbnb's refusal to release complete transaction data and the need to develop alternative spatial analytic techniques as well as by Airbnb's aggressive public relations tactics which include commissioning favorable studies and engaging in protracted legal battles with cities.

Despite these difficulties, empirical studies have begun to shed light on the issue of impact, finding positive correlations between the density of Airbnb listings and increases in rent and house prices, and discussing the relation between STRs, displacement and gentrification. These studies do not form a cohesive body of work. They use different methodologies, focus on different aspects of the housing market and are embedded in differing theoretical perspectives. Some are located in tourism publications, others in planning, economic and/or policy journals. Others are the products of government agencies, local authorities and think tanks, and remain unpublished. One of our objectives is to bring this scattered body of empirical work together within the broader perspective of financialization.

The city and city studies. Although Airbnb can be found in all sizes and types of localities, it has been an urban phenomenon from the start, taking advantage of the rise in urban tourism as cities have competed for visitors and tourism has become a major component of the urban economy (Hoffman et al. 2003).[3] Airbnb listings have been concentrated in cities and it is in cities where its negative externalities have been most visible. Moreover, it is in cities – the regulatory unit for land use, housing and the governance of much of everyday life – where the conflict over Airbnb and its consequences plays out. Cities have become a battleground for proponents and opponents of Airbnb.

To gain a more in-depth understanding of these processes, we have constructed a series of case studies of major cities in the US, Australia and Germany. In the US, we have chosen four iconic cities – New York, San Francisco, Los Angeles and Boston. The narrative structure of case studies is particularly adept at capturing the dynamics of these ongoing struggles. Although all the cities we studied ultimately passed measures to regulate Airbnb, the timing and the specific nature of the regulations have varied. Moreover, the struggles to regulate and to enforce regulations are ongoing.

Our US studies suggested that Airbnb's origin, trajectory and impact, were products of specific aspects of US housing markets and post-crisis conditions. To better understand the relevance of these factors, we turned to a comparative perspective to see whether Airbnb's trajectory and impact were similar or different elsewhere. We chose Australia and Germany, two countries with differing housing tenures, policies and cultures, and countries whose housing markets were differently impacted by the GFC. As in the United States, we have focused on large cities that are also major magnets for tourism: Melbourne and Sydney in Australia, and Berlin and Munich in Germany. In examining these cases, we follow the same format as with the US: we describe the structure of the housing/home finance system, look at the impact of the GFC on housing markets, examine the impact of Airbnb and STRs on housing and neighborhoods, and look at the local regulatory response.

The map of the book

We have divided this book into two parts. Part One consists of three chapters that focus on the US experience. Chapter 1 sets the stage by giving a brief history of the sharing economy and the evolution of its "poster-child" Airbnb – from renting out "underutilized" space to co-developing multi-family apartments for STRs – as a form of platform capitalism whose business model encourages real estate speculation and commercialization. Claiming to help financially stressed homeowners and renters, Airbnb was well positioned to exploit the social and economic transformations wrought by the GFC. We trace the increasing financialization of housing and, in the aftermath of the housing bubble, changes in housing tenure in the US – the growing number of renters and rentiers – and changes in the rental sector. We conclude by describing a rapidly growing multibillion-dollar STR sector, driven by venture capital funds, investors and commercial operators.

Chapters 2 and 3 address the contested claim that Airbnb and STRs negatively impact residential housing and neighborhoods. Chapter 2 takes up the issue of data. Protected by Section 230 of the 1996 Communications Decency Act, access to data lies at the heart of the Airbnb phenomenon. The chapter provides case studies of the data wars waged in four iconic American cities – New York, San Francisco, Los Angeles and Boston – where the majority of residents are renters and housing markets are stressed. While the struggle to assess Airbnb's impact on their housing and neighborhoods and to draft effective regulatory policies have played out somewhat differently in each city, the four cities ultimately passed regulatory legislation, which in some cases required the platforms to provide limited data. Although Airbnb made some concessions, it has not given authorities in any city the data they need to easily and efficiently monitor and enforce regulations. Moreover, the narratives are inconclusive and the data wars are ongoing as Airbnb's litigious behavior results in long, costly legal battles. The lack of adequate data that impedes regulatory enforcement also creates costly externalities for cities.

In Chapter 3, we discuss the available evidence of Airbnb's impact on housing and neighborhoods, both the structural and cultural effects. The empirical evidence suggests that Airbnb and STRs have had a significant impact on the long-term rental market, contributing to rising rents, house prices and lack of availability. This impact is not distributed evenly throughout the city but tends to be concentrated in inner city and trendy neighborhoods where these effects are magnified. In these neighborhoods, Airbnb fuels displacement of long-term residents and has been accused of promoting racialized gentrification and "touristification." We discuss Airbnb's role in marketing neighborhoods as part of its claim to enable visitors to live like a local and note the particular vulnerability of vertical communities in high-rise buildings where STRs compromise security as well as quality of life. Airbnb turns localities into battlegrounds, challenging local control over taxes, zoning and housing regulations,

What happens when the model moves abroad? In Part Two we look beyond the United States at Australia and Germany, countries which have differing housing systems and have been differently affected by the GFC. Chapter 4 focuses on Australia, Airbnb's "most penetrated market." Like the US, Australia is a nation of homeowners with a highly financialized housing system. Relatively unscathed by the GFC, an investor-driven building boom in Melbourne and Sydney made for a surplus of vacant central city apartments and an open house for Airbnb. Examining Airbnb's trajectory in these two major cities, we find that residents have been less concerned about rising rents then the loss of amenities. Although the cities eventually enacted regulation, regulatory efforts have primarily taken the form of codes of conduct, addressing behavioral issues, and have been mild, leaving enforcement to residents and their housing associations. The New South Wales regulations (Sydney) remain to be implemented as of spring 2020.

In Chapter 5 we turn to Germany, one of Airbnb's least penetrated markets and a counterpoint to Australia. Unlike the US and Australia, Germany is a nation of renters with a tradition of legal protection for tenants and well-organized tenant associations. As in Australia, the GFC had only minor effects on the German housing market and, in contrast to both the US and Australia, financialization came late and primarily to the large rental sector. For our city studies, we chose Berlin and Munich, both major tourist cities facing severe housing crises. Although Airbnb made early inroads in these cities, local authorities and residents were skeptical about Airbnb and its claims. Responding to the concerns about the loss of residential housing, the cities used existing housing laws that protect residential housing from "misuse" to regulate STRs. While empirical data was relatively sparse, local authorities were less concerned with the number of STRs than with the principle – the misuse of residential housing.

In the concluding chapter, we return to the second narrative: the emergence of a hybrid real estate sector featuring new actors, with ever more sophisticated digital technology and fueled by venture capital. The chapter describes this sector and discusses its implications for housing equality and insecurity. Although this sector may provide more options for owners and investors in residential housing, the ability to pick and choose between tenure options adds to the existing insecurity of rental households as they confront rising rents and low vacancy rates. Given the importance of a well-functioning housing system to social and political stability, we question whether these developments can provide the needed financial and social support, and note that housing is back on the political agenda.

Notes

1 Although Airbnb is one of a number of hosting platforms, we focus on Airbnb as the pioneer, template and largest homesharing platform. Studies typically use Airbnb because third-party sources supply scraped data from its website.
2 A notable exception is the recent article by Cocola-Gant (2019).
3 Brian Chesky, one of Airbnb's founders, has repeatedly asserted that Airbnb is not to be confused with a vacation rental company, with "houses on the beach like my parents used to rent" (Knowledge@Wharton 2017).

References

Cocola-Gant, Augustin and Ana Gago. 2019. Airbnb, Buy-to-let Investment and Tourism-driven Displacement: A Case Study in Lisbon. *Economy and Space*. https://journals.sagepub.com/doi/full/10.1177/0308518X19869012

Hoffman, Lily M., Susan S. Fainstein and Dennis R. Judd. 2003. *Cities and Visitors: Regulating People, Markets, and City Space*. Malden, MA: Blackwell Publishing.

Knowledge@Wharton. 2017. The Inside Story Behind the Unlikely Rise of Airbnb. https://knowledge.wharton.upenn.edu/article/the-inside-story-behind-the-unlikely-rise-of-airbnb/

PART ONE
The American experience

1
THE SHARING ECONOMY, AIRBNB AND THE FINANCIALIZATION OF HOUSING IN THE UNITED STATES

A brief history of the sharing economy

Airbnb, an offshoot of the private equity-fueled tech sector and a poster child of the "sharing" economy, emerged during the first decade of this century. Using information technology to create an online marketplace for goods and services and an economic model that emphasized access over ownership, the sharing economy appeared at a time when the Global Financial Crisis (GFC) of 2008 raised questions about the viability of the market economy and seemed to promise a solution to many of society's problems.

Historically speaking, providing access or sharing is an old concept. People have always shared goods and services both collectively and individually, whether driven by needs (economic insecurity, lack of access) or ideological motivations (religious, political, communitarian) or some combination of the two. They have bartered, shared or rented land, housing, equipment, clothing and other possessions as well as services using local channels such as cooperatives or simply by word-of-mouth. What was new was the use of sophisticated information technology to create a globally connected online marketplace in which digital platforms matched different groups of users and providers. This exponentially increased the size and scale as well as the ease and security of traditional transactions.

The buzz about the sharing economy started in the tech and business sector, which gave birth to a variety of internet-based businesses. It was popularized by the publication of Botsman and Rogers' book, *What's Mine is Yours: The Rise of Collaborative Consumption* in 2010, and validated in March 2011, when *Time* magazine placed "sharing" among the top ten ideas that would change the world for the better. If ownership "had just about ruined the country," then as *Time* proclaimed in a headline: "Today's Smart Choice: Don't Own. Share" (Walsh 2011).

At its debut, cheerleaders promoted an optimistic, even utopian narrative that spoke of "doing good, building social connections, saving the environment, and providing economic benefits to ordinary people" (Schor 2014). Proponents claimed that the sharing economy decentralized production, allocated supply and demand more efficiently, and promoted social interaction and trust by putting owners and users into direct contact. It was "a feel-good story in which technological and economic innovation ushered in a better economic model" (Schor 2014, See also: Hamari et al. 2016, Sundrarajan 2017).

Within a relatively short time, however, a more discerning appraisal of the concept, the model, and the consequences began to appear. As platforms began to serve diverse functions, observers questioned the kinds of transactions that should be included in the sharing economy. Distinguishing sites that utilized assets (Airbnb) from those which offered labor and services (Uber), re-circulated goods (eBay) or performed some combination of these activities (Etsy), several scholars suggested the need to reserve different terms for different functions (Schor and Fitzmaurice 2015), Schor (2017) and Botsman (2015). Some debated the appropriateness of using "sharing" to refer to monetized transactions, pointing out the inherent contradictions in the concept (Kalamar 2013). By the ten year mark, it was becoming obvious that the term "had expanded and morphed" and was being widely applied to businesses without reference to their underlying model (Rinne 2018). Everyone wanted to be included because sharing was a warm, fuzzy concept connoting an anti-consumerist style and socially beneficial objectives.

As it entered the mainstream in 2013 and 2014 and the number of studies multiplied, the sharing economy was subject to increasing criticism directed at its relationship with and effects on the market economy. Several platforms quickly become "unicorns" – start-ups valued at more than $ 1 billion by private investors who funded their growth – leading some to argue that these successful for-profit platforms had "co-opted what began as a progressive, socially transformative idea" (Schor 2014, 10). Airbnb fit this description; it was a recipient of venture capital funding and followed the venture capital business model which encouraged start-ups to "grow aggressively – faster than the competition, faster than regulators" (Griffith 2019).

While some saw an inherent paradox – that the sharing economy was part of the capitalist economy while claiming to be an alternative (Richardson 2015) – others went further. Relabeling the sharing economy "platform capitalism," Srnicek located it squarely within the evolution of capitalism and argued that it was the "only business model adequate to the digital age" (2017). Like all forms of capitalism, platform capitalism tends toward monopolistic positions and needs to continuously expand extraction and control into new areas. According to Srnicek, the sharing economy model is "the most hyped-up type of platform;" it is a "lean" platform and thus "the most unsustainable."

Critics also pointed to the sharing economy's "dark side" (Malhotra and Van Alstyne 2014). Instead of a path to sustainability, greater economic opportunity and a decentralized and more equitable economy, they noted the emergence of unregulated market places reinforced by a neoliberal paradigm, new forms of inequality and exploitation, and the emergence of a new precariat (Martin 2016; Murillo et al. 2017; Morozov 2013; Caldararo 2014; Scholz and Schneider 2016; Standing 2011).

This was only the beginning. Although it is not yet certain to what extent the platform-based economy or specific platforms will be reined in, these companies have currently become targets of widespread criticism. In the US and Europe, scrutiny has moved beyond media and academia to legislative bodies and courts where the issues range from concerns about data privacy and content, to labor exploitation and anti-trust violations.

Airbnb's evolving model – from tourism disruptor to housing disruptor

Airbnb is a case in point. Frequently cited as the prototype of the sharing economy as well as a major commercial and financial success, Airbnb's trajectory illustrates both the initial rhetoric of the sharing economy as well as the subsequent criticism of these technologically enabled platforms. Its iconic "origins" story, described in the Introduction, is of two roommates paying a high rent in San Francisco's tight housing, who decide to rent out the floor of their San Francisco apartment and advertise online; thus, Airbnb was born.

Legitimation is central to this story for although homesharing was not new, it had negative connotations for both users and hosts. Airbnb's promotion of alternative accommodations as a more authentic, experiential type of travel proved to be inspired marketing. It removed the rooming house stigma and made short-term rentals (STRs) fashionable, even sexy, for potential travelers. To overcome the "classic urban challenges of mass anonymity and a lack of strong social bonds" and to foster trust in sharing private space with strangers, Airbnb's website and app provided users with tools to rate their experiences (Davidson and Infranca 2018).

Viewed by the travel and tourism industry as a "disruptor," an innovation that upsets existing markets and arrangements, Airbnb has changed travel permanently and, many say, for the better. The company's slogan – "Book rooms with locals rather than hotels" – has appealed to visitors looking for alternatives to hotels and for more authentic travel experiences. It has made travel less expensive, more family friendly, and as Airbnb has claimed, it has made cities "bigger," expanding the tourist locale beyond a central hotel district to a diverse number of neighborhoods, many of them places without traditional hotels (Clampet 2014). For many travelers this relaxed localized style has itself become an inducement to further travel (Thompson 2018).

But to date, Airbnb continues to evolve, expanding and diversifying beyond its homesharing origins to compete directly with major full-service online travel platforms, such as Expedia and Booking.com. Within a decade, the company has grown from offering shared rooms to offering a wide range of accommodations – vacation rental homes, timeshares, luxury villas, traditional bed-and-breakfasts, boutique hotels and even treehouses. It also offers local tours and experiences.

Moreover, Airbnb has been moving beyond the tourism industry to real estate and has put forward plans to expand from the digital economy to production and ownership (Wilson 2018). According to Srnicek (2017), this evolution is inevitable because lean digital platforms such as Airbnb, which minimize the costs of ownership, are less viable in the long run unless they broaden their activities and acquire assets. An early venture was Airbnb's Friendly Buildings program (2016) which provided a way for landlords, property managers and homeowners' associations to manage hosting in multifamily buildings. Airbnb then partnered with Newgard Development Group to co-brand luxury rental apartments with hotel-style amenities such as front desks and concierge – Niido Powered by Airbnb. Announcing this project in 2017, Airbnb's Chris Lehane, noted that Niido was "designed in part to help tenants afford the rising costs of rent" (Quackenbush 2017). Niido will be followed by similar new developments under the rubric Natiivo, in Austin, Texas, and Miami, Florida. Since these condo buildings will be licensed as hotels, owner/investors can rent the units on Airbnb all year long and "not worry about any municipal limitations on homesharing placed on traditional residences" (Sisson 2019). In 2018, Airbnb announced plans to design affordable housing to accommodate STRs. According to Joe Gebbia, one of the founders, the Backyard Initiative "is not just about housing but about rethinking the home" (Wilson 2018). This suggests that "the company that disrupted hotels wants to do the same for housing" (Riquier 2018).[1]

This trajectory raises the question of whether it is appropriate to view Airbnb's impact on the housing market as some sort of unforeseen or unanticipated consequence. Writing in the *Atlantic Monthly*, Derek Thompson said: "The platform is unwittingly producing a subsidy of tourists paid for by nonparticipating urban dwellers who bear the cost of higher rental prices" (2018). Alternately, we suggest that Airbnb's impact on housing could have been anticipated from the start by looking at its business model.

Airbnb's business model and housing

What does Airbnb's business model have to say about housing? Like much of the sharing economy, the Airbnb business model makes money on the use of other people's assets, namely residential space. It treats the home as a financial asset to market STRs, extracting a share of the profit from hosts and visitors in return for providing an easy-to-use payment system and access to a global marketplace.

While the home has always been a financial asset and, used as collateral, a potential source of capital that can be leveraged by incurring debt as with a second mortgage or home equity loan, the Airbnb model allows residents to generate revenue without incurring debt. The model also differs because it applies to renters as well as homeowners. Moreover, the institutionalization of the STRs as a new revenue source and an attractive business opportunity has reinforced the exchange value of housing.

Adopting the rhetoric of the sharing economy, Airbnb's business model is based on motivating people to monetize their "underutilized" assets – rooms, apartments, houses – for the temporary use of visitors. Assuming these assets are spare rooms, or houses and apartments unused when the owner is on vacation, Airbnb proposes to put this excess or idle capacity to use. As Frenken and Schor (2017) point out, the meaning of underutilization is key to the controversy about homesharing platforms because STRs are not necessarily owner-occupied or even the primary residence of the host. For example, if a person buys a second home or apartment as an investment, with the sole purpose of renting it out to visitors, this property cannot be classified as underutilized; it then becomes a commercial lodging site.

Beyond the fiction of underutilization, housing differs from other assets, such as cars or tools. As a place of habitation, it is universally perceived to be a necessity or a human right, not an indulgence. Housing is also relatively fixed, represents a large investment of time and money, and cannot be quickly replaced. For these reasons, housing is typically subject to numerous protective regulations that apply to its utilization, safety and construction.

At the same time, housing stock is also flexible in that one can switch from owner-occupied to renter-occupied and from long-term to short-term rental depending upon local laws and regulations. Herein lies the threat that homesharing platforms and STRs pose to the residential housing market. As we will discuss in more detail in the following chapters, multi-unit hosts and commercialized sites have become an ever growing segment of Airbnb's listings and profit, suggesting that a significant share of housing stock has shifted from the residential to the more lucrative short-term market as individual and corporate investors park their capital in residential housing. Given the inherently flexible nature of housing, the new and more lucrative short-term rental market lures owners and investors and promotes speculation to the detriment of residential housing.

Since profit and growth depend on an ever-increasing supply of hosts and listings which must be managed and serviced, commercialization and professionalization are part and parcel of the business model. The need for more hosts and listings, as noted earlier, has led Airbnb to partner with multi-family real estate owners, developers and property managers. It has also lured investors and created a professionalized ecosystem.

The Airbnb model also benefits from the tech industry's well-known freedom from regulation. Drawing upon Section 230 of the 1996 Communications Decency Act, which gave the digital economy a free pass in accord with the neoliberal *Zeitgeist* of the time, Airbnb argues that they are merely "intermediaries" or third parties and have no control over hosts or guests. This uncertain legal status has allowed them to flaunt many of the existing laws that regulate traditional tourist accommodations and, perhaps more importantly, to challenge the ability of cities to enforce municipal housing, safety and fire codes, and collect transient occupancy taxes.

Although Airbnb's rhetoric has emphasized the cultural and social as well as the economic aspects of homesharing as a "win-win" situation for all participants and for society at large, this is not a winning situation if our focus is the impact on housing markets and localities. By incentivizing the transformation of residential real estate into tourist accommodations, Airbnb and STRs directly and indirectly affect housing costs, availability and neighborhood milieu. While the hotel industry has been able to respond to the challenges posed by Airbnb by offering similar accommodations and amenities, it is important to emphasize that the housing market is much less flexible. Indeed, it is in the already fragile and contested housing markets of cities that Airbnb has the potential to do far greater damage.

The launch of Airbnb in 2008 coincided with the second worst financial crisis in American history, a crisis that began in the US housing market and quickly became global. To better understand Airbnb's threat to the housing market, we need to look at how the housing bubble destabilized the housing market in the US, setting the stage for the emergence of homesharing platforms and the boom in STRs.

Financialization and the financial crisis

At the heart of the crisis was the hyperfinancialization of housing. Prior to the financial crisis and the Great Recession that followed,[2] housing tenure in the US was characterized by the state-sponsored promotion of a "home of one's own." This was the American Dream – an ideology and business model based on long-term, low-interest mortgages backed by the federal government. Owner-occupied tenure was basically available to the non-minority middle-class with steady incomes. Rentals were negatively perceived, limited to urban areas and relatively few in number. Riding this housing finance model during the 1970s, the US achieved one of the highest rates of homeownership among the industrialized nations, 64.4 % in 1980; at the height of the housing bubble in 2004, the rate reached a high of 69.2 % (US Census 2018).

The undermining of this model is the story of the financial crash and the Great Recession of 2008. It had a major impact upon housing as well as upon the opportunities and expectations of the general population, in particular, the generation of millennials – those born between 1981 and 1996, who came of age with the internet (Dimock 2019).

Financialization, defined in terms of the increasingly active role of financial institutions and processes, is not new to housing. In the US, beginning in the 1930s, financial institutions have been the basis for widespread homeownership. The US government began to promote homeownership as part of the New Deal, using a government sponsored institution, Fannie Mae, to facilitate the process. The initial US mortgage model separated the origin of the loan from the ultimate funding source: local Savings and Loans (S&Ls) originated the 30-year fixed-rate mortgage according to standardized criteria, and Fannie Mae purchased and insured the loans and issued government bonds.

This home-finance system worked well through the 1970s until the late 1980s when inflationary pressures and rising interest rates produced a liquidity crisis for the S&Ls, the traditional mortgage lenders. Burdened by low-interest, long-term loans, over one thousand S&Ls failed and government-sponsored institutions, like Fannie Mae and Freddie Mac kept the mortgage market afloat. This shock, together with the demands of large US banks and investment firms for less regulation to compete in an increasingly globalized marketplace, led both the Reagan and Clinton administrations to deregulate financial institutions, which in turn, allowed new actors to engage in mortgage lending. This ushered in a period of rapid and dramatic change in the mortgage markets, marked by the increasing extent of and changing nature of financialization. According to economic historian Adam Tooze: "Between the 1990s and the outbreak of the crisis in 2007, American housing finance was turned into a dynamic and destabilizing force by a fourfold transformation – the securitization of mortgages, their incorporation into expansive and high-risk strategies of banking growth, the mobilization of new funding sources and internationalization" (2018, 43).

Securitization, commonly regarded as the main culprit in the 2008 crisis, was first introduced by the government-backed institutions in the 1970s in the form of mortgage-backed securities to off-load the risk of volatile rates by pooling mortgages and selling shares in the pool directly to investors. Securitization basically made the seemingly immoveable house into a financial product that could be packaged and sold globally. This meant that during the 1980s – a period of rapid de-industrialization in the US – attempts to halt foreclosures "through no fault of one's own," came up against a new reality; there were no local lenders to appeal to since the mortgages had already left home (Heisler and Hoffman 1987; Hoffman and Heisler 1989).

Compared to the earlier mortgage model with its strict criteria, securitization reduced the lender's incentive to carefully monitor the loan (Tooze, 50). As newly deregulated private actors entered the mortgage arena and wanted to increase the number and flow of mortgages to pool, they created new instruments, such as adjustable rate mortgages (ARMS) which replaced the 30-year fixed rate, as well as subprime instruments which eased, then abandoned, lending requirements such as credit worthiness and down payments.

These actors also created more abstract investment vehicles – structured financial products, such as collateralized mortgage obligations or CMOs, which enabled the pooling and marketing of high-risk mortgages – the so-called subprimes. In effect, the banks had built "an integrated mortgage securitization business" from originating loans to selling them packaged as financial products (Tooze, 55). Requiring only a continual input of mortgages, it was a highly profitable business model and a seemingly winning proposition for buyers and investors as well as financiers since house prices were assumed to climb by 5 % each year. People were buying homes and apartments to flip in order to realize the capital gains.

Demand was also high as US mortgage-based securities became a gold standard for individual and corporate investors, internationally and nationally. There was demand from pension and insurance funds as well as private wealth funds; foreign money flooded in from emerging nations such as China. The dot.com bubble of the late 1990s led many investors to abandon the stock market and turn to real estate, further fueling the hunger for real estate and mortgage-backed securities. The mortgage market, according to Aalbers, had been "transformed from being a facilitating market for homeowners to a tool for facilitating global investment" (2016, 11).

Government policy also played into the build-up of the housing bubble. In 2004, President Bush called for an "ownership society," encouraging homeownership among the low-income/minority population by inducing the banks to lower rates and ease mortgage requirements – the so-called subprime instruments. By 2006, 70 % of new mortgages were subprime or other types of unconventional loans made to be pooled and securitized by the banks (Tooze, 63).

When interest rates rose and housing prices fell in late 2006–2007, the mortgage default rate began to go through the ceiling, threatening to take with it not only US financial institutions but the interconnected global financial marketplace that had placed its trust in the US residential housing market. This raises a question – how did the transformations of the US housing market shape the expectations of the generation affected by the financial crisis?

Post-crisis, a nation of renters and rentiers

The lack of affordable housing has been an ongoing issue in the US, pre-dating the Great Recession. A product of policy and practice, it was exacerbated by the retreat from subsidized housing for low-income families in the 1970s and 1980s as privatization and austerity prevailed. Ironically, providing low-income households with vouchers for use in the private sector intensified the pressure on low-cost housing, as did the back-to-the city movement in the 1990s when much affordable rental stock in urban areas was converted to condominiums and co-ops. New construction did not alleviate the lack of supply, because builders built for the high end of the market since prices seemed to rise annually, interest rates remained low and national and international demand remained strong. That said, the lack of affordable housing has been aggravated in the aftermath of the Great Recession.

While the housing market has bounced back, there has been a dramatic shift in housing tenure. As homeownership has declined, the number of households that rent has risen. At the peak of the housing bubble in 2004, 69.2 % of Americans owned their homes, a figure which dropped to 63.7 % in 2016, the lowest since 1965. Homeowners are also aging. Households 65 and older were the only age group that had higher homeownership rates in 2017 than in 1987. Homeownership rates declined for all other age groups, with millennials showing the steepest decline (JCHS 2018).

Today more US households are renting than at any point in the last 50 years – close to the 1965 high of 37 % (Cilluffo et al. 2017). This shift has been fueled in part by the massive number of mortgage foreclosures during and after the GFC. Between 2006 and 2012, approximately eight million families lost their homes to foreclosure, and homeowners lost $ 7 trillion in home equity (Ellen and Dastrup 2012). In the aftermath, rising house prices, more restrictive lending criteria, student debt, less secure employment and/or the changing preferences of millennials, who came of age with the sharing economy and grew up in the shadow of the GFC, have contributed to the decline of homeownership.[3]

Given the number of foreclosures and the post-crisis rise in home prices, the rise in renting is not unexpected. However, it reverses a long-standing trend. For most of the period since the Second World War, as owner-occupied tenure has grown, rental housing has accounted for a declining share of US housing tenure and has not attracted private builders except to the high end of the market. These trends have not been restricted to the US but have been observed in other "homeownership societies" such as Great Britain and Australia. In Britain, Guy Standing refers to "Generation Rent" (2017) and Forrest and Hirayama give similar data on renting for the younger generation in Australia and Japan (Forrest and Hirayama 2015; *The Economist* 2020).

This is not to say that homeownership should have been put on a pedestal and propped up by governmental policies in the past nor that homeownership should be a goal for the future; rather, in the post-crisis scenario, the reality and expectations about housing tenure as well as the material meaning of housing have begun to change. Indeed, a special report in *The Economist* speaks of the "end of an era" and refers to "the obsession with homeownership" as a "horrible blunder" (2020).

The demographic composition of renters has changed as their numbers have changed. Renters today include an increasing proportion of wealthier and better educated households, more families and all age groups. A recent study found that renter households making more than $ 75,000 increased by 45.1 % between 2010 and 2018 (JCHS 2020). This demographic shift has been accompanied by a corresponding change in social status. Whereas in the recent past, rental tenure was generally perceived to be a waystation to homeownership or a tenure for low-income households, the social status of the renter has been upgraded.

However, although renters now include a larger share of high-income households, rents have risen faster than incomes, particularly in the large metropolitan areas where most jobs are located. Renters, who represent a majority of households in most large cities, continue to face tight housing markets with historically low vacancy rates, and, compared to homeowners, renters still pay a larger share of their income for housing at all income levels. Not surprisingly an increasing percentage of renters are cost-burdened (spend over 30 % of income on rent). According to the 2020 JCHS report, in most metro areas at least 40 % of renters are cost-burdened and in some locations the figure is as high as 56 %.

At the same time, the rental sector has been transformed. There are new owners, new and different rental stock, and increasing investment by financial corporations. The steady growth of income and wealth inequality has meant that those with the assets to purchase residential real estate as an investment, have become rentiers, drawing income from multiple properties. Landlordism, according to Standing (2017) has become a hallmark of what he refers to as "global rentier capitalism" and is typically subsidized by the neo-liberal state through favorable interest rates and tax policies.[4]

As the rental sector has become more attractive for domestic and international investors, ownership and management has changed. In contrast to the traditional owners – the developers and property-owning/management companies who dealt solely with real estate, typically in specific cities and regions, and who took a long-term view of their properties – these new actors are private equity funds and financial firms not previously involved in real estate and whose focus is primarily on short-term profit. Institutional/corporate ownership of rental property has increased as the percentage of individual owners has dramatically declined. Attracted to what has become a global market, investors are betting that "the renter class that swelled after last decade's housing crash is here to stay" (Dezember 2019). These trends have given rise to a growing academic literature on the effects of a more financialized ownership and management structure on tenants (among others see Aalbers 2017; IJUR 41(4) 2017; Fields 2017). The overall conclusion is that it has contributed to shelter instability as evidenced by higher eviction rates and other negative tenant practices.

As might be expected, renewed interest in rental housing has created demand for new construction and new types of rental stock, reversing several decades of relative decline. Between 2008 and 2018, 87 % of new rental construction consisted of large multifamily buildings and single-family homes. As noted, this has focused on the higher end of the market with the construction of less expensive small and mid-size units remaining essentially flat. The most noted development has been the creation of a rental market in single-family homes by corporate investors who bought up hundreds of thousands of foreclosed homes and repurposed them as rental housing (Fields 2018; Dezember 2019; Raymond et al. 2016). Given the success of this profitable new market segment, developers now build specifically for the single-family rental market.

It was in this post-crisis scenario that Airbnb entered the story. Airbnb's founders were among those directly affected by the Great Recession. Both the impetus for innovation and the market niche were San Francisco's tight housing and lodgings markets. A product of the chaotic economic climate and the neoliberal *Zeitgeist* that celebrated individual entrepreneurship and technical innovation and saw government regulation as an outdated barrier, Airbnb marketed itself to travelers as an inexpensive way to travel, to hosts as a solution to high rents and mortgages, and rode the perfect storm.

But the story does not end there. The high and increasing number of households who rent, together with the transformation of rental housing, have made the growing short-term rental market a significant housing issue. This is particularly true for cities where most residents are renters and where STRs have a direct impact on the long-term rental market.

An emerging short-term rental sector

By legitimating and institutionalizing the short-term rental, Airbnb jump-started a new and growing market in STRs. As a Forbes journalist noted, "it was only a matter of time before a new breed of entrepreneur unsatisfied with renting out one spare bedroom or vacant property would look for more leverage and scale in an expanding Airbnb ecosystem" (Myler 2017). This has occurred on a global basis, and although Airbnb continues to stress that most of its listings are from hosts renting out a single room or residence, the evidence shows that it is the hosts who offer multiple units who make up a disproportionate share of Airbnb's listings and profit in the US and elsewhere. Moreover, entrepreneurs with one or two apartments are at a disadvantage. According to former Airbnb chief financial officer Laurence Tosi, "Short-term rentals are a scale business in which only the largest and most sophisticated players can thrive" (Sumers 2019).

While Airbnb is the largest and most visible platform, it is not the only player in the short-term rental market. This multibillion-dollar sector has grown exponentially in recent years as hotels and multifamily real estate, which initially opposed STRs, have begun to converge on this market, offering new models, some of which are designed to evade local regulations. Airbnb has actively encouraged, promoted and invested in this expanding ecosystem. In addition to the initial businesses that grew up around Airbnb – the professional greeters, laundry and cleaning services, and decorators – an expanding ecosystem now supports the short-term rental market. There are now services "that replicate and in some cases even expand the hotel model" to deliver liquor and provide spa treatments and child care (Allen 2019). There are also online full-service management companies and consultants who help the investor identify optimal locations or help buildings (and even cities) manage Airbnb-related conflict. Complaints from cities and residents notwithstanding, the industry view is that despite the growing pains, short-term rentals will persist because "demand always wins and someday, short-term rentals will change the way we look at space forever" (Jensen 2018).

★ ★ ★

This chapter has described a feedback cycle which starts with Airbnb treating the home as an asset to incentivize STRs. As the evidence will show, STRs have contributed to rising rents, rising house prices and the decreasing availability of long-term rentals as well as to displacement and gentrification. But there is another loop to this cycle: by incentivizing the home as an asset, STRs have encouraged real estate investment and speculation, creating a growing short-term rental sector which bodes further transformative change for housing. We will return to this topic in our concluding chapter.

Notes

1. There is evidence that Airbnb and STRs are influencing the design of homes and apartments. In Melbourne, Australia, with micro-apartments (Alexander 2018) and in the US, homebuilder Lennar introduced a popular model called NextGen in 2011 designed with an attached one-bedroom suite and hotel-style door that can be closed off from the main house (Jackson 2018).
2. The Great Recession is a term commonly used to refer to the aftermath of the financial crisis and refers to the period from December 2007 to June 2009.
3. The millennial generation refers to the generation born between 1981 and 1996.
4. A good example are the recent changes in US tax policy that have supported investor-owned residential real estate and the commercialization of STRs. The 20 % pass-through tax deduction, a central component of President Trump's tax-cut legislation in 2017, allows Airbnb hosts who do not occupy their property at any point during the year to claim the 20 % deduction on rental income. This does not apply to moms-and-pops sharing under- or unutilized space (Tankersley 2019).

References

Aalbers, Manuel B. 2016. *The Financialization of Housing: A Political Economy Approach*. New York: Routledge.

Aalbers, Manuel B. 2017. The Variegated Financialization of Housing. *International Journal of Urban and Regional Research* 41(4): 542–554.

Alexander, Jacqui. 2018. Domesticity On-Demand: The Architectural and Urban Implications of Airbnb in Melbourne, Australia. *Urban Science*. September 12. www.researchgate.net/publication/327613688_Domesticity_On-Demand_The_Architectural_and_Urban_Implications_of_Airbnb_in_Melbourne_Australia

Allen, Peter. 2019. How the Sharing Economy Is Transforming the Short-term Rental Industry. *Knowledge@Wharton*. February 14. https://knowledge.wharton.upenn.edu/article/short-term-rentals-the-transformation-in-real-estate-and-travel-set-to-check-in/

Botsman, Rachel. 2015. Defining the Sharing Economy: What Is Collaborative Consumption – And What Isn't? www.fastcoexist.com/3046119/defining-the-sharing-economy-what-iscollaborative-consumption-and-what-isnt

Botsman, Rachel and Roo Rogers. 2010. *What's Mine Is Yours: The Rise of Collaborative Consumption*. New York: Harper Collins.

Caldararo, Niccolo Leo. 2014. Empty Housing in America, Housing Needs, Shadow Banks and the Sharing Economy. June 30. https://ssrn.com/abstract=2460987 or http://doi.org/10.2139/ssrn.2460987

Cilluffo, Anthony, A.W. Geiger and Richard Fry. 2017. More U.S. Households Are Renting than at any Point in 50 Years. July 19. www.pewresearch.org/fact-tank/2017/07/19/more-u-s-households-are-renting-than-at-any-point-in-50-years/

Clampet, Jason. 2014. 6 Ways Airbnb Changed Travel and the Vacation Rental Industry. July 31. https://skift.com/2014/07/31/6-ways-airbnb-changed-hospitality-and-the-vacation-rental-industry/

Davidson, Nestor M. and John Infranca. 2018. The Place of the Sharing Economy. In Nestor M. Davidson, Michele Finck and John J. Infranca (eds.) *Cambridge Handbook on the Law of the Sharing Economy*. Cambridge: Cambridge University Press, 205–219.

Dezember, Ryan. 2019. Wall Street's Big Landlords Are So Hungry for Houses They're Building Them. *The Wall Street Journal*. January 3. www.wsj.com/articles/wall-streets-big-landlords-are-so-hungry-for-houses-theyre-building-them-11546511401

Dimock, Michael. 2019. Defining Generations: Where Millennials End and Post-Millennials Begin. *Pew Research Center*. Washington, DC. www.pewresearch.org/fact-tank/2018/03/01/defining-generations-where-millennials-end-and-post-millennials-begin/

The Economist. 2020. The Horrible Housing Blunder: Why the Obsession with Home Ownership Is So Harmful. *A Special Report*. January 18–24. www.economist.com/leaders/2020/01/16/home-ownership-is-the-wests-biggest-economic-policy-mistake

Ellen, Ingrid Gould and Samuel Dastrup. 2012. Housing and the Great Recession, the Russell Sage Foundation and the Stanford Center on Poverty and Inequality. October. https://furmancenter.org/files/publications/HousingandtheGreatRecession.pdf

Fields, Desiree. 2017. Unwilling Subjects of Financialization. *International Journal of Urban and Regional Research* 41(4): 588–603.

Fields, Desiree. 2018. Constructing a New Asset Class: Property-led Financial Accumulation after the Crisis. *Economic Geography* 94(2): 118–140. http://unequalcities.org/wp-content/uploads/sites/17/2019/01/Fields-Desiree-Constructing-a-new-asset-class-final.pdf

Forrest, Ray and Yosuke Hirayama. 2015. The Financialization of the Social Project: Embedded Liberalism, Neoliberalism and Home Ownership. *Urban Studies* 52(2): 233–244. https://doi.org/10.1177/0042098014528394

Frenken, Koen and Juliet Schor. 2017. Putting the Sharing Economy into Perspective. *Environmental Innovation and Societal Transitions* 23(June): 3–10. https://doi.org/10.1016/j.eist.2017.01.003

Griffith, Erin. 2019. More Start-Ups Are Telling Venture Capitalists to Get Lost. *The New York Times*. January 13. www.nytimes.com/2019/01/11/technology/start-ups-rejecting-venture-capital.html

Hamari, Juho, Mimmi Sjoklint and Antti Ukkonen. 2016. The Sharing Economy: Why People Participate in Collaborative Consumption. *Journal of the Association for Information Science and Technology* 67(9): 2014–2059.

Heisler, Barbara Schmitter and Lily M. Hoffman. 1987. Keeping a Home: Changing Mortgage Markets and Regional Economic Distress. *Sociological Focus* 2(3) (August): 227–241.

Hoffman, Lily M. and Barbara Schmitter Heisler. 1989. Home Finance: Buying and Keeping a House in a Changing Financial Environment. In Elizabeth Huttman and W. van Vliet (eds.) *Handbook of Housing and the Built Environment in the United States*. Westport, CT: Greenwood Press, 149–165.

International Journal of Urban and Regional Research (IJUR). 2017. Symposium on the Variegated Financialization of Housing 41(4).

Jackson, Candace. 2018. The New American Dream Home Is One You Never Have to Leave. *The New York Times*. October 13. www.nytimes.com/2018/10/13/opinion/sunday/real-estate-housing-market-dream-home.html

Jensen, Jeremiah. 2018. In the Pipeline: Short-term Rentals Are the Future of Commercial Real Estate. August 8. www.housingwire.com/articles/46393-in-the-pipeline-short-term-rentals-are-the-future-of-commercial-real-estate

Joint Center for Housing Studies of Harvard University (JCHS). 2020. America's Rental Housing 2020. www.jchs.harvard.edu/americas-rental-housing-2020?embargo=ZIzrezGk_nJs2QUiZrFCt2wTZOi9IbP_Olx7TgX9lqQ

Joint Center for Housing Studies of Harvard University (JCHS). 2018. The State of the Nation's Housing 2018. http://jchs.harvard.edu/state-nations-housing-2018

Kalamar, Anthony. 2013. Sharewashing Is the New Greenwashing. *OpEd News*. www.opednews.com/articles/Sharewashing-is-the-New-Gr-by-Anthony-Kalamar-130513-834.html

Malhotra, Arwind and Marshall Van Alstyne. 2014. The Dark Side of the Sharing Economy and How to Lighten It. *Communications of the ACM* 57(11): 24–27.

Martin, Chris. 2016. The Sharing Economy: A Pathway to Sustainability or a Nightmarish form of Neoliberal Capitalism? *Ecological Economics* 121: 149–159.

Morozov, Evgeny. 2013. The "Sharing Economy" Undermines Workers' Rights. *Financial Times*. October 14. www.ft.com/cms/s/0/92c3021c-34c2-11e3-8148-00144feab7de.html#axzz42ealhVqf

Murillo, David, Heloise Buckland and Esther Val. 2017. When the Sharing Economy Becomes Neoliberalism on Steroids: Unravelling the Controversies. *Technological Forecasting and Social Change* 125: 66–76.

Myler, Larry. 2017. Some Airbnb Hosts Producing Job-Quitting Cash With This Emerging Business Model. *Forbes*. September 7. www.forbes.com/sites/larrymyler/2017/09/07/some-airbnb-hosts-producing-job-quitting-cash-with-this-emerging-business-model/#514b13c821ef

Quackenbush, Casey. 2017. Airbnb Apartment Complexes Could Soon Be Coming to the U.S.- Thanks to $200 Million Investment. *Fortune*. December 19. https://fortune.com/2017/12/19/airbnb-niido-branded-apartments-investment/

Raymond, Elora, et al. 2016. Corporate Landlords, Institutional Investors, and Displacement: Eviction Rates in Single Family Rentals, Community & Economic Development

Discussion Paper, No. 04–16. *Federal Reserve Bank of Atlanta.* December. www.frbatlanta.org/-/media/documents/community-development/publications/discussion-papers/2016/04-corporate-landlords-institutional-investors-and-displacement-2016-12-21.pdf

Richardson, Lizzie. 2015. Performing the Sharing Economy. *Geoforum* 67: 121–129.

Rinne, April. 2018. The Dark Side of the Sharing Economy. *World Economic Forum.* January 16. www.weforum.org/agenda/2018/01/the-dark-side-of-the-sharing-economy/

Riquier, Andrea. 2018. Will Airbnb Move from Home-sharing to Home-building? *Market Watch.* November 29. www.marketwatch.com/story/will-airbnb-move-from-home-sharing-to-home-building-2018-11-29

Scholz, Trevor and Nathan Schneider (eds.). 2016. *Ours to Hack and to Own: The Rise of Platform Cooperativism, A New Vision for the Future of Work and a Fairer Internet.* New York: OR Books.

Schor, Juliet B. 2014. Debating the Sharing Economy. *Great Transition Initiative.* www.greatrransition.org/publication/debating-the-sharing-economy

Schor, Juliet B. 2017. Does the Sharing Economy Increase Inequality Within the Platform Providers? *Cambridge Journal of Regions, Economy and Society* 10(2): 263–279. https://doi.org/10.1093/cjres/rs047

Schor, Juliet B. and Connor J. Fitzmaurice. 2015. Collaborating and Connecting: The Emergence of the Sharing Economy. In L. Reisch and J. Thogersen (eds.) *Handbook of Research on Sustainable Consumption.* Cheltenham: Edward Elgar, 410–425.

Sisson, Patrick. 2019. New Hotel and Homesharing Hybrid Creates Investment Vehicle for Airbnb. *Curbed.* July 2. www.curbed.com/2019/7/2/20679910/airbnb-hotel-miami-austin-natiivo-niido

Srnicek, Nick. 2017. *Platform Capitalism.* Malden, MA: Polity Press.

Standing, Guy. 2011. *The Precariat: The New Dangerous Class.* London: Bloomsbury.

Standing, Guy. 2017. *The Corruption of Capitalism: Why Rentiers Thrive and Work Does Not Pay.* London: Biteback Publishing Ltd.

Sumers, Brian. 2019. What'll It Take to Survive in Short-term Rentals: Former Top Airbnb Exec. *Skift.* December 5. https://skift.com/2019/12/05/whatll-it-take-to-survive-in-short-term-rentals-former-top-airbnb-exec/

Sundrarajan, Arun. 2017. *The Sharing Economy: The End of Employment and the Rise of Crowd-Based Capitalism.* Boston: MIT Press.

Tankersley, Jim. 2019. Trump Administration Spells Out Who Wins and Loses from New Tax Break. *The New York Times.* January 18. www.nytimes.com/2019/01/18/business/trump-administration-business-tax-break.html

Thompson, Derek. 2018. Airbnb and the Unintended Consequences of 'Disruption.' *The Atlantic Monthly.* February 17. www.theatlantic.com/business/archive/2018/02/airbnb-hotels-disruption/553556/

Tooze, Adam. 2018. *Crashed: How a Decade of Financial Crises Changed the World.* New York: Viking.

US Census. 2018. Quarterly Residential Vacancies and Homeownership. www.census.gov/housing/hvs/files/currenthvspress.pdf on homeownership rates, p. 9.

Walsh, Bryan. 2011. Today's Smart Choice: Don't Own. Share. *Time Magazine.* March 17. http://content.time.com/time/specials/packages/article/0,28804,2059521_2059717_2059710,00.html

Wilson, Mark. 2018. Exclusive: Airbnb Will Start Designing Houses in 2019. *FastCompany.* November 28. www.fastcompany.com/90271599/exclusive-airbnb-will-start-designing-houses-in-2019

2
CITIES, DATA AND DATA WARS

> We cannot understand, or even investigate, a subject about which nothing is known.
> *(Pasquale 2015, 1)*

Access to data lies at the very heart of the Airbnb phenomenon. As Pasquale argues, the obfuscation of data is part of the *modus operandi* of many businesses, particularly in the tech industry, and is the source of power and revenue. Before there was systematic data, anecdotal accounts of Airbnb's negative impact on housing markets and localities began to appear. Residents noted the proliferation of lock boxes, tourists with rolling suitcases in residential areas and the proliferation of trash and loud parties. Local politicians and affordable housing advocates noted that contrary to Airbnb's claims that most hosts shared their space, the majority of listings appeared to be whole units without a host present. Moreover, a significant number of listings seemed to be commercial or investment units rented full-time, and while they were not the majority of listings – a point constantly repeated by Airbnb – they represented a large and growing share of Airbnb's revenue and listings.

Existing use of zoning to separate residential and commercial areas made rentals for fewer than 30 days – short-term rentals (STRs) – basically illegal in residential neighborhoods. Some localities such as New York City also specifically restricted STRs in residential buildings. Sooner or later local authorities would have to catch up with this *fait accompli* and consider how to regulate STRs, but to do this, they would need data.

During Airbnb's first few years of operation, the only available data were its own positive reports, written by in-house research to bolster the platform's claims, among them: the growing number of hosts who earned needed income, the beneficial impact of hosts and guests on the local economy, the platform's geographic effect in dispersing visitors and the positive experience of the host/visitor encounter.

These reports typically included a line or two of simple statistics (percentages and numbers) along with the stories and testimonials of delighted hosts and guests. The statistics were neither backed by full reports nor verified by third parties.

To support their claims, Airbnb also commissioned studies from "embedded researchers" or "sympathetic research organizations" which used the data to paint a similarly positive image and claim that Airbnb had little or no negative effect on the housing market (Sperling 2013; Rosen et al. 2013; HR&A Advisors 2012). But without access to the raw data, one could not refute this reassuring portrait.

As a privately held for-profit corporation, Airbnb has not been required to disclose operational or financial data. The company's typical stance has been to release selected data, deny requests for independent review and fight attempts to require the submission of actual transaction records. Although a public stock offering – an Initial Public Offering or IPO – is expected, one critic has argued that "remaining private" is a tactical strategy that allows tech companies to minimize public scrutiny and maximize flexibility as they expand to scale (Slee 2016).

However, the most significant barrier to accessing data and public accountability has been the platform's ability to shelter behind Section 230 of the 1996 Communications Decency Act. This act famously gives online platforms legal immunity from posted content by explicitly stating that they not be treated as publisher or speaker. Airbnb also uses the First and Fourth Amendments to protect its data on the basis of privacy (disclosing the personal data of hosts) and protection from unreasonable search and seizure. The Stored Communications Act (SCA) offers platforms additional protection from disclosing confidential customer information without legal process.

Airbnb's refusal to make their data publicly available has given rise to alternate methods of accessing Airbnb data – both individual data scraping and third-party datasets – and to self-styled "data activists" such as Tom Slee and Murray Cox, who have scraped transaction data from the company website and provided independent analyses.[1] Slee, a critic of the sharing economy and author of *What's Yours is Mine*, has posted data on Airbnb's activity in 99 cities on his website. Cox, who began tracking Airbnb activity in his Brooklyn, New York, neighborhood, founded InsideAirbnb in 2016. In 2019, the platform had data and visualizations on over 80 cities worldwide. Cox provides information to and works with city officials and affordable housing organizations in the US and abroad. Cities, such as New York, San Francisco, Barcelona and Paris, have requested his help, and he maintains his website through payment from researchers, cities and hotel trades organizations. Self-described as "Airbnb's watchdog," Cox considers himself a housing activist who believes that housing is a human right, not a commodity (Carville 2019a, 3).

In contrast, the most widely used third-party data set, AirDNA (founded in 2015) is an investment tool that follows the performance of Airbnb listings worldwide and identifies the most profitable investment locations. Although Airbnb's transaction data was accurate up until the fourth quarter of 2015, Airbnb then altered the platform to make it impossible to distinguish bookings from blocked dates. Going forward, AirDNA developed a model to estimate occupancy rates and revenue (BJH Advisors 2016). Although AirDNA is technically independent of

Airbnb, as a business, AirDNA is dependent on the success of Airbnb and has been known to come to its defense in debates about the interpretation of data (Ferre-Sadurni 2018).[2]

To date, most local authorities and academic researchers, rely on third-party data provided by either AirDNA or Murray Cox's InsideAirbnb. However, these alternate sources of data are not perfect. Most are snapshots taken within a specific time frame rather than a continuous stream of data. For researchers trying to assess Airbnb activity in a given locality, the major constraint is that Airbnb's public-facing website does not provide host-specific information such as name, address and telephone number. This makes it difficult to identify illegal rentals and commercial operators. Researchers and third parties who have developed webscraping techniques to retrieve this data have resorted to estimating and modeling the missing information by extracting zip codes, using the number of user reviews, updates to host calendars, average length of stays and other spatial analytic techniques.

Airbnb has been quick to criticize studies that use third-party scraped data for overestimating transactions, failing to collect accurate occupancy or utilization rates, and using asking price rather than transaction price in their calculations (Coles et al. 2017). In response to these criticisms, NYC Comptroller Scott Stringer has aptly and succinctly replied: "Airbnb needs to stop distracting and release the raw data" (NYC Comptroller 2018b).

Assessment is also complicated by the fact that most of the empirical studies are, to varying degrees, the work of interested parties. In describing the studies in this chapter, we indicate – to the best of our knowledge – whether they were funded by, sponsored by or otherwise part of a known agenda. Some studies have been directly commissioned by the hotel and leisure industry and by unions and non-profit organizations as well as by Airbnb. To date, there are few independent and/or academic studies that focus directly on the impact on housing and communities.

Cities and data wars

Given these challenges, it is not surprising that empirical studies have been slow to appear.[3] It is also not surprising that some of the earliest and most systematic studies were initiated by local governments and affordable housing advocates to gather empirical data for policy purposes. We found that we could not discuss how cities responded to Airbnb and STRs without talking about the local struggles surrounding the data.

The emergence and rapid growth of STRs have made cities the battleground for opponents and proponents of STRs by virtue of their authority to control land use and housing and because they constitute the most immediate site for the governance of everyday life. The CEO of Host Compliance, a consulting company which helps city governments draft and enforce STR ordinances, has called Airbnb's bitter struggles with local authorities, "a city-by-city, block-by-block guerrilla war" in which the platform "fight[s] every one of these battles like it is the most important battle they have" (Ulrik Binzer, quoted in Martineau 2019a, 3).

While many large and small cities have become Airbnb battlegrounds, we have focused on four major US cities where Airbnb has a strong presence: New York, San Francisco, Los Angeles and Boston. These cities share certain characteristics that make the threat posed by STRs particularly acute:

- They are among the ten most expensive cities in the US with rising house and rent prices that make them increasingly unaffordable for the middle class
- They have diverse and thriving economies and, while they have benefitted from the exponential growth in urban tourism, tourism is not their major industry or defining characteristic
- The back-to-the-city movement has been particularly strong in these coastal cities, adding additional pressure to the housing market
- Unlike many US cities where homeownership remains the dominant form of housing tenure, the majority of residents are renters

In each of these cities, the rapid growth of Airbnb provoked a backlash that captured the attention of governmental, business and civic actors as well as some academics.

One of the first issues local authorities faced was that most Airbnb listings were illegal in terms of existing zoning restrictions and/or other laws protecting housing. By ignoring existing laws and norms – a hallmark of the aggressive platform disruptors – Airbnb undermined local governance. In this context, the ongoing attempt to assess the impact of Airbnb and STRs can be seen not only as part of the effort to forge viable policies to protect housing and neighborhoods but as a means to retain local control.

Whether the initial response was oppositional or accommodating, sooner or later the cities found they needed to regulate STRs, and to do so, they needed empirical data. This has led to what we refer to as data wars. The data wars have been characterized by empirical studies, often carried out by interested parties, presenting conflicting statistical and qualitative evidence; by political campaigns for and against legislation led by proponents and opponents; and through legal tussles to gain and/or deny access to data. These struggles have played out somewhat differently in each city depending on such factors as the nature of the housing stock, existing regulations and local politics.

New York City, tough on Airbnb

> We believe Airbnb vs. NYC is the defining fight of the sharing economy and some understanding of how the platform is being used will help clear up the laws as they change.
>
> *(Clampet 2014a)*

As Airbnb's second largest US market, a major tourist destination, and a "luxury city" experiencing a critical need for affordable housing, New York City (NYC) was a likely candidate to challenge Airbnb for access to data. Historically, NYC has been supportive and protective of its housing. According to Ellen and O'Flaherty, it has more subsidized housing, more rent regulation, greater local spending on housing and a more heavily regulated housing market than most other cities (2013, 307).

NYC is also a vertical city with distinctive housing stock. "It is the only major metropolitan area in which a majority of the housing units are located in buildings with five or more units" (Ellen and O'Flaherty 2013, 296). In 2009, 44 % of New Yorkers lived in a rental building with five plus units as compared to 34 % in Los Angeles, the second largest US city, and 19 % in Chicago. Looking at renter households, with the exception of Miami, NYC had the highest share of renter households – 68 % in 2016. Boston had 65 %, Los Angeles, 64.1 %, and San Francisco, 62.1 % (Zillow 2018).

NYC has laws governing rentals – "rent regulation" – as do Los Angeles and San Francisco. Given the nature of the typical housing stock, rent regulation covers buildings with six or more apartments built before 1974, together with units subsidized under other tax abatement programs. Approximately half of NYC's rental housing is protected by rent stabilization or rent control. Only San Francisco has a similarly high number of protected rental units.

Airbnb came to NYC in 2009. Shortly afterwards, New York State (NYS) amended its 1954 Multiple Dwelling Law (MDL) to clarify existing ambiguity about the occupancy of Class A multiple dwellings (three or more units) which constitute the majority of NYC's housing stock.[4] The amended law, which went into effect July 2011, stated that in Class A multiple dwellings, units could only be used for permanent residence. The law defined "resident" as a natural person or family (not a corporate entity) and "permanent" as 30 days or more. Although Airbnb lobbied against the bill which it felt was targeted at their business model, NYS argued that the impetus for revision – to stop unethical landlords from turning residential housing into illicit hotels – existed prior to Airbnb's arrival. The press noted that the revised ordinance still allowed Airbnb to offer genuine home-sharing – i.e., permanent residents could have a paying visitor for fewer than 30 days as long as they were present.

Airbnb basically ignored the MDL, neither warning hosts about the law nor culling illegal listings. Meanwhile its listings in NYC grew exponentially and by 2013, there was a backlash against what was now obvious: a majority of all Airbnb entire home/apartment listings were illegal as they were in apartment buildings of three or more units, a category which, as noted earlier, represents most of the city's buildings. Moreover, commercial hosts were using the platform for multiple listings. Enforcement began to pick up in 2011 as NYC's Office of Special Enforcement (OSE), issued 1897 violations for illegal conversions of residential buildings into hotels (Clampet 2013).

Media steps into the data gap. When NYS Attorney General Eric Schneiderman asked Airbnb for data so NYS could assess the situation and was told it was too much of a burden, Skift, an online media and information source for the travel industry, did a "data dive." It asked Connotate, a data extraction firm, to examine

Airbnb listings in NYC for January 2014. The results, published online by Skift in early 2014, showed that, despite Airbnb's claim that most hosts shared their home, less than 2 % of listings were for shared space; 66 % were for entire home/apartment, which in NYC meant that most of these listings were illegal (Clampet 2014a). Although the number of hosts with one listing (88 %) roughly tallied with what Airbnb had claimed, the 12 % with two or more unique listings accounted for 30 % of the total inventory on the site. Skift/Connotate also did an in-depth look at the top ten hosts with multiple units including one management company which listed 80 units. Skift commented:

> These are the hosts that Airbnb would rather not talk about, and the New York State Attorney General may like to have a chat with. They're the hosts that don't appear in Airbnb case studies or show up in marketing materials. . . . They don't fit the narrative of the sharing economy mainly because they operate on Airbnb like entrepreneurs.
>
> *(Clampet 2014b)*

The first major empirical study of Airbnb impact was initiated by Attorney General Schneiderman. Schneiderman subpoenaed Airbnb's transaction records in late 2013 for detailed transaction information and, after a long legal tussle, Airbnb shared anonymized data, without names or addresses. Airbnb acknowledged deleting some 2,000 transactions shortly before presenting the data to NYS and noted noncommittally that the deleted hosts represented "bad actors."

The resulting report presented a "snapshot of short-term rentals in NYC from January 1, 2010 through June 2, 2014" that radically differed from Airbnb's official picture of its activity (NYS AG 2014). Among the findings: 72 % of the STRs appeared to be in violation of the MDL. The report underlined the dominance of commercial hosts, conservatively defined as hosts with more than two unique units; it provided evidence of displacement of long-term rentals, measured by units booked for STRs for half the year or more; gave evidence of illegal hostels; and showed that the listings clustered in three gentrifying districts.

In an attempt to be more "transparent," Airbnb released data in December 2015 on NYC transactions for the previous year. In February 2015, however, Cox and Slee, who had independently compared their scraped data with the Airbnb set, wrote a report showing that Airbnb had scrubbed over 1,000 listings of potential commercial operators from the released data (Cox and Slee 2016). At first Airbnb denied the claim, then apologized, arguing that it had deleted listings to illustrate its policy of "One Host, One Home" and project more accurate figures going forward.

In July 2015, New York Communities for Change (NYCC) and Real Affordability For All (RAFA), two of the city's leading housing advocacy organizations, released a report lending additional support to the NYS Attorney General's findings (NYCC and RAFA 2015). The report showed that Airbnb listings consumed a significant share of the housing market in NYC's least affordable neighborhoods where the supply of affordable housing was already limited and where rents increased by more than the citywide average, raising the specter of gentrification.

In June 2016, two anti-Airbnb organizations – the Housing Conservation Coordinators and Mobilization For Youth (MFY) Legal Services – commissioned BJH Advisors to study the impact of Airbnb's STRs on the traditional rental market in NYC (BJH Advisors 2016). The study created a new category – Impact Listings – which required listings to meet three criteria: entire apartment/home, regular short-term and commercial. The rationale given for the conservative estimate was: "Impact Listings are likely to have the strongest effect on the residential market because given the three criteria it is extremely unlikely that hosts of Impact Listings live in the units they rent. This implies that these units have been removed from the residential rental market" (BJH Advisors 2016, 17).

The carefully designed study found that Airbnb listings continued to defy the MDL, that commercial use (defined by hosts with multiple listings and number of days per year available) was pervasive and that listings were disproportionately concentrated in a few neighborhoods in Manhattan and Brooklyn.

In October 2016, the NYS legislature passed tough new provisions to the NYS MDL and the NYC Building Code, which prohibited all forms of advertising of dwelling units in Class A multi-family buildings for any use other than permanent residence. The provisions authorized fines of up to $ 7,500 and turned the enforcement of illegal listings over to the NYC Mayor's Office of Special Enforcement (OSE). The intent was to fine Airbnb and other platforms that violated the MDL.

Airbnb criticized NYC for being beholden to the hotel unions and responded to the "advertising law" by filing lawsuits against both the city and the state, arguing that the platform was not responsible for content and that the law violated its constitutional rights. To the surprise of some, Airbnb settled out of court with NYC and NYS, with NYC agreeing to impose fines against site users – not platforms – and to focus on those operating illegal hotels. Airbnb also launched its conciliatory "One Host, One Home" policy in NYC in 2016, although the policy still ran afoul of the MDL.

Refusing to be completely stymied by legal tactics and legal gray areas, NYC amped up enforcement. Given Mayor de Blasio's focus on affordable housing, it was not surprising that Airbnb activity was on his radar; his administration dramatically increased the budget of the OSE and expanded from 11 to 48 the number of staff tracking down illegal hotels. The result has been continuing media coverage of particularly egregious commercial hosts, which in turn, has underlined the need for accurate data.

In response to Airbnb's claims that it was growing much faster in predominantly black neighborhoods than citywide, data activist and Airbnb watchdog, Murray Cox examined Airbnb's impact on NYC's 72 predominantly black neighborhoods, including a case study of Bedford-Stuyvesant (2017). Using a dataset from InsideAirbnb and facial recognition software and methodology similar to that used by researchers at Harvard Business School to racially code hosts (Edelman et al. 2017), Cox found that in NYC's 72 predominately black neighborhoods, hosts were five times more likely to be white; that the white hosts earned over three times as much total revenue as black hosts; and that displacement and disruption were more likely to affect black residents.

Adding to this ongoing controversy, two members of Airbnb's own data science team – their chief economist and the team manager – co-authored a paper with three New York University researchers which looked at Airbnb usage in NYC neighborhoods between 2011 and 2016 (Coles et al. 2017). The study compared the relative profitability of STRs to long-term rentals (the conversion incentive) and examined whether Airbnb listings concentrated or dispersed visitors overtime. It concluded that STRs were less profitable than commonly assumed and that Airbnb spread visitors to less central residential neighborhoods.

Meanwhile, research efforts and lobbying by all the interested parties increased as the likelihood of regulatory action peaked during the winter of 2017 and spring 2018.

The first study, by David Wachsmuth at McGill University's School of Urban Planning, was commissioned by the Hotel Trades Council and the AFL-CIO and was co-sponsored by several NYC community, housing and tenant advocacy organizations which lobbied against Airbnb. Wachsmuth et al. (2018) examined Airbnb activity in the NYC metropolitan region from September 2014 to August 2017 using AirDNA data and a "new spatial methodology" to locate listings. The study found that almost 90 % of entire home reservations were illegal under NYS law. It found evidence of "ghost hotels" (multiple rented rooms in a single apartment) and estimated the proportion of the increase in median long-term rent attributable to Airbnb activity by neighborhood. The report also described racialized effects, including the gentrification of predominantly black neighborhoods.

In April 2018, NYC Comptroller Scott Stringer's Office released a study of Airbnb's impact on the city's rents from 2009–2016 (NYC Comptroller 2018a). Using AirDNA data, the study found that Airbnb listings were correlated with rising rents citywide, particularly in some densely impacted neighborhoods. The study also estimated the monetary impact on New Yorkers in terms of the monthly increase in rent by neighborhood as well as the aggregate annual increase.

Airbnb launched a multipronged attack on the NYC Comptroller's report, calling it a "false report" and saying that the comptroller had gone after the company in cahoots with the hotel industry (Bredderman 2018). AirDNA sprang to Airbnb's defense, questioning the comptroller's methods and conclusions and stating that the comptroller did not purchase the public access data, did not ask for their advice and incorrectly interpreted the data (Ferre-Sadurni 2018). The main criticism – that NYC conflated listings with actual occupancy – was again at issue because Airbnb obscured the actual transaction data.

The release of the comptroller's report started "a seven-week, seven-figure television ad buy targeting the Democratic politician as an enemy of middle-class New Yorkers who earn extra cash with short-term sublets through the website" (Bredderman 2018). Comptroller Springer countered with a televised town hall meeting, hosted and paid for by anti-Airbnb groups. ShareBetter, a coalition of anti-Airbnb groups backed by the hotel industry, mailed the findings of the McGill

University Study and the NYC Comptroller's report to 100,000 households in zip codes with the densest Airbnb listings. In 2018, Airbnb was listed as one of the top ten biggest lobbying spenders in NYC (Lewis 2019).

The NYC Comptroller's report was used to support NYC's first effort to regulate Airbnb, the Airbnb disclosure law. The law was passed unanimously by the City Council in July 2018, signed by the mayor in August and went into effect in February 2019. Its intent was to make it easier for the city to crack down on illegal listings by requiring Airbnb and similar platforms to disclose host names, addresses and other transaction details to the city on a monthly basis. The law also established substantial fines for non-compliance – $ 1,500 per listing or the total amount of fees collected during the preceding year – if the platforms did not provide the requisite information.

Bloomberg News referred to the new ruling as "one of its biggest blows in the company's 10-year history" and predicted it would dramatically cut NYC's 52,000 Airbnb listings (Zaleski 2018). Airbnb blamed the city's powerful Hotel Trades Council for pressuring the city council to pass the legislation[5] then turned around and, together with HomeAway, sued NYC for violating its constitutional rights. In January 2019, a federal judge issued a temporary injunction on the NYC law, arguing that it was too broad but encouraging NYC to subpoena specific hosts. In February 2019, NYC issued a subpoena demanding information from Airbnb for over 17,000 apartment listings possibly being used as de-facto hotels. Mayor de Blasio called this an attempt to force Airbnb to "come clean about what they're actually doing in this city" (Martineau 2019b).

In January 2019, Wachsmuth et al. came out with a follow-up to their 2018 report. Publicized by the sponsoring anti-Airbnb groups, New York Communities for Change and Tenants PAC (2019), the report was a response to the court-ordered temporary injunction on NYC's Airbnb disclosure law and emphasized the costs of the injunction: more Airbnb listings, more commercial operators, greater rent increases and the loss of additional housing. The report estimated that, over the next year, as many as 10,800 additional residential units could be diverted for use as STRs.

Although the legal battle for access to data continues, NYC has scored several partial victories. Airbnb responded to NYC's February 2019 subpoena of over 17,000 listings by giving the city redacted data minus the necessary user-specific information. The city and Airbnb reached a court-ordered agreement that permitted NYC's OSE to request user-specific data for the 17,000 plus listings with the proviso that it do so within a one-year window and only if it could show relevance to an investigation (DeGregory 2019). Airbnb also agreed to share anonymized data on all listings between January 1, 2018, and February 18, 2019, that potentially violated NYS's housing ordinance, according to specific criteria listed in the subpoena, and in two stages: initially anonymized and, if warranted, user-specific (Martineau 2019b).

However, one cannot speak of more than a partial victory as judicial decisions throughout the country span a variety of outcomes. Moreover, the legal battles illustrate the exorbitant amount of time and effort required for the city to enforce its housing ordinance in the absence of user-specific data and platform accountability. Not every city could or would do what NYC does by way of enforcement and follow-through. The city's position is that Airbnb is simply being made to follow the rules and hopes to set a precedent for other cities that seek to regain municipal authority. Director of NYC's OSE, Christian Klossner, said of the rulings: "The recent decisions and court-ordered settlement prove that when the city sends a subpoena, short-term rental platforms have to turn over data" (McDonough 2019).

Airbnb has also attempted to end-run NYC, a tactic it has successfully used elsewhere, by initiating favorable legislation at the state level.[6] The platform co-authored a bill that would reform NYS occupancy laws to permit apartment rentals for fewer than 30 days as long as tenants register with the state. This effort failed when progressive Democrats took control of the state legislature.

At the same time, Airbnb has attempted to "make peace" with NYC before a public stock offering supposedly set for 2020. In May 2019, Airbnb agreed to ban listings of subsidized or rent-controlled housing in NYC. Airbnb also extended an invitation to meet with one of its most vocal detractors, data activist Murray Cox, who supplies the OSE monthly statistics detailing the types of listings, price and number by zip code, and who is seen as enabling NYC's tough stance. In a media account of the meeting, it seems that neither side was willing to compromise (Carville 2019b).

As of April 2020, Airbnb's lawsuit, which put NYC's data disclosure law under a preliminary injunction, has been temporarily put on hold, and Airbnb and NYC have begun to negotiate an agreement (Carville and Larson 2020). Whether or not this succeeds, there is pressure on Airbnb to settle its decade-long fight with NYC, as the city, with its strict regulations, vigorous enforcement and 55,000 listings (of which approximately two-thirds are illegal) stands in the way of a successful public stock offering.

San Francisco, Airbnb's "hometown"

Known for its spectacular setting and the iconic Golden Gate Bridge, its history as the center of the 1960s cultural revolution and as a liberal bastion, San Francisco has long been a popular destination for international tourism. Beginning in the mid-1990s, the city has been identified with the growing tech industry, becoming "a locational and metaphorical extension of Silicon Valley" (McNeill 2016, 494).[7] In the process, the city has become whiter, richer and more unequal.[8] Today San Francisco is the most expensive city in the US.

San Francisco's population of 884,000 is small compared to New York, ranking the city thirteenth among American cities. While skyscrapers and multi-story high rises dominate the skyline of NYC, San Francisco's skyline is characterized by a cluster of high rises in the central business district. In residential areas, long-standing zoning laws limit the height of buildings to 40 feet and restrict the number of units within a building to no more than three (Fisher 1962; Oatman-Stanford 2018).

According to the San Francisco Planning Department's 2017 Housing Report, 32 % of the city's housing stock consists of single family homes, 30 % of are "low density" (two to nine units) and 38 % are higher density (ten plus units), a distribution that has been relatively stable over the past five years (San Francisco Planning Department 2018). While 35 % of the city's residents are homeowners, the majority (65 %), are renters and of these, 60 % live in rent-controlled buildings. Even rent-controlled apartments have become unaffordable for households earning less than 80 % of median income (Brinklow 2018).[9]

While San Francisco's housing crisis is acute, it has been long in the making. In the face of rapid economic growth and job creation, zoning regulations, such as the limits placed on the height of buildings together with the slow rate of new construction, have contributed. Between 2012 and 2016, the San Francisco metropolitan area added 373,000 jobs but permitted the construction of only 58,000 new housing units (Clark 2017).

Not surprisingly, affordable housing and homelessness have been important political issues that gained increased attention with the rapid growth of Airbnb. Although Airbnb listings in the city grew exponentially from the start, under existing zoning laws, rentals for fewer than 30 days were considered commercial businesses and therefore not allowed in residential neighborhoods or buildings. Since these laws were widely ignored this meant that most STRs in the city were technically illegal.

Supported by media reports, city legislators began to hold forums about the "airbnbfication" of the city, but the scale of Airbnb's impact was hard to measure.[10] The only available data came from Airbnb's website and a 2012 study that Airbnb commissioned from HR&A Advisors, a consulting firm. This report cited Airbnb's "transformative benefits" claiming that the company had generated $ 56 million in direct and indirect spending in the past year and had distributed visitor spending throughout the city (HR&A Advisors 2012).

In short, there were no independent studies of Airbnb's effects on the city's housing market despite the rising rate of evictions and the complaints from local residents that dominated much of the political debate (Said 2014a). In an attempt to diffuse mounting criticism, Airbnb sponsored a study in 2014 by "a noted UC Berkeley professor and housing expert," Ken Rosen, which concluded that media reports of renters and landlords benefiting financially represented isolated cases and not the market as a whole (Airbnbcitizen 2014).[11] Tenants Together, a statewide organization for renter's rights, came to a different conclusion. They published a report claiming that "serial speculators," incentivized by Airbnb, were the driving force behind most of the Ellis Act evictions in the city (Kwong 2014; Tenants Together 2014).[12]

As the debate heated up, *The San Francisco Chronicle* published the first independent report in 2014, entitled "Airbnb's Impact on San Francisco" (Said 2014b). The report, which was based on an analysis commissioned from Connotate Inc. and used data scraped from Airbnb's website on May 19, 2014, found that most listings were for entire houses/apartments which appeared to be rented full-time.

While the majority of hosts had a single listing, 10 % had multiple listings and the top ten hosts controlled 5.2 % of all listings on the platform. Furthermore, the listings were concentrated in a few neighborhoods.

The *Chronicle* report provided the impetus for the city to act. In October 2014, six years after Airbnb had begun to operate in San Francisco, the Board of Supervisors voted to legalize and regulate STRs.[13] Although the legislation had been in the making for almost two years, it had run into a range of legal and policy issues (Said 2014a). The final version, the San Francisco "Airbnb Law," applied to all buildings with one or more residential units owned or rented by permanent residents – those living in their units for at least 275 days per year. It specified that owners of multi-unit buildings could only rent the unit in which they reside, and that although individual bedrooms could be rented, each must be listed separately. Eligible hosts (permanent city residents) had to register with the city's Planning Department, get liability insurance, pay transient occupancy tax and pledge to abide by the law. While there were no time limits for hosted units, un-hosted STRs were limited to 90 calendar days per year. Violations were subject to a daily fine that increased for repeat offenders. The law did not require platforms to track listings; instead it placed the responsibility upon the hosts.

Although it placed a few limits on Airbnb's activities, the law made Airbnb legal in the city. After the passage of the ordinance, Airbnb expressed its support: "The legislation that moved forward tonight will give regular people the right to share the home in which they live and make it fair to share in San Francisco . . . this vote was a great victory for San Franciscans" (Wohlsen 2014). Affordable housing advocates and long-time city residents, however, expressed their disappointment as several proposals that would have toughened the legislation had failed to pass. The law went into effect in February 2015. Responding to continued criticism from affordable housing advocates, the Board of Supervisors passed an amendment the following summer creating the Office of Short-Term Rentals (OSTR) to enforce the law,. A second amendment that would have limited STRs to 75 days instead of 90 days per year and that required Airbnb to file quarterly reports to the city failed to pass.

Without relevant data from Airbnb and by relying on hosts to self-report, the law was basically unenforceable. Responding to continued concerns about the adequacy of regulation, Supervisor David Campos commissioned a report from the Budget and Legislative Analyst to get a more accurate picture of Airbnb's impact on the city's long-term rental market. As measured by the low rate of host registrations (only 9.5 % had registered by May 2015), the supervisors felt that the law was being ignored, and that in order to move forward, they needed a systematic assessment.

Airbnb did not respond to the city's request for anonymized listings and booking data. Although Supervisor Campos wanted to subpoena the necessary data from Airbnb (Pershan 2015), the office of the Budget and Legislative Analyst decided to turn to third-party data and chose to work with InsideAirbnb's Murray Cox, who provided a December 2014 webscrape. The report was released in May 2015 (San Francisco Budget and Legislative Analyst 2015). To determine the extent to which Airbnb listings were removing housing units from the long-term rental market, the report distinguished between "casual hosts" (hosts who occasionally make their residence available for supplemental income) and "commercial hosts" (hosts who make entire units available "who probably do not live there and use it as a means of generating income"). Focusing on "commercial hosts" who were assumed to be those most responsible for removing units from the long-term rental market, the report estimated that almost a third of listings were commercial. These figures were particularly high in six neighborhoods.

Airbnb panned the report and released a memorandum threatening the city: it would lose the $ 416,000 a month in taxes that Airbnb was collecting from hosts if the city reduced the cap from 90 to 60 days. Ultimately the board was convinced that any meaningful law required that Airbnb hand over its data to the city for verification and enforcement (Carson 2015). Meanwhile affordable housing advocates, tenant and labor organizations, and local politicians who had lobbied for more rigorous regulation and enforcement turned to the ballot initiative to bypass the legislation.[14] They collected signatures to put Proposition F – the "Airbnb initiative" – on the November 2015 ballot. The measure proposed a more stringent limit of 75 nights per year, tightened provisions regarding hotel taxes and city codes, and mandated revenue reports to the city by both hosts and platforms every three months. One particularly controversial provision was that neighbors and other interested parties could initiate private action lawsuits if they suspected that the laws were being violated.

Proposition F was defeated (55 to 45) after an acrimonious struggle in which the proponents of the measure, who spent $ 1.5 million, were clearly outgunned by Airbnb, which spent over $ 8 million dollars on TV ads, lobbying, phone calls and the mobilization of hundreds of hosts who went door-to-door. Although it was defeated, the battle over proposition F galvanized the city and placed the issue of STRs front and center in the news for several months. San Franciscans also reelected Aron Peskin – a long-term housing and anti-Airbnb activist and former member of the Board of Supervisors – to the Board of Supervisors.

In May 2016, the Board of Supervisors submitted a follow-up report to assess changes in Airbnb activity since 2015 and to consider additional regulation and more effective enforcement (San Francisco Budget and Legislative Analyst 2016). Prior to completing the report, Airbnb and Tripadvisor had provided listing data to the office of the Budget and Legislative Analyst. While Airbnb's data indicated multiple listings for some hosts, the data did not include needed information on frequency of bookings or number of registered hosts; to get better data they had to go back to InsideAirbnb's webscrapes.

The new report showed an overall increase in listings with a more rapid increase in the neighborhoods with previously high numbers of listings. Although the data indicated a number of hosts with multiple listings, the analysis could not identify their exact number. And although there was a city-wide increase in the number of listings, the majority of listings were concentrated in the six neighborhoods identified in 2014. In short, the study indicated that the Airbnb Law had little effect on reining in Airbnb activity in San Francisco.

In response to these findings, the Board of Supervisors, now strengthened by a progressive majority, voted unanimously to toughen the law in June 2016. They demanded that Airbnb and other platforms only publish listings that included an official registration number. Sites that did not comply could face fines of up to $ 1,000 daily. Airbnb and HomeAway responded by suing the city, claiming the law violated the Communications Decency Act, Section 230. Following a year-long legal battle and three-month court-ordered mediation, Airbnb and HomeAway settled with the city in May 2017.

The final agreement was said to represent a significant victory for the city. It made the platforms responsible for registration and enforcement as well as for providing the city with the listing id, claimed registration number and expiration date, and the zip code of hosts on a monthly basis. However, the platforms do not provide precise addresses. To ensure compliance, the platforms are required to submit a monthly affidavit verifying that all hosts are registered with the city and are required to deactivate listings found in violation. To audit this report, the city makes use of monthly scraped data from InsideAirbnb.

Eligible hosts have to get a business license, register their unit with the city and take out $ 500,000 of liability insurance. Existing hosts were given a 240-day window during which Airbnb would help them register. Rather than having to register in person, new hosts were given the option of sending their details to Airbnb to forward to the city. Hosts must provide quarterly reports of rental activity to the OSTR.

After a decade of legal wrangling, San Francisco became the first city to succeed in getting Airbnb to release limited transaction data. The law also requires the platform to participate in registration through a pass-through model and to remove the illegal listings identified by the city. Airbnb played down the significance of these concessions, taking pains to emphasize that the company was interested in forging agreements with cities worldwide (Said 2017). Chris Lehane, Airbnb's policy chief, even expressed satisfaction with the agreement: "We're incredibly proud to be a San Francisco company. This company could not have been founded in any other city. The energy and the vision and the creativity that exists in San Francisco helped create the big idea that became Airbnb" (Lehane as quoted in Carson 2017). After all San Francisco was Airbnb's hometown.

The immediate effect of the agreement was that Airbnb listings in San Francisco dropped by half, from roughly 8,900 listings to 4,000. In an interview on the local CBS station, Kevin Guy, director of the OSTR noted: "That's a substantial number that represents a real dramatic shift" (CBS SF BayArea 2018) The city also began to show that it was serious about enforcement and examples of serial violators were publicized in the media (Said 2018). In the words of one journalist: "While the city drew a hefty amount of criticism for letting Airbnb take over our rental market fairly un-regulated for its first few years, it appears that San Francisco's now making up for lost time" (Sawyer 2018).

At the same time, an online long-term rental service, HotPads, reported that the number of new long-term rental units on the market in San Francisco jumped six-fold in the week after the new law was implemented, but returned to normal levels soon thereafter as the new units were quickly absorbed. According to Joshua Clark, HotPads economist, "San Francisco has struggled with a housing shortage for a long time now . . . and even with a spike in new rental listings, we aren't seeing a lasting change in overall on-market rental inventory levels, likely because there continues to be strong demand for rentals in the city" (quoted in Thompson 2018).

In a 2018 report to the Board of Supervisor's Government Audit and oversight Committee, the OSTR reported statistics on the office's activities to date. The report stated that the office had focused its enforcement efforts on "high volume hosts with multiple listings and rentals with quality of life impact for neighbors," that there had been a significant increase in applications for short-term rental permits and that a significant number had been rejected.

While the San Francisco story has been widely hailed as a success, tenant rights advocates remain cautious as the agreement does not allow city regulators access to Airbnb's enormous data source. The city must still rely on self-reporting by the platforms and by the hosts to make sure that they are following the law. As long as the tech industry can hide behind laws such as Section 230 that protect their source of power, which is data, this may be as good as it gets.

Los Angeles, reluctant regulator

For urbanists, Los Angeles (LA) has been the prime example of the postmodern city, a decentralized sprawl of single-family suburban development and congested freeways, a testament to mid-twentieth century auto culture. For visitors, it is a gateway city which welcomed 50 million tourists in 2018 and will host the Summer Olympics in 2028. It is also the home of Hollywood and the entertainment capital of the world, where one in every six persons works in the creative industries. LA overtook NYC as Airbnb's largest US market in 2018, and along with NYC, it is the only US city that ranks in the top ten Airbnb listings worldwide (L.A. Biz 2018).

LA is also one of the costliest cities in the US as well as the city with the second largest homeless population after NYC. Lack of affordable housing has been a long-term challenge for the city, reflected in the high cost of homes and rents. And although rising rents and stagnating wages are a nationwide issue, LA seems to have had a more intransigent problem, as witnessed by relatively lower homeownership rates and relatively more households that rent (Chiland 2018a).

Over time, LA has increasingly become a city of apartments and renters. In 2018, the city had the third highest share of renter households among US cities, closely following behind NYC and San Francisco, with 64.1 % of households renting (Zillow 2018). LA's rental vacancy rate of 2.7 % is among the lowest of any major metropolitan area in the US while its rents are among the highest. In 2017, 58 % of LA renters were "rent-burdened," spending 30 % or more of household income on rent, and half of them were "severely burdened," spending over 50 % of income on rent (Chiland 2017). The financial crisis of 2008 contributed to the present situation by adding 100,000 former homeowners to an already stressed rental market (Ellen and O'Flaherty 2013, 296; Lee 2016).

Outside of high-rise areas such as the downtown, Century City, and Warner Center among others, LA is commonly characterized as a city of single-family homes, of "ranch houses and Craftsman bungalows" (Chiland 2018b). LA initiated land-use zoning early in the twentieth century, to separate residential and industrial areas, and in the following decades tightened height, density, parking and lot restrictions to give precedence to homeowners (Whittemore 2012). On a listing of "pricey cities" by their share of single-family housing, 57 % of LA residential properties were single-family, compared to 49 % for San Francisco, 14 % for Boston and 1 % for Manhattan (Rosenberg 2018).

Discussing the Trump administration's policy shift – from integrating low-income housing into high-income neighborhoods to relaxing restrictive zoning codes to make it easier and less costly to build new housing – Ben Carson, Secretary of the Department of Housing and Urban Development (HUD), blamed the LA housing crisis on the strict zoning that created its single-family suburban neighborhoods and continues to stymie development (Kusisto 2018). Almost half of all developable land in the city is restricted to single-family homes (Chiland 2018b). Responding to changing HUD policy directives and its own affordability crisis, LA passed a law in January 2017 making it easier for homeowners to build granny flats or second units on their property.[15]

Like NYC and San Francisco, LA has a rent stabilization ordinance that covers all units with two or more apartments built before 1978. This includes mobile homes and hotels and motels if occupied by the same tenant for 30 plus days (Ellen and O'Flaherty 2013). The ordinance requires that units be registered, regulates rent increases and lists legal reasons for eviction. A California state law, the 1985 Ellis Act, allows landlords to evict tenants in rent-controlled units if they are planning to "go out of the rental business" (Tenants Together 2014). The city's rent-stabilized housing stock is the second largest in the US and represents 82 % of all rental units.

Thus, the stage was set for potential conflict as Airbnb and STRs became a widespread phenomenon in LA between 2009 and 2014. By 2018, Airbnb listings in LA had surpassed the number of listings in NYC. Despite the fact that an Airbnb presence was illegal in low-density residential areas and that converting a rental apartment into a business was against the terms of most residential leases, Airbnb provided new incentives for conversions, both legal and illegal, by owners of multi-family buildings. Frequently noted in the local media, neighborhoods such as Venice and Silver Lake were up in arms about the conversions.[16] Over the course of several years, there were heated discussions about the booming short-term rental market as anecdotal and empirical evidence began to document the negative impact on housing and as residents formed groups to protect their housing and neighborhoods.

City officials and advocates of affordable housing – organizations such as Los Angeles Alliance for a New Economy (LAANE) – were among the early critics who, along with the hotel industry and hotel workers union, called for a level playing field. Like NYC and San Francisco, LA was home to a well-organized and politically influential labor movement, but the struggle over Proposition F in San Francisco had shown opponents how much Airbnb was willing to invest in fighting regulation. Moreover, as they had done in San Francisco, Airbnb was busy mobilizing its host community. As Chris Lehane, head of Airbnb's global policy, said:

> If you just look at the numbers – the size, depth and breadth of our community – it's 100,000 plus in L.A. and growing, growing very quickly. . . . It's a real constituency. There is a real Airbnb/homesharing voter bloc.
> *(Lehane quoted in Zahniser 2017, 4)*

Airbnb initiated talks with Mayor Eric Garcetti in late 2014, as it had done in other cities, whetting the city's appetite by proposing to collect Transient Occupancy Tax (TOT) for STRs. Airbnb promoted such agreements, which they refer to as Voluntary Collection Agreements (VCAs), because they knew that cities were hungry for revenue and because they saw these agreements as a step towards legalization. LA, which had been particularly hit by the economic recession, faced a continuing "structural deficit" with high pension costs consuming funds for public services and new constraints in the form of financial commitments and forfeited revenue. The city was looking for new sources of funding (Zahniser 2017).

In his 2015 State of the City address, Mayor Garcetti spoke favorably about a proposal to collect the TOT and said he would use some of the tax revenue to build affordable housing (Bergman 2015). However, not everyone favored this plan. During the summer of 2015, the LA City Council voted to hold off negotiating the tax agreement arguing that a TOT would put "the wagon before the horse" and that the budget committee first needed to draft a more comprehensive plan for regulating homesharing platforms. Thus began several years of debate and discussion during which there was intensive lobbying by Airbnb. The platform spent approximately $ 1.3 million on lobbying between 2014 and 2018.

In the interim, the city, which was anxious to collect the occupancy tax (TOT) while discussion about regulation continued, reached a three-year agreement with Airbnb to collect a 14 % TOT on STRs for stays of 30 days or fewer, effective August 1, 2016. Although some headlines proclaimed that LA was "one step closer to regulation," the agreement was to be a trial run.[17]

Meanwhile, empirical data began to appear. The first major empirical report on the impact of STRs on LA's housing market was sponsored by LAANE, a well-known advocacy organization and leader of LA's progressive movement, and written by Roy Samaan. Using data scraped from Airbnb's website, Samaan gives a "snapshot" of Airbnb activity in LA on October 17, 2014 (2015a).[18] The study undermined several of Airbnb claims, finding that the platform significantly understated the size and scope of its offerings; there was significant commercial activity as well as evidence of the conversion of rent-controlled apartments into hotels. As was the case with NYC and San Francisco, the report also found that listings were concentrated in several of the most popular neighborhoods and that the density of listings was associated with higher median rents and lower vacancy rates.

Venice, the neighborhood with the highest concentration of Airbnb listings in 2014, was an epicenter for this type of activity, and the LAANE report gave several illustrative examples of Airbnb incentivizing conversion. In a sales brochure for the Morrison Apartments – a 21-unit building covered by rent stabilization – the broker, Coldwell Banker Commercial, suggests that a prospective owner could double net revenue by converting the building into Airbnb units. The report also documents the gradual conversion of an historic Venice apartment building, the Waldorf, into a *de facto* hotel as long-term residents leave and the owner shifts apartments to STRs (Samaan 2015a, 16–18).[19] Overall, the study concluded that Airbnb exacerbated LA's lack of affordable rentals (Samaan 2015a).

In a follow-up study five months later, Samaan (2015b) used publicly accessible sources to look at a broad range of STR operators along with Airbnb, a total of 19 platforms. The report found that the short-term rental industry was more than twice as large as the earlier March estimate and that Airbnb's short-term rental listings, which represented 65 % of all short-term rental listings in LA, had increased by 32 % since March 2015. Moreover, commercialized activity (professional landlords) had grown even though Airbnb had responded to media reports and local protests by removing some of the largest "bad actors." The report concluded that STRs negated LA's attempts to create new housing by removing the equivalent of two-thirds of new construction over a four-year period.

Airbnb responded to the LAANE report with a study that claimed to be a collaboration between its data scientists and members of the UCLA Luskin School of Public Affairs, namely Paavo Monkkonen. The report found that STRs made up only a small share of the region's housing inventory and that it did not incentivize conversion from long-term to short-term rental. In an introduction to the report, Monkkonen argues that the focus on Airbnb's impact distracts us from other more important causes of the affordability crisis.

Commenting on this report, the L.A. Times pointed out that "Airbnb may have misrepresented the study" by insinuating that it was a UCLA study. Monkkonen, in an interview with the L.A. Times, added that he neither conducted the study nor worked on the data but merely wrote an introduction (Hiltzik 2015). In an exchange between Samaan, the author of the LAANE report and Airbnb, Samaan said: "I would caution against taking at face value a company study based on data no one can see." The article concluded: "None of this will make the jobs of city planners or lawmakers any easier as they ponder how to regulate the striking expansion of short-term rentals" (Hiltzik 2015).

In February 2016, Dayne Lee, at the Harvard Law School, published a thorough descriptive analysis of Airbnb's impact on LA's affordable housing market, collecting and synthesizing the existing legal, statistical and secondary sources including the 2015 LAANE reports. Lee concluded that Airbnb contributed to an increase in rents in neighborhoods where listings were dense, substantially reduced the aggregate supply of housing stock and incentivized illegal conversions as well as the "hotelization" of entire buildings. Lee also suggested that Airbnb activity was correlated with gentrification, residential segregation and the displacement of low-income and minority tenants. The net effect was a citywide reduction in affordable housing (Lee 2016).

Lee's study illustrates the close relationship of research to impending regulatory policy. Based on his findings, Lee questioned Mayor Garcetti's proposed TOT agreement with Airbnb. The Mayor proposed to levy a 14 % occupancy tax on STRs and use the projected $ 5 million annual revenue to build affordable housing (Bergman 2015). Lee showed that the projected revenue would fund only 16 affordable units whereas Airbnb rentals had removed 7,316 units; it also did not address the effects of gentrification or rent increase (Lee 2016, 245).

One of the sticking points in the city council's several years of effort to draft regulations was the number of rental days per year – the "cap" on STRs. Airbnb was opposed to any cap so as to maximize the earnings potential of hosts. Affordable housing advocates initially suggested 60 days to minimize the incentive to switch rentals from long-term to short-term and the city planners initially proposed 90 days, but the mayor's appointed Planning Commission chose a 180-day cap.

Responding to the heated debate over the "cap," InsideAirbnb's Murray Cox issued a report in August 2016 entitled "Airbnb vs Rent: City of Los Angeles." Examining Airbnb listings by neighborhood, he demonstrated that it took an average of only 83 nights to earn more on Airbnb than renting out long-term for one year. Concluding that the proposed 180-day cap would provide a significant financial incentive to shift rental units from long-term to short-term, he argued for "a complete ban on entire home rentals or a low cap combined with data sharing and platform accountability" (Cox 2016).

Airbnb weighed in, citing the potential impact of regulation on the city's tax revenue. In the spring of 2017, after the city comptroller cautioned that the city could face a deficit of $ 224 million and before the mayor released his budget for the 2018 fiscal year, Airbnb wrote to city officials estimating the effect of each potential cap on tax revenue. If the bill capped rentals at 180 days per year, the city would lose $ 15 million of the expected $ 37 million in occupancy taxes; if the cap were 60 days, it would lose $ 24 million annually (Reyes 2017a). In early December 2018, shortly before regulations were passed, Airbnb announced that it had remitted more than $ 100 million in transient occupancy tax to the city between August 2016 and December 2018, revenue that went into the city's general fund to help cover the cost of services, such as street repair and trash removal, as well as $ 5 million put aside for affordable housing for the homeless (Sentinel News Service 2018). In other words, there was significant political "pressure to adopt looser regulations to avoid hurting the city's bottom line" (Reyes 2017b).

After three years of deliberation and many public meetings, the Los Angeles City Council finally passed an Airbnb ordinance in December 2018, legalizing and regulating STRs (LA Short-Term Rental Ordinance 2018). The ordinance permits STRs *only* in a primary residence where the host lives for at least six months per year and forbids STRs in any rent-stabilized unit or accessory dwellings built after January 2017. However, it caps the rentals at 120 days per year and provides for extended homesharing (any resident who has been registered for at least six months and has been issued no more than one citation in three years can apply to rent for all 365 days). Hosts are required to register with the LA City Planning Department and pay a registration fee. The ordinance makes Airbnb and other platforms responsible for keeping track of occupancy and registration and for providing transaction information (name, location, number of days) on a monthly basis. It also subjects both platforms and hosts to fines – $ 1000 per day for platforms and $ 500 per day for hosts – for failing to require registration numbers on ads or refusing to submit host data. Because the TOT remained in effect, there was no mention of taxes.

In the aftermath of the law's passage, media headlines offered alternate readings: some called it a win for hosts and Airbnb, while others saw it as "cracking down" on the short-term rental market in LA. Mike Bonin, the councilmember who co-introduced the bill, spoke of it as a compromise in a bitter struggle in one of the world's largest short-term rental markets. He said that while it "doesn't satisfy anybody 100 percent," the regulations tried to strike a balance between good and bad STRs – to accommodate hosts who "share their homes to make their ends meet" and punish "rogue hotel operators who are robbing the residents of this city of rental housing, making gentrification worse and making the affordable housing crisis worse" (Nota 2018).

The ordinance took effect July 1, 2019, but the city postponed enforcement until November 1. During the intervening period, Airbnb continued to lobby. There was a last minute attempt to amend the law to allow residents to host in rent-stabilized apartments.[20] The city council considered a second ordinance supported by Airbnb, to allow STRs in second homes, referred to as "vacation rentals." And, there were other complications related to enforceability under the Coastal Act.

A few months later, there was controversy about the effect of the ordinance. While the city cited a significant drop in the number of listings, others argued that the city was not enforcing the ordinance. A hotel industry study indicated that Airbnb listings in LA had increased from 2018 to 2019 (CBRE 2020). A report by David Wachsmuth at McGill University, sponsored by anti-Airbnb supporters, noted that the decrease was most likely a result of Airbnb's removing blacklisted rent-stabilized units from a list supplied by the city, and that the units removed "were no more likely to be in violation of the principal residence regulations than the ones which remained on the platform." This suggested that the targeted removals were "disproportionately actual homes sharing operations while commercial operators violating the City's regulations have by and large remained active on the platform" (Wachsmuth 2019).

It seems that LA's reluctance to act is in part driven by the need for tax revenue. However, a potentially equal and opposing driver may be the city's need to house its enormous homeless population and protect its housing from conversion or loss. As is the case elsewhere, nothing is set in stone: Airbnb and other platforms may present legal challenges, intensive lobbying will persist and the Airbnb law will likely be reviewed within six months to a year to fine-tune its operation.

Boston, an Airbnb frontier plays catch-up

Boston, one of the most historically significant US cities and the center of a dynamic metropolitan area, is home to major universities, medical research and a thriving technology sector. It is also the state capital of Massachusetts and one of the country's top ten tourist destinations. On the city's website, Mayor Martin Walsh states that what distinguishes Boston is not its skyline but "its proud, vibrant neighborhoods." Boston's downtown is a mix of high-rise and low masonry buildings; the diverse housing stock in residential neighborhoods includes the triple-decker – a style of housing dating from the nineteenth century and found throughout New England.

As in San Francisco, employment and population growth have coincided with a lagging housing supply, making Boston one of the most expensive large American cities. The city ranks fourth after San Francisco, New York and Los Angeles. Like San Francisco, New York and Los Angeles, Boston is a city of renters. In 2017, only 35.2 % of the population lived in owner-occupied units whereas 65 % were renters (Acitelli 2019; Zillow 2018). According to the Greater Boston Housing Report Card (Bluestone and Hussey 2017), the average rent in the city's central neighborhoods increased 55 % between 2009 and 2017. In 2015, only 2.6 % of apartments were vacant (Logan 2015).

Unlike San Francisco and NYC, Boston does not have rent control laws; Massachusetts outlawed rent control in a 1994 referendum. However, the 1994 Massachusetts law requires property owners who do not occupy their unit and wish to rent to register with the city annually and pay a registration fee. If a property is rented to four or more unrelated persons, the landlord must get a lodging house license, register as a business and pay taxes. To insure they are up to code, all rental properties are subject to inspections by the city's Inspectional Services Department (ISD) every five years.

Airbnb first offered STRs in Boston in 2009 and listings grew rapidly. As was the case in other cities, the Boston Zoning Code made Airbnb illegal in most residential neighborhoods (Jimenez 2017). Compared to our other cities Boston has been slow to respond to Airbnb and has moved forward cautiously. There was a general feeling that existing rental regulations would cover STRs. Despite the facts that the Boston's Airbnb listings had increased by 63 % between July 2013 and July 2014 (Teitell 2014), that most listings violated existing zoning laws, and that multi-unit rentals did not register and pay hotel taxes as required, in July 2014 the city instructed the ISD not to fine residents who rent short-term (Vaccaro 2014).

Beginning in 2014, City Councilor La Mattina, who represented East Boston and North End, neighborhoods where Airbnb had a strong presence, began to call for a council hearing on STRs but without success (Annear 2014). In August 2015, the *Boston Globe*, using third-party data, reported that while 85 % of Airbnb hosts listed a single property, 15 % listed two or more properties, and quoted Councilor La Mattina's concern that "investors [are] buying up properties so they can use them for Airbnb" (Rocheleau 2015).

Still, it took another year for the city council to finally hold a hearing. Following a contentious debate, the council decided to "proceed with utter caution" (Herndon 2016). While city officials continued to study the issue, two economists from the University of Massachusetts, Boston, undertook an independent empirical investigation "on the short-term effects of the growth of Airbnb in Boston neighborhoods on the rental market" (Horn and Merante 2017, 14). One of the earliest empirical studies in the US, this carefully designed study examined the impact of Airbnb on rents and house prices in Boston between September 2014 and January 2016. It found that Airbnb directly impacted asking prices for long-term rentals and decreased the supply of residential housing, an impact that was more pronounced in census tracts with the highest percentage of listings. As in other cities, Horn and Merante found that while commercial operators were the minority (less than one-fifth of all hosts), they controlled almost half of Airbnb listings.

In an earlier working paper which the city council consulted in their deliberations, the researchers suggested that should the growth of Airbnb continue at the current annual rate of 24 %, the increase in the asking rent would more than double by 2019; they concluded by urging policy makers to respond by regulating and taxing STRs (Merante and Horn 2016, 22). In short, the Boston City Council had access to solid empirical data from an independent academic source.

Concerned about the city's slow response, Community Labor United, a coalition of grassroots groups and labor unions, undertook a modest study to investigate the prevalence and growth of commercial STRs in Boston (Jimenez 2017). The report, which used data from Tom Slee's website, focused on commercial STRs defined as "whole unit rentals not used as a primary residence" and found that although commercial hosts represented the minority of hosts, they controlled almost one-third of all listings, almost half of the total revenue, and were concentrated in specific neighborhoods.

Citing previous comparative data from AirDNA, the report also indicated that financial incentives to use properties as STRs were particularly strong in Boston. This was likely due to the lack of regulation, a factor noted by investor guides such as AirDNA. Given the unregulated environment and past growth rates, the report suggests that the number of commercial operators will continue to grow in the future and concludes by urging the city to regulate STRs and enforce regulation.

In February 2018, the Alliance of Downtown Civic Organizations (ADCO), a coalition of nine civic downtown organizations representing 20 % of the city's population, released a detailed report on the impact of Airbnb and other STR platforms in the city (ADCO 2018a, 2018b, 2018c). Since its founding in 2014, ADCO had raised concerns about the rapid increase of commercial STRs, particularly in the downtown neighborhoods they represented.

Using data from tomslee.com, ADCO detailed the rapid growth of Airbnb listings between the fourth quarter of 2015 and the second quarter of 2016. This growth outpaced other cities during the same period and was considerably higher in popular downtown neighborhoods where listings more than doubled. Almost two-thirds of all listings were for entire homes/apartments and most of these were defined as "investor controlled." The report also noted that the share of investor-controlled listings were considerably higher than in NYC and San Francisco.

These studies, together with the lobbying of anti-Airbnb groups, were instrumental in the city council's decision to finally regulate Airbnb and other home-sharing platforms. After three years of deliberation and several proposals, the city council voted 11 to 2 to regulate STRs on June 2, 2018. Mayor Walsh signed the new law two weeks later stating that his goal "has always been to responsibly incorporate the growth of the home-share industry . . . by striking a fair balance between preserving housing while still allowing Bostonians to benefit from this new industry" (City of Boston 2018a).

To accommodate the city's distinctive housing stock, the Boston Airbnb law identifies three types of units which can be legally rented on a short-term basis: limited share units (private rooms in the owner's primary residence when the owner is present); homeshare units (whole units available for an STR at the primary residence where the owner resides at least nine months of the year); and owner-adjacent units (an owner-occupied two- or three-family building, in which the owner lists a single secondary unit as a short-term rental). The new law bans all renters and investment owners (owners of units they do not reside in) from STRs.

Like the San Francisco law, the Boston law regulates both hosts and platforms. Eligible hosts must register with the city and pay an annual registration fee. They must include their registration number on platform listings and post the number in their unit. The law makes the ISD responsible for maintaining a database of all registered hosts and specifies that hosts who fail to register will face a daily fine. In addition, hosts must notify neighbors within 300 feet about hosting. The law also makes Airbnb and other platforms accountable for listing registration numbers, providing a monthly report of all listings to the ISD which includes location, type of listing, registration number and occupancy data. Platforms which illegally list hosts are subject to a fine of $ 300 per night (City of Boston 2018b).

According to City Councilor Michelle Wu, who was instrumental in leading the fight for regulation and who was subjected to personal attacks from Airbnb and its supporters, the ordinance would likely return between 2,500 to 4,000 units to the residential housing stock, relieve some of the pressure on housing prices and increase supply (Enwemeka 2019).

In November 2018, Airbnb responded to the Boston law by suing the city in federal court. It called the new regulation "draconian" and claimed that the provision that required the platform to police listings and pay fines violated state and federal law. Although the new ordinance went into effect January 1, 2019, implementation remained partial pending the outcome of the lawsuit.

In early May 2019, a US District judge ruled to block the city from requiring that Airbnb and other platforms provide information on the number of days each month the rental was occupied, but upheld the provisions regarding registration, the eligibility of hosts and the city's right to impose a $ 300/per day fine on illegal listings. Airbnb responded that the judge should have gone further in blocking the ordinance (Fox 2019).

In August 2019, the City of Boston and Airbnb reached an agreement that required hosts to enter registration numbers on the website or be removed. Airbnb agreed to share some data with the city: host identity, registration number, URL, type of rental unit and zip code (Enwemeka 2019). Both Mayor Walsh and Airbnb, as they had in San Francisco, expressed satisfaction with the agreement. Immediately following enactment of the law in January 2020, the number of listings on Airbnb's website dropped one-third from 5,500 in December of 2019 to 3,780. At the same time 1,978 people attempted to register with the ISD. ADCO's Ford Cavallari cautioned that this would not be the end of the story as "determined operators who know how profitable short-term rentals can be will keep seeking ways to quietly continue" (quoted in Cotter 2020). An analysis by ADCO indicates that the overwhelming majority of the new listings were corporate operators with multiple listings, who had been taking advantage of a loophole in the ordinance exempting hospital and executive stays.

In December 2018, Massachusetts passed a statewide law to tax and regulate Airbnb and other STRs. The law, which had been in the making for two years, went into effect July 1, 2019. Strongly opposed by Airbnb, it mandated a minimum of 5.7 % tax on STRs (cities and towns can add an additional tax) and required that hosts who rent more than 14 days a year must register with the state STR registry and obtain $ 1 million in liability insurance. Mayor Walsh welcomed the law as an "additional complementary tool" (Enwemeka 2019) and City Councilor Wu noted that the legislation would "bolster what the city is trying to do" (Lane 2018).

Slow to get on the regulatory bandwagon, the Boston STR market has been noticeably investor driven. When Boston finally regulated STRs in 2019, it had the advantage of being the latecomer, able to learn from the victories and defeats of other cities. The city tried to emulate San Francisco's "success." But although the Boston ordinance specifically bans renters from subletting for STRs and investors from listing on Airbnb, investors have been able to take advantage of loopholes in the law.

Cities as battlegrounds

As can be seen, the struggles to assess Airbnb's impact on housing and neighborhoods and to draft effective regulatory policies have played out somewhat differently in each city.

Airbnb posed a particular threat to NYC's high-rise housing stock. An existing NYS housing ordinance prohibiting STRs in multiple dwelling units, meant that Airbnb's arrival raised early alarms and the state quickly authorized a study to gather empirical data. NYC's Disclosure Law, currently blocked by a court injunction, requires platforms to provide the transaction data needed to enforce the city's housing regulations and defend its housing, much of which is rent-stabilized or rent-controlled. Unlike other cities, NYC has not semi-legalized STRs by entering into tax agreements. The strong presence of hotel industry lobbies reinforced by affordable housing organizations and the city's current political administration has contributed to NYC's tough stance on regulation and enforcement. All stakeholders, however, are under pressure. As many have noted, coming to an agreement with NYC is crucial for Airbnb's forthcoming public stock offering.

As Airbnb's hometown, San Francisco found itself caught between tech-friendly politicians and lobbies and its socially conscious constituents and activist history. Although the city's acute housing pressure raised early awareness of Airbnb's effects on housing, it still took several years for the city to act. When Airbnb challenged the city's regulation, the court ordered both sides to negotiate an agreement. Ultimately both sides made concessions: in return for legalizing STRs, Airbnb and other platforms agreed to provide some data to city authorities and monitor compliance on their platforms. Frequently cited as a success, Airbnb gained political and social cachet by cooperating with its hometown.

Although a progressive city with a strong labor movement, LA had been hard hit by the economic recession. Looking for needed revenue, the city first let Airbnb in the door by making an interim agreement to collect transient occupancy taxes. When LA finally passed an Airbnb ordinance in 2019, it was more lenient than similar regulations in San Francisco and Boston, capping STRs at a generous 120 days per year, with a liberal exemption for residents in good standing. Enforcement has been slow and problematic, due in part to the importance of Airbnb's tax revenue to the city's bottom line.

Boston was a latecomer in recognizing that Airbnb and STRs posed a threat to the city's housing and its neighborhoods. Late to regulate, the city has become a frontier for investors and commercial operators. By the time the city began to seriously address regulation, commercial operators already had a significant presence, greater than in New York or San Francisco. Moreover, Boston's Airbnb's listings per population were among the highest in the world. The city's belated response was to legalize STRs with a regulatory framework requiring data and platform compliance. Although the regulation bans investors, the 21-plus day loophole provides a back door.

These city narratives are not conclusive. Reports from numerous cities show that the processes of regulation and implementation are prolonged by seeking agreements as well as by legal challenges and by the difficulties of enforcement (Martineau 2019a). Airbnb has used a variety of strategies to gain legal status and block demands for accountability and information. They have whet the appetite of cities by offering to collect local occupancy taxes, agreeing to participate in some online regulation such as monitoring listings and, in a few cases, agreeing to disclosure clauses, although the reliability and completeness of the data is in question. Moreover, Airbnb's litigious reputation intimidates local authorities and results in long, costly legal battles. When stymied at the city level, Airbnb has pursued favorable legislation at the state level as in New York, Tennessee and Texas.

This brings us back to the issue of data. Although several data-sharing requirements have been upheld in the courts, at the time of this writing Airbnb has not given authorities in any city the data they need to easily and efficiently monitor and enforce regulations or study impact. In Pasquale's terms, cities are still dealing with a "black box" (2015).

San Francisco, often referred to as the best-case scenario for platform accountability, illustrates some of the continuing difficulties. By institutionalizing STRs, the platform has created an incentive for hosts to circumvent regulation. After San Francisco's law went into effect, the number of fraudulent applications submitted to the OSTR, rose dramatically, resulting in the rejection of 45 % of applications for false residency claims alone (Shaban et al. 2019). This made for a significant backlog for the staff of six, who, in addition to conferring with the platform on a weekly basis, had to visit the potentially illegal units, nearly tripling the time it took to register to an average of nine months. In the meantime, the applicant was free to rent out short-term. According to Omar Masry, senior analyst at OSTR, "There is an ongoing challenge for people who want to game the system and not play by the rules" (Shaban et al. 2019). He added that even after Airbnb deregisters a listing, hosts often re-register using false names, set up shell companies and list on multiple platforms. This is particularly true for commercial actors, who are the chief focus of enforcement efforts and the most difficult violators to root out.

Although the agreement requires platforms to delete the illegal listings submitted to them by the city and to submit monthly reports of listings, the city must go through Airbnb's monthly reports of listings to check compliance, a task made difficult and time-consuming by the fact that Airbnb provides only zip codes, not exact addresses, and omits other essential information. While the city cannot verify that the platform has actually removed all illegal listings, it can and does use third-party data services to "audit" the relative accuracy of Airbnb data. This means that enforcement remains challenging and time-consuming for city authorities, depending upon the complaints of neighbors and third-party data scraping. Observers have suggested that Airbnb could do this much more easily and efficiently with an algorithm.

Ironically, the digital platform, which owes its business model to technology, creates costly externalities for cities. Confronted by a large global corporation with seemingly unlimited resources, city authorities can find themselves overwhelmed and outmatched.

Notes

1 Webscraping is a technique used to extract and compile data from publically available websites beyond what is visible to the public.
2 In 2018, AirDNA publically criticized a report by NYC Comptroller Stringer which was used to support regulatory legislation, citing "flawed conclusions" in the use of data.
3 David Dann et al. (2018) reviewed 118 published journal articles about Airbnb in the areas of tourism, information management, law and economics between 2013 and 2018. Seventeen articles dealt with economic issues, of which five dealt with impact on housing.
4 NYS's Multiple Dwelling Law, which prohibits STRs, actually dates back to 1929.
5 Airbnb charged that 15 of the 51 City Council members had received campaign contributions from the hotel industry.
6 When Nashville sought to prohibit "mini hotels," Airbnb successfully lobbied the Tennessee state legislature to prohibit cities from banning STRs. Texas provides another example of Airbnb's shift from city (Austin) to state (Martineau 2019a).
7 Most of the iconic tech companies started in San Francisco and have their headquarters there – among them: Airbnb, Craigslist, Dropbox, Lyft, Pinterest, Salesforce Twitter and Uber.

8 According to a 2015 study "An Equity Profile of the San Francisco Bay Area Region" by Policy Link, San Francisco is the only county in the central Bay Area where ethnic and racial diversity is decreasing as lower-income and working-class people are forced to leave the city.
9 San Francisco's rent control law, which dates to 1979, capped annual rent increases to 7 % and applies to all multi-family structures.
10 According to Statistica.com, in 2013 per capita listings of Airbnb in American cities were highest in San Francisco.
11 Kenneth Rosen is chair of UC Berkeley's Fisher Center for Real Estate and Urban Economics, a school that receives financial support from corporate executives and real estate groups. The data for the study is not available.
12 The Ellis Act is California state law (1985) that allows landlords to evict tenants if they go out of the rental business.
13 Airbnb refers to these tax agreements as voluntary collection agreements or VCAs. Portland, Oregon, was the first US city to sign a VCA with Airbnb in 2014. The agreement effectively legalized Airbnb in the city. As of 2019, there were about 300 VCAs nationwide and 500 internationally (Martineau 2019a).
14 California is one of 26 states in the US that allows citizens to pass legislation using the initiative process. Once a measure passes, it can only be changed by going back to the ballot box.
15 In spring 2019, several bills to allow more intensive development near transit and to prevent steep rent hikes and evictions either failed or faced stiff opposition in the state legislature.
16 Keep Neighborhoods First, for example, was founded as a grassroots coalition of neighbors, tenants and affordable housing advocates to address the problems created by the proliferation of commercial STRs.
17 For a critical discussion of the transient occupancy tax agreements (VCAs) that Airbnb has entered into with cities in the US and abroad, see Martineau (2019a).
18 Samaan (2015a) assumes that whole-unit STR listings were listed year-round on Airbnb, although it is likely that some of these units were occupied by the host for part of the year.
19 The fight against illegal conversions in Venice continues with a May 2019 protest that successfully stopped the conversion of the Ellison, a 58-unit rent-stabilized apartment building (Keep Neighborhoods First 2019).
20 Rent-stabilized apartments make up the bulk of LA apartments built before October 1, 1978, and amount to approximately 600,000 apartments.

References

Acitelli, Tom. 2019. Boston Homeownership Has Increased, But City Still Overwhelmingly One of Renters. *Crushed Boston*. January 17. https://boston.curbed.com/2019/1/17/18185570/boston-homeownership-vs-renter

Airbnb. 2014. Airbnb's Positive Impact in Boston. https://blog.atairbnb.com/airbnbs-positive-impact-boston/

Airbnbcitizen. 2014. Policy News. February 13. www.airbnbcitizen.com

Alliance of Downtown Community Organizations (ADCO). Memo. 2018a. Why ADCO Supports Mayor Walsh's Revised Short-term Rental Ordinance. June1. https://drive.google.com/file/d/1dKaj4oioqIh0tqHw2GmG7eI_xKQ_mCuT/view

Alliance of Downtown Community Organizations (ADCO). 2018b. Alliance Releases Follow up Report on Short-term Rentals. June 1. https://drive.google.com/file/d/1cuIG7sqgd0ZGRMLGDUyUyPdbVtbtiuHH/view

Alliance of Downtown Community Organizations (ADCO). 2018c. Airbnb Density by Zipcode. December 2. https://drive.google.com/file/d/1o_EYz2uKIea0D4gHqNUQWlflN4Q54728/view

Annear, Steve. 2014. City Councilor Wants to Discuss Possible Airbnb Regulation. *Boston Magazine*. August 18. www.bostonmagazine.com/news/2014/08/18/airbnb-regulations-boston-hearing/

Bergman, Ben. 2015. Garcetti Wants Airbnb to Help Solve L.A.'s Affordability. *Crisis*. April 16. www.scpr.org/news/2015/04/16/51042/garcetti-wants-airbnb-to-help-solve-la-s-affordabi/

BJH Advisors. 2016. Shortchanging New York City: The Impact of Airbnb on New York City's Housing Market. www.hcc-nyc.org/documents/ShortchangingNYC2016FINALprotected_000.pdf

Bluestone, Barry and James Hussey. 2017. Greater Boston Housing Report Card. https://cssh.northeastern.edu/policyschool/wp-content/uploads/sites/24/2017/11/GBHRC-2017-POWERPOINT.pdf

Boston, City of. 2018a. Mayor Walsh Signs Short-Term Rental Ordinance. June 15. www.boston.gov/news/mayor-walsh-signs-short-term-rental-ordinance

Boston, City of. 2018b. Ordinance Allowing Short-term Rentals. June 13. www.boston.gov/sites/default/files/document-file-08-2018/short-term_rental_ordinance.pdf

Boston, City of Mayor Martin Walsh. Neighborhoods. n.d. www.boston.gov/neighborhoods

Bredderman, Will. 2018. Hotel Industry, Activists and Comptroller Go to War with Airbnb. May 8. www.crainsnewyork.com/article/20180508/REAL_ESTATE/180509894/hotel-industry-activists-and-comptroller-scott-stringer-go-to-war-with-airbnb

Brinklow, Adam. 2018. More than 60% of SF Rents Are Rent Control. *Curbed*. July 12. https://sf.curbed.com/2018/7/12/17565192/housing-needs-trends-report-rent-control-san-francisco

Carson, Biz. 2015. The Fight Between Airbnb and San Francisco Just Got Nastier. *SF Gate*. May 15. www.sfgate.com/technology/businessinsider/article/The-fight-between-Airbnb-and-San-Francisco-just-6267230.php

Carson, Biz. 2017. Airbnb Declares a Truce in Its Lawsuit Against Its Hometown San Francisco. *Business Insider*. May 1. www.businessinsider.com/airbnb-settles-lawsuit-with-san-francisco-2017-5

Carville, Olivia. 2019a. Meet Murray Cox, the Man Trying to Take Down Airbnb. *Bloomberg News*. May 23. www.bloomberg.com/news/articles/2019-05-23/meet-murray-cox-airbnb-s-public-enemy-no-1-in-new-york

Carville, Olivia. 2019b. New York Is Standing Between Airbnb and an IPO. *Bloomberg News*. September 19. www.bloomberg.com/news/articles/2019-09-19/airbnb-ipo-why-new-york-city-is-making-investors-nervous

Carville, Olivia and Erik Larson. 2020. Airbnb Is in Settlement Talks with New York Over Data Law. *Bloomberg News*. February 14. www.bloomberg.com/news/articles/2020-02-14/airbnb-says-it-s-in-settlement-talks-with-new-york-over-data-law

CBRE Research. 2020. Short-Term Rentals. www.cbre.us/research-and-reports/Short-Term-Rentals-A-Maturing-US-Market-Its-Impact-on-Traditional-Hotels-January-2020

CBS SF BayArea. 2018. 6,000 Short-Term Rentals Disappear From San Francisco Almost Overnight. January 17. https://sanfrancisco.cbslocal.com/2018/01/17/san-francisco-short-term-rental-supply-disappears/

Chiland, Elijah. 2017. 58% of LA Tenants Are Spending Too Much on Rent. *Curbed*. November 13. https://la.curbed.com/2017/11/13/16635946/rent-cost-los-angeles-income-percent

Chiland, Elijah. 2018a. LA's Rate of Homeownership Is One of the Lowest in the Nation. *Curbed*. August 9. https://la.curbed.com/2018/8/9/17665124/los-angeles-homeowner-rate-renter-population

Chiland, Elijah. 2018b. Single-family Homes Cover Almost Half of Los Angeles – Here's How that Happened. *Curbed*. September 10. https://la.curbed.com/2018/9/10/17827982/single-family-houses-los-angeles-zoning-rules-explained

Clampet, Jason. 2013. Airbnb's Growing Pains Mirrored in New York City, Where Half Its Listings Are Illegal Rentals. *Skift*. January 7. https://skift.com/2013/01/07/airbnbs-growing-pains-mirrored-in-new-york-city-where-half-its-listings-are-illegal-rentals/

Clampet, Jason. 2014a. Airbnb in NYC: The Real Numbers Behind the Sharing Story. *Skift*. February 13. https://skift.com/2014/02/13/airbnb-in-nyc-the-real-numbers-behind-the-sharing-story/

Clampet, Jason. 2014b. The 10 Airbnb Super-Hosts that Rule New York City. *Skift*. February 13. https://skift.com/2014/02/13/the-10-airbnb-super-hosts-that-rule-new-york-city/

Clark, Patrick. 2017. Why Can't They Build More Homes Where the Jobs Are? *Bloomberg News*. June 23. www.bloomberg.com/news/articles/2017-06-23/why-can-t-they-build-more-homes-where-the-jobs-are

Coles, Peter, Michael Egesdal, Ingrid Gould Ellen, Xiaodi Li and Arun Sundararajan. 2017. Airbnb Usage Across New York City Neighborhoods: Geographic Patterns and Regulatory Implications. October 12. https://papers.ssrn.com/sol3/papers.cfm?abstract_id=3048357

Cotter, Sean Philip. 2020. Boston Airbnb Listings Drop by a Third After.... *Boston Herald*. January 14. www.bostonherald.com/2020/01/14/boston-airbnb-listings-drop-by-a-third-after-agreement-kicks-in/

Cox, Murray. 2016. Airbnb vs Rent: City of Los Angeles. August 30. http://insideairbnb.com/airbnb-vs-rent-city-of-la/

Cox, Murray. 2017. The Face of Airbnb: New York City, Airbnb as a Racial Gentrification Tool. *InsideAirbnb*. March 1. http://insideairbnb.com/reports/the-face-of-airbnb-nyc.pdf

Cox, Murray and Tom Slee. 2016. How Airbnb's Data Hid the Facts in New York City. *InsideAirbnb*. February 10. http://insideairbnb.com/reports/how-airbnbs-data-hid-the-facts-in-new-york-city.pdf

Dann, David et al. 2018. Poster Child and Guinea Pig-insight from a Structured Literature Review on Airbnb. *International Journal of Contemporary Hospitality Management* 31(1): 474–495. https://doi.org/10.1108/IJCHM-03-2018-0186

DeGregory, Priscilla. 2019. Airbnb Gives NYC Information on 17,500 Rental Listings. May 24. https://nypost.com/2019/05/24/airbnb-gives-nyc-information-on-17500-rental-listings/?utm_source=email_sitebuttons&utm_medium=site%20buttons&utm_campaign=site%20buttons

Edelman, Benjamin, Michael Luca and Dan Svirsky. 2017. Racial Discrimination in the Sharing Economy: Evidence from a Field Experiment. *American Economic Journal: Applied Economics* 9(2): 1–22.

Ellen, Ingrid Gould and Brendan O'Flaherty. 2013. How New York and Lost Angeles Housing Policies Are Different – And Maybe Why. In David Halle and Andrew A. Beveridge (eds.) *New York and Los Angeles: The Uncertain Future*. New York: Oxford University Press, 286–309.

Enwemeka, Zeninjor. 2019. New Short Term Rental Rules Take Effect in Boston. *WBUR Radio*. January 1. www.wbur.org/bostonomix/2019/01/01/airbnb-boston-ordinance

Ferre-Sadurni, Luis. 2018. Report on Airbnb in New York Made "Crucial Errors," Data Provider Says. May 4. www.nytimes.com/2018/05/04/nyregion/airbnb-new-york-report-errors.html

Fisher, Clyde. 1962. Land Use Control Through Zoning: The San Francisco Experience. *Hastings Law Journal* 13(3): 322–343. https://repository.uchastings.edu/cgi/viewcontent.cgi?article=1690&context=hastings_law_journal

Fox, Jeremy. 2019. Judge Blocks Part of Boston's Airbnb Ordinance. *Boston Globe*. May 4. www.bostonglobe.com/metro/2019/05/04/judge-blocks-parts-boston-airbnb-ordinance/Efi8VodgI4dhxSZqV0v5zL/story.html

Herndon, Astead. 2016. City Council to Take up Airbnb Regulations. *Boston Globe*. October 19. www.bostonglobe.com/metro/2016/10/19/city-council-take-airbnb-regulations/q1td0KKmrkwz0kpZrGkJ5L/story.html

Hiltzik, Michael. 2015. No Surprise: That Airbnb Study of Rentals in L.A. Isn't What It Seems. September 30. www.latimes.com/business/hiltzik/la-fi-mh-airbnb-study-of-rentals-20150930-column.html

Horn, Keren and Mark Merante. 2017. Is Home Sharing Driving up Rents? Evidence from Airbnb in Boston. *Journal of Housing Economics* 38: 14–24.

HR&A Advisors. 2012. The Transformative Benefits of Airbnb and the Sharing Economy. December 7. www.hraadvisors.com/hra-report-reveals-transformative-benefits-of-airbnb-and-the-sharing-economy/

Jimenez, Sarah. 2017. The Growth of Commercial Short-term Rentals. How Boston Can Protect Affordable Housing and Quality of Life. *Community Labor United*. September. www.forworkingfamilies.org/sites/default/files/publications/images/clu_shorttermrental_report_prf7.jpg

Keep Neighborhoods First. 2019. Time Is Running Out: Help Save the Ellison. May 9. https://mail.google.com/mail/u/0?ik=e6dccaefb5&view=pt&search=all&permthid=thread-f%3A1633063219334533066%7Cmsg-a%3Ar2217465951361589029&simpl=msg-a%3Ar2217465951361589029&mb=1

Kusisto, Laura. 2018. HUD Moves to Shake Up Fair-Housing Enforcement. *Wall Street Journal*. August 13. www.wsj.com/articles/hud-moves-to-shake-up-fair-housing-enforcement-1534161601

Kwong, Jessica. 2014. Report Claims Speculators Are Behind Most Ellis Act Evictions in SF. *San Francisco Examiner*. April 4. www.sfexaminer.com/news/report-claims-speculators-are-behind-most-ellis-act-evictions-in-sf/

L.A. Biz. 2018. New York and L.A. Only US Cities in Top 10 Airbnb Listings. August 7. www.bizjournals.com/losangeles/news/2018/08/07/new-york-and-la-only-us-cities-in-airbnb-list.html?s=print

Lane, Ben. 2018. Massachusetts Enacts New Laws Taxing and Regulating Short-term Rentals. *Housing Wire*. December 31. www.housingwire.com/articles/47810-massachusetts-enacts-new-laws-taxing-and-regulating-short-term-rentals

Lee, Dayne. 2016. How Airbnb Short-Term Rentals Exacerbate Los Angeles's Affordable Housing Crisis: Analysis and Policy Recommendations. *Harvard Law & Policy Review* 10: 229–253. http://harvardlpr.com/wp-content/uploads/2016/02/10.1_10_Lee.pdf

Lewis, Rebecca C. 2019. New York City's 10 Biggest Lobbying Spenders. *City and State New York*. March 4. www.cityandstateny.com/articles/politics/new-york-city/everything-you-need-know-about-nycs-top-10-lobbyists.html

Logan, Tim. 2015. Boston Is Nation's Second Tightest Rental Market. *Boston Globe*. July 31. www.bostonglobe.com/business/2015/07/31/boston-nation-second-tightest-rental-market/P3pjOfldD5yDAzMOWl1j7J/story.html

Los Angeles, City and County [LA]. 2018. Short-term Rental Ordinance. http://clkrep.lacity.org/onlinedocs/2014/14-1635-S2_ord_draft_12-07-2018.pdf

Martineau, Paris. 2019a. Inside Airbnb's "Guerrilla War" Against Local Governments. *Wired*. March 20. www.wired.com/story/inside-airbnbs-guerrilla-war-against-local-governments/

Martineau, Paris. 2019b. Airbnb and New York City Reach a Truce on Homesharing Data. *Wired*. May 24. www.wired.com/story/airbnb-new-york-city-reach-truce-on-home-sharing-data/

Merante, Mark and Keren Horn. 2016. Is Home Sharing Driving up Rents? Evidence from Airbnb in Boston. *Department of Economics*. University of Massachusetts. Working Paper 2016-3.

McDonough, Annie. 2019. Airbnb's New York City Legal Battles. *City and State New York*. June 2. www.cityandstateny.com/articles/policy/technology/airbnbs-new-york-city-legal-battles.html

McNeill, Donald. 2016. Governing a City of Unicorns: Technology Capital and the Urban Politics of San Francisco. *Urban Geography* 37(4), 494–513. https://doi.org/10.1080/02723638.2016.1139868

New York City, Office of the Comptroller, Scott Stringer [NYC Comptroller]. 2018a. The Impact of Airbnb on NYC Rents. April. https://comptroller.nyc.gov/reports/the-impact-of-airbnb-on-nyc-rents/

New York City, Office of the Comptroller, Scott Stringer. 2018b. City Comptroller's Response to Airbnb Guest Commentary. May 23. www.citylandnyc.org/city-comptrollers-response-to-airbnb-guest-commentary/

New York Communities for Change and Real Affordability for All [NYCC and RAFA]. 2015. Airbnb in NYC: Housing Report. www.sharebetter.org/wp-content/uploads/2015/07/AirbnbNYCHousingReport1.pdf

New York State, Office of the Attorney General, Eric T. Schneiderman. (NYS AG). 2014. Airbnb in the City. https://ag.ny.gov/pdfs/AIRBNB%20REPORT.pdf

Nota, Alexa. 2018. Los Angeles City Council Bans Traditional Vacation Rentals. *VRMintel*. December 15. www.vrmintel.com/los-angeles-city-council-bans-traditional-vacation-rentals/

Oatman-Stanford, Hunter. 2018. Demolishing the California Dream: How San Francisco Planned Its Own Housing Crisis. *Collectors Weekly*. September 21. www.collectorsweekly.com/articles/demolishing-the-california-dream/

Pasquale, Frank. 2015. *The Black Box Society: The Secret Algorithms that Control Money and Information*. Cambridge, MA: Harvard University Press.

Pershan, Caleb. 2015. Planning Department Won't Force Airbnb to Share Records. *SFIST*. April 27. https://sfist.com/2015/04/27/planning_department_wont_force_airb/

Policy Link San Francisco. 2015. An Equity Profile of the San Francisco Bay Area Region. https://nationalequityatlas.org/sites/default/files/documents/bay-area-profile/BayAreaProfile_21April2015_Final.pdf

Reyes, Emily Alpert. 2017a. Airbnb Warns that L.A.'s Budget Could Suffer from Restricting Short-term Rentals. *Los Angeles Times*. April 18. www.latimes.com/local/lanow/la-me-ln-airbnb-budget-20170418-story.html

Reyes, Emily Alpert. 2017b. With Garcetti's Budget Relying on Millions from Airbnb, Will L.A. Still Clamp Down on Short-term Rentals? *Los Angeles Times*. May 3. www.latimes.com/local/lanow/la-me-ln-airbnb-money-20170503-story.html

Rocheleau, Matt. 2015. Lawmakers Worry Owners Taking Advantage of Airbnb. *Boston Globe*. August 24. www.bostonglobe.com/metro/2015/08/23/some-boston-housing-now-used-like-hotels-via-airbnb/deDVVOZf6EYYBmxDyWWHfJ/story.html

Rosen, Kenneth, Randall Sakamoto and David Bank. 2013. Short-Term Rentals and the Impact on the Apartment Market. *Rosen Consulting Group*. October 13. www.rosenconsulting.com

Rosenberg, Mike. 2018. Rapidly Growing Seattle Constrains New Housing Through Widespread Single-family Zoning. May 3. www.seattletimes.com/business/real-estate/amid-seattles-rapid-growth-most-new-housing-restricted-to-a-few-areas/

Said, Carolyn. 2014a. Airbnb Profits Prompted S.F. Evictions, Ex-tenant Says. *SFGate*. January 22. www.sfgate.com/bayarea/article/Airbnb-profits-prompted-S-F-eviction-ex-tenant-5164242.php

Said, Carolyn. 2014b. Window into Airbnb's Hidden Impact on S.F. *San Francisco Chronicle*. June. www.sfchronicle.com/business/item/Window-into-Airbnb-s-hidden-impact-on-S-F-30110.php

Said, Carolyn. 2017. Airbnb Settles Lawsuit with San Francisco. *Governing: The State and Localities*. May 2. www.governing.com/topics/urban/tns-airbnb-lawsuit-san-francisco.html

Said, Carolyn. 2018. San Francisco Fines Airbnb Landlords $2.25 Million for Illegal Rentals. *San Francisco Chronicle*. November 5. www.sfchronicle.com/business/article/SF-fines-Airbnb-landlords-2-25-million-for-13364513.php

Samaan, Roy. 2015a. Airbnb, Rising Rent, and the Housing Crisis in Los Angeles. March. www.laane.org/wp-content/uploads/2015/03/AirBnB-Final.pdf

Samaan, Roy. 2015b. Short-Term Rentals and L.A.'s Lost Housing. August 24. www.laane.org/wp-content/uploads/2015/08/Short-Term_RentalsLAs-

San Francisco, City and County, Board of Supervisors, Budget and Legislative Analyst, [SF Budget & Legislative Analyst]. 2015. Policy Analysis Report. https://sfbos.org/sites/default/files/FileCenter/Documents/55575-BLA.ShortTermRentals%20040716.pdf

San Francisco, City and County, Board of Supervisors, Budget and Legislative Analyst, [SF Budget & Legislative Analyst]. 2016. Short Term Rentals 2016 Update. https://sfbos.org/sites/default/files/FileCenter/Documents/55575-BLA.ShortTermRentals%20040716.pdf

San Francisco Planning Department. 2018. San Francisco Housing Inventory 2017. https://default.sfplanning.org/publications_reports/2017_Housing_Inventory.pdf

Sawyer, Nuala. 2018. S.F. Fines Two Airbnb San Francisco Host $5.5. Million for Illegal Rental. *San Francisco Weekly*. May 2. www.sfweekly.com/news/s-f-fines-two-airbnb-hosts-5-5m-for-illegal-rentals/

Sentinel News Service. 2018. City of Los Angeles Has Collected $100 Million in Taxes from Airbnb Hosts and Airbnb. *Los Angeles Sentinel*. December 6. https://lasentinel.net/city-of-los-angeles-has-collected-100-million-in-taxes-from-airbnb-hosts-and.html

Shaban, Bigad, Michael Bott and Michael Horn. 2019. San Francisco's Attempts to Uproot Unregistered Vacation Homes on Airbnb. August 20. www.nbcbayarea.com/news/local/san-francisco-unregistered-vacation-homes-surge-fraudulent-short-term-rental-applications/150739/

Slee, Tom. 2016. The Sharing Economy's Dirty Laundry. www.jacobinmag.com/2016/03/uber-airbnb-sharing-economy-housing-tech/

Sperling, Gene. 2013. How Airbnb Combats Middle Class Income Stagnation. www.cedarcityutah.com/wpcontent/uploads/2015/07/MiddleClassReport-MT-061915_r1.pdf

Teitell, Beth. 2014. Online Bookings Bring Steady Cash, Unexpected Twist. *Boston Globe*. July 15. www.bostonglobe.com/lifestyle/style/2014/07/14/bed-bath-and-boston-all-over-town-people-are-earning-big-bucks-renting-out-their-spaces-airbnb/oIJu7pd7WeCBw3D7IUqApK/story.html

Tenants Together. 2014. The Speculator Loophole: Ellis Act Evictions in San Francisco. March 24. www.antievictionmappingproject.net/ellisreport.html

Thompson, Lauren. 2018. After San Francisco's New Short-Term Rental Regulations, Listings Increase But Prices Hold Steady. *Hotpadsblog*. February 19. https://hotpads.com/blog/san-francisco-short-term-rental-regulations/

Vaccaro, Adam. 2014. Boston Mulling Airbnb Regulations, Won't Fine Hosts in Meantime. *bNews*. www.boston.com/news/business/2014/07/09/boston-mulling-airbnb-regulations-wont-fine-hosts-in-meantime

Wachsmuth, David. 2019. STRs in Los Angeles: Are the Nov. 2019 Regulations Being Enforced? December. https://static1.squarespace.com/static/5ccdda1b93a6321152025235/t/5dfa9b765e268a0ad6e7ba03/1576704887313/STR_UPG_McGIll.pdf

Wachsmuth, David, David Chaney, Danielle Kerrigan, Andrea Shillolo and Robin Basalaev-Binder. 2018. The High Cost of Short-Term Rentals in New York City. A Report from the Urban Politics and Governance Research Group, School of Urban Planning, McGill University. January. www.politico.com/states/f/?id=00000161-44f2-daac-a3e9-5ff3d8740001

Wachsmuth, David, Jennifer Combs and Danielle Kerrigan. 2019. The High Cost of Short-Term Rentals in New York City. A Report from the Urban Politics and Governance Research Group, School of Urban Planning McGill University. www.sharebetter.org/wp-content/uploads/2019/01/Impact-of-New-STR-Regs-2019.pdf

Whittemore, Andrew H. 2012. Zoning Los Angeles: A Brief History of Four Regimes. *Planning Perspectives* 27(3): 393–415. http://doi.org/10.1080/02665433.2012.681140

Wohlsen, Marcus. 2014. San Francisco's New Housing Rules Are the Best Things to Happen to Airbnb. *Wired*. August 8. www.wired.com/2014/10/san-franciscos-new-limits-best-thing-happen-airbnb/

Zahniser, David. 2017. Even in a Booming Economy, L.A. City Hall Faces Daunting Budget Challenges. *Los Angeles Times*. August 3. www.latimes.com/local/politics/la-me-la-city-budget-20170803-htmlstory.html

Zaleski, Olivia. 2018. Airbnb's NYC Bookings Could Be Cut in Half by New Rule. *Bloomberg News*. July 24. www.bloomberg.com/news/articles/2018-07-24/airbnb-s-nyc-bookings-could-be-cut-in-half-by-new-rule

Zillow. 2018. Share of Renters Rise in Each of the 50 Largest U.S. Cities. www.bloomberg.com/graphics/2020-airbnb-ipochallenges/; http://zillow.mediaroom.com/2018-08-08-Share-of-Renters-Rise-in-Each-of-the-50-Largest-U-S-Cities

3
THE AIRBNB EFFECT, CHALLENGES TO HOUSING AND LOCALITIES

The impact of Airbnb on housing and localities is at the heart of this book. While the regulatory struggles over short-term rentals (STRs) have played out in the local press, the consequences for housing and neighborhoods have remained fragmented and less visible. In this chapter, we synthesize the available empirical evidence drawing upon the studies described in the previous chapter. We look first at housing effects, then – given the spatial concentration of Airbnb listings – at the consequences for the social and structural fabric of neighborhoods, and last, at the ongoing challenges faced by local authorities as they struggle to preserve housing, neighborhood milieu and local control.

Housing effects

Although they use differing data sets and methodologies, the existing empirical studies share several important conclusions concerning the effects of Airbnb on housing and localities. They document the associated rise in rents and house prices, the decrease in the availability of residential rental units, the disproportionate presence of commercial operators and the concentration of listings in certain neighborhoods.

Residential rents. In New York City, San Francisco, Los Angeles and Boston, cities where most residents are renters and where rising rents and low vacancy rates have created an affordability crisis, the studies have focused primarily on the impact of STRs on the residential or long-term rental market.[1] The studies all show a positive correlation between an increase in Airbnb listings in a given area and an increase in asking rents for long-term rentals (NYS AG 2014; Lee 2016; Horn and Merante 2017; Samaan 2015a, 2015b; NYC Comptroller 2018; BJH 2016; Barron et al. 2018).

Some of the studies also quantify the rent increase. In Boston, Horn and Merante (2017) find that from September 2015 to January 2016, an increase of one standard deviation in Airbnb listings relative to total housing units is associated with an increase in mean asking rent of 0.4 % or $ 93.00 per month in 2015. They estimate that if Airbnb's growth rate continued for three years, "Boston's mean asking rents in January 2019 would be as much as $178 a month higher than in the absence of Airbnb activity."

Barron et al. (2018) find similar results for the 100 largest metropolitan areas: an increase of one standard deviation in listings between 2012 and 2016 was associated with a 0.54 % increase in rents. In an interview with *The Wall Street Journal*, one of the authors, Edward Kung, placed these figures in a larger context, noting that although the numbers sounded "small," rents rose about 2.2 % annually in the 100 areas and home prices rose by an average of 4.8 % annually during this period (Ward 2017).

Looking at NYC, several reports also put a number on the rent increase. Wachsmuth et al. (2018) calculate that Airbnb likely increased the median long-term rent by 1.4 % over the 2014–2017 period. For the median NYC tenant this translates into $ 375 more in 2017 and into even more in some neighborhoods. A study by the NYC Comptroller's Office (2018), which used the proportion of Airbnb listings in a given census tract as its independent variable, estimates that 9.2 % of the citywide increase in rents between 2009 and 2016 was attributable to Airbnb, a total of $ 616 million.

It is important to unpack the logic of these studies. As we know, housing is a recognizably complex phenomenon, and many endogenous as well as exogenous factors can affect housing price and availability in a given locality. Most of the studies at the neighborhood or census tract level attempt to control for demographic effects such as income and education, as well as neighborhood amenities, such as crime rates, restaurants, building permits and so forth. But while studies try to pinpoint the exact nature of the relationship between Airbnb listings and the rise in rents, it is impossible to rule out the possibility that the relation is spurious and that other factors may be driving both Airbnb usage and rents. This means that all findings are ultimately estimates of the relationship.

There is also an assumption in these studies about the mechanism linking the increased number of Airbnb listings to increases in long-term or residential rents. The researchers suggest that the growth of Airbnb's easy-to-use STR market removes residential housing stock by incentivizing a shift from the long-term to the short-term market. It is this shift that drives up residential rents because the same amount of demand faces a more limited supply of rental stock. But here too, the exact relationship is unknown as rents are based on a variety of factors.

Some observers suggest that the Airbnb effect on rents is small in terms of the overall number of housing units in a given city. However, Barron et al. (2018) and those who follow their methodology and logic use census level vacancy rates as the critical factor in estimating the number of residential units removed from the long-term housing supply. They have shown that at the census tract or neighborhood level, small differences in vacancy rates are quite significant.

Barron et al. underline the consequences for residents seeking housing: "In the median zip code, a local resident looking for a long-term rental unit will find that about 1 in 8 of the potentially available homes are being placed on Airbnb instead of being made available to long-term residents" (Barron et al. 2018, 19). In neighborhoods where there is a high concentration of Airbnb listings, the ratio is worse for the would-be renter. Kung, one of the authors, adds: "For neighborhoods in the 90th percentile, where the number of Airbnb listings is very high, it's almost one for one, where for every one unit listed on Airbnb, you see one unit listed on the long-term market" (Ward 2017, 4). Speaking of LA, Lee reminds us: "In tight housing markets with near-zero vacancy rates, a sudden reduction in supply naturally increases rents, particularly because neither the market nor the public sector can swiftly add to the housing stock" (2016).

Availability of long-term rentals. Most studies find that Airbnb has removed a significant number of residential rental units from the housing market. In Boston, Horn and Merante (2017) find that a one standard deviation increase in Airbnb listings relative to total housing units is correlated with a 5.9 % decrease in the number of units offered for long-term rental.

Drawing upon several local studies, Lee (2016) concludes that Airbnb has exacerbated LA's affordable housing crisis by incentivizing both the conversion of long-term rentals to STRs for the tourism market as well as the "hotelization" of entire properties. Samaan (2015b) concludes that STRs undermine LA's attempts to produce more housing. The report estimates that STRs removed 11 units per day, approximately 63 % of new housing construction over a four-year period and cost LA renters over $ 464 million.

In San Francisco, the Board of Supervisor's 2015 report calculates that Airbnb rentals have removed approximately 15 % of housing units from the long-term market and in neighborhoods such as the Mission District, estimates the figure may be as high as 40 %.

The NYC studies underline similar negative effects on housing stock. As early as 2013, the NYS Attorney General's report found that over 4,600 entire house/apartment units were booked as private STRs for three or more months of the year and of these, half were booked for six months, making them unavailable for use by long-term residents. Most of the units were in popular neighborhoods in Brooklyn and Manhattan. Moreover, the share of revenue from these types of units increased over time from 18 % in 2010 to 38 % in 2013 (NYS AG 2014, 12–13).

In estimating the loss of rental units in NYC, the BJH Advisors report is particularly conservative. The study creates a new category, "Impact Listings," which must meet three criteria (entire apartment or home, commercial, and short-term listing) and argues that these listings are most likely to be removed from the residential rental market (BJH 2016). It concludes that in 2015, Impact Listings constituted 16 % of all listings in NYC. If available on the rental market, the listed units would increase the number of vacant rental units citywide by 10 % and the low vacancy rate, currently between 3.4 % and 3.6 %, would rise to 4.0 %. These findings are even more dramatic at the macro-neighborhood level. For example, if the 687 Impact Listings in the West Village/Greenwich Village/Soho were available on the rental market, the report estimates that the vacancy rate for these neighborhoods would increase from 2.9 % to 5 %.

Wachsmuth et al., who examine frequently rented entire homes/apartments in NYC over the 2014–2017 period, estimate that Airbnb likely removed 7,000 to 13,500 units from NYC's long-term rental market (2018). They also find 4,700 "ghost hotels" (private room listings in a single apartment or building), which remove another 1,400 units from the long-term market.[2] As to incentive, they note: "The median host of a frequently rented entire-home/apartment listing earned 55 % more than the median long-term rent in its neighborhood" in 2017 (2018, 27). In their follow-up 2019 report, they project that, should the federal injunction against the NYC Airbnb regulation remain in place during the following year, the STR market would continue to commercialize, and between 1,800 to 10,800 additional units could be removed from long-term housing.

Wachsmuth and Weisler (2018) provide a theoretical explanation for these processes. They argue that Airbnb creates a "new" rent gap – the difference between the revenue from long-term and short-term rents – which encourages conversions. Other studies have looked at the conversion incentive in switching from short-term to long-term rental markets, including Cox (2016), Jimenez (2017), NYCC and RAFA (2015).

House prices. Two of the studies examine the impact of Airbnb on house prices: Horn and Merante (2017) and Barron et al. (2018). Both indicate that the dynamic market in STRs exerts upward pressure on property values. In their study of metropolitan areas, Barron et al. find that a 1 % increase in Airbnb listings is associated with a 0.026 % increase in house prices in the median owner-occupancy rate zip-codes and suggest that two mechanisms are at work; the increase in rental income from STRs is capitalized into house prices, and more directly, by enabling homeowners to generate extra income on unused capacity, there is an increase in the price-to-rent ratio.[3]

Interestingly, both studies found that the correlation between Airbnb listings and the increase in rents and home prices is moderated by the proportion of owner-occupied rentals in a given zip code. This is consistent with the contention that absentee landlords are shifting their homes from the long-term to the short-term rental market.

Estimating the overall effect of STRs on housing, Barron et al. point out:

> In aggregate, the growth in home-sharing through Airbnb contributes to about one-fifth of the average annual increase in U.S. rents and about one-seventh of the average annual increase in U.S. housing prices. By contrast, annual zip code demographic changes and general city trends contribute about three-fourths of the total rent growth and about three-fourths of the total housing price growth.
>
> *(Barron et al. 2019)*

Commercial operators. Arguably, the most important issue for localities has been the presence and rapid growth of commercial and/or professional operators defined as non-resident hosts offering multiple units. They include individual investors, landlords of multi-family properties as well as management companies. When the listings cluster in a building, it becomes a *de facto* hotel.

Although the majority of hosts are individuals with one listing, the studies all document the disproportionate presence of these commercial operators in terms of their share of listings and Airbnb revenue. The studies have also shown that, overtime, STRs in a given locality tend to become increasingly commercialized, and that commercial operators are the fastest growing segment of the market and key to Airbnb's profit.

Two hotel industry sponsored studies of multiple cities, including New York City, San Francisco, Los Angeles and Boston, support these conclusions. A study of commercial activity in 14 cities between 2014 and 2016, which looked at the activity of two overlapping groups of commercial users – multiple unit operators renting out two or more units and full-time operators renting their units 360 or more days per year, found that 40 % of Airbnb revenue in the 14 cities came from those commercial hosts (O'Neill and Ouyang 2016). The CBRE study of the activity of "entire-home, multi-unit hosts" in 13 cities 2014–2016 found that hosts with two or more units accounted for nearly 32 % of the 1.8 billion Airbnb revenue in the US; that this was the fastest growing segment of the market and a "key driver of Airbnb growth" (2017).

In San Francisco, the 2014 study commissioned by *The San Francisco Chronicle*, finds that two-thirds of the 5,000 listings on the platform are for entire houses or apartments that appear to be rented full-time. The San Francisco Board of Supervisor's study (2015) finds that 31 % of listings in 2014 are of hosts who list entire units and probably do not reside there. The follow-up study, based on 2015data finds that the majority (57 %) of listings were for entire un-hosted units.

In Los Angeles, Lee (2016) cites numerous sources on absentee owners including Samaan (2015a) and Kudler 2015) and notes that in 2014, 64 % of Airbnb listings were for units never occupied by owners and managed by companies contracting with decorators and cleaners.

In Boston, several studies document the strong presence of commercial hosts whose share of listings range from a relative low of 12 % (Jimenez 2017), to 18 % Horn and Merante (2017), to a high of 60 % (ADCO 2018).[4] These commercial operators control a disproportionate number of listings: Horn and Merante find that commercial operators control half of the listings, and Jimenez finds that the top 50 operators have 1,000 listings (2017). Moreover, the share of commercial operators is considerably higher in certain neighborhoods; in the nine downtown communities represented by ADCO, the average is 85 % with a high of 93 % in Chinatown. The report also notes that the percentage of investor-controlled listings in Boston is far higher than in NYC and San Francisco; that the listings are more geographically concentrated than in San Francisco; and that per population, they are among the highest in the world.

The biggest issue in NYC has been the commercial usage of the platform. Between 2010 and 2015, Airbnb listings skyrocketed from 1,000 to over 43,000, and commercial usage increased along with the listings. Looking at Airbnb listings between 2010 to 2014, and using a conservative definition of commercial usage, the NYS Attorney General found that while 94 % of hosts offered at most two unique units, the remaining 6 % (with 3 or more unique listings) dominate the platform, with 36 % of bookings and 37 % of host revenue (2014). The report also identifies a class of large commercial users, over 100 operators who each control 10 plus units and accept 47,103 STRs. The top 12 NYC operators each earn over $ 1 million, and the highest-earning commercial operator administered 272 unique Airbnb listings and received $ 6.8 million in revenue (NYS AG 2014).

Between 2014 to 2017, Wachsmuth et al. (2018) found that commercial operators in NYC with multiple entire home/apartment listings or large portfolios of private rooms comprised 12 % of hosts but earned over 28 % of the revenue. By 2017, the top 10 % of hosts earned 48 % of all Airbnb revenue. In a follow-up report in 2019, Wachsmuth et al. hypothesize that if the NYC Airbnb law, currently under a federal injunction, were not put into effect, commercial operation would increase from 16.7 % to 18.5 % of all entire-home listings by 2020 (2019).

In short, commercial hosts are primarily responsible for Airbnb's negative effects on housing. Unlike mom-and-pop hosts who may rent out their apartment while on vacation, it is the commercial hosts, real estate owners and investors incentivized by the passive revenue stream, who remove entire units from the long-term rental market. Not surprisingly, they have been the focus of regulation.

The results of San Francisco's efforts to regulate STRs lend support to the causal chain of logic described earlier. In San Francisco, Airbnb listings decreased by 52 %, from 8,740 in August 2018 before regulation to 4,191 in January 2019, after the law went into effect. At the same time, the number of rentals offered on long-term or residential rental sites, such as HotPads and the Zillow Group, surged after the ordinance went into effect in January 2019. According to Joshua Clark, Hot-Pads economist, "the large number of people who got lopped off Airbnb changed to advertising as long term rentals" (Said 2018).

Although Airbnb has justified its resistance to releasing data by arguing that it is protecting the privacy of its hosts, an equally important factor is its reluctance to make public that a large part of its revenue is derived from commercial operators. When criticized about the disproportionate role played by commercial operators, Airbnb's typical response is to minimize the problem and say that it represents "a minority of bad actors."

Spatial concentration and neighborhood effects

Most importantly, the studies show that Airbnb listings are not distributed throughout the city but tend to be concentrated in a minority of neighborhoods. These neighborhoods include those close to the central city, near tourist attractions, restaurants and public transportation as well as areas that have been gentrifying.[5] This has been the case in each of the four cities we have discussed. Although the cities use different indicators to measure concentration, most use the number of Airbnb listings and host revenue.

In NYC, the many existing studies show that listings cluster in a number of central and gentrifying neighborhoods in Manhattan and Brooklyn. The NYS Attorney General's study finds that over 40 % of Airbnb revenue for 2010–2014 went to just three Community Districts in Manhattan (the Lower East Side/Chinatown, Chelsea/Hell's Kitchen and Greenwich Village/Soho) while less than 3 % of the total revenue went to the three outer boroughs, Queens, Staten Island and the Bronx (NYC AG 2014). Examining Airbnb listings for entire home/apartments by zip code for the same time period, the NYCC and RAFA (2015) study finds that 20 % of NYC listings concentrate in only four of NYC's 145 zip codes (East Village, West Village, Williamsburg, Brooklyn and the Lower East Side). The BJH report (2016) finds that 90 % of Airbnb listings in 2015 are concentrated in the boroughs of Manhattan and Brooklyn and that 53 % of these listings are clustered in five macro-neighborhoods. Wachsmuth et al.'s comparison of Airbnb's listings from 2016 to 2017 shows more growth in gentrifying areas in Brooklyn and northern Manhattan (2018).

In LA, Samaan's analysis of a "snapshot" of Airbnb listings for October 17, 2014, finds that nine of LA's 95 neighborhoods accounted for 73 % of Airbnb revenue for the city, the top two being Venice and Hollywood (2015a). Lee describes Airbnb's concentration in seven of the city's densest, most affluent and gentrifying neighborhoods – Venice, Downtown, Miracle Mile, Hollywood, Hollywood Hills, Echo Park and Silver Lake. Despite housing only 8 % of city residents, these neighborhoods account for almost half of Airbnb listings and 69 % of its revenue in 2014 (2016, 235).

Although Airbnb listings in San Francisco can be found throughout the city, the listings are highly concentrated in six of the city's 28 neighborhoods. In 2015, the Inner Mission neighborhood accounted for 16 % of the total city listings; high concentrations were also found in Haight-Ashbury, Castro, Russian Hill, Soma and Portrero Hill. Together, these six neighborhoods accounted for 61 % of the listings in the city (San Francisco Budget and Legislative Analyst 2016).

The ADCO study in Boston, which defines concentration in terms of the "density of listings per acre," finds that the overall density per acre for the city was 0.14 with a high of 1.26 in the North End, followed closely by Beacon Hill with 1.06, Back Bay with 1.04 and Chinatown with 1.03 (ADCO 2017). All nine ADCO neighborhoods show densities above the average, and the lowest, the West End, still recorded double the city's average density. The report concludes that the downtown neighborhoods which represented 20 % of the city's population were "most affected by the rapid rise of Airbnb and other short-term rentals" (ADCO 2018).

While Airbnb has touted the fact that its listings can be found scattered throughout a given city, spatial concentration remains the rule. Despite some dispersal of tourists away from the traditional hotel and tourist district, STR listings can be found in traditional residential areas where they have created new concentrations. Thus, although the "hot spots" may shift over time, the listings remain concentrated and threaten to "touristify" traditionally residential areas of a city.

Displacement and gentrification

Why does spatial concentration matter? In neighborhoods with a high density of Airbnb listings, the negative effects on housing affordability and availability are magnified. These negative effects are structural as well as social. By structural, we refer to the displacement of long-term renters due to rising rents or eviction and the loss of residential (often rent-controlled) housing through conversion to STRs.

Take the findings of the NYS Attorney General's Report, that the top 20 zip codes for Airbnb listings in Brooklyn were all zip codes in which the average rent increased by at least 32 % between 2002 and 2014. The report explains what this means to a given neighborhood by noting that in Williamsburg, Brooklyn, over 70,000 people applied for affordable housing in a new seven-story building with just 38 units in 2013, and that the Lower East Side – another Airbnb "hot spot" – was one of the city's ten least affordable neighborhoods due to the high rent burden. Needless to say, these areas are predominantly minority/low-income albeit gentrifying neighborhoods.

Racialized gentrification. Faced with evidence that people of color encounter discrimination as users of Airbnb (Edelman et al. 2017), Airbnb has advertised the benefits of STRs to African-American neighborhoods (Bredderman 2018). Yet studies of Airbnb's impact on minority/low-income neighborhoods suggest that STRs not only contribute to gentrification in general but, more specifically, to racialized gentrification.

Looking at the impact of STRs on majority black neighborhoods in Brooklyn, Cox (2017) finds that the economic benefits are skewed as well as the disadvantages. Airbnb hosts in these neighborhoods are five times more likely to be white, and white hosts receive three times more revenue. Moreover, the residents of majority minority areas are six times more likely to be affected by housing loss and neighborhood disruption, in part because Airbnb listings in these locations earn more than double the median long-term rent.

These findings are confirmed by Wachsmuth et al. who identify a pattern of "racialized" gentrification in NYC neighborhoods with disproportionate shares of either total Airbnb activity or new growth – hot spots such as Bedford-Stuyvesant and East New York (2018). Together with the work of Cox (2017), these findings suggest that Airbnb activity in majority minority neighborhoods is taking long-term rentals off the market, increasing rents and disproportionately benefitting the resident white population.

In LA, Lee (2016) argues that Airbnb reduced neighborhood integration by incentivizing hotelization, particularly though the conversion of rent-controlled units into STRs and by driving out low-income/minority renters. Lee also notes that since digital access and property are unequally distributed along racial and socioeconomic lines at the start, the winners remain the same, and Airbnb exacerbates existing social-economic inequality.

Airbnb-fueled gentrification. Although "tourism gentrification" is not new (Gotham 2005), many find that Airbnb and STRs are creating a distinctive type of gentrification. They argue that spatial concentration of STR listings is at the root of what is referred to as "Airbnb-fueled gentrification" (Peck and Maldonado 2017). Although some observers believe that Airbnb in and of itself causes gentrification, the evidence suggests that it is a contributing factor that accelerates the process. Visitors are unlikely to choose STRs in low-income/minority neighborhoods that are not already gentrifying or gentrified. From the perspective of the host, such areas offer relatively inexpensive opportunities for investing in the housing market. As we have seen earlier, some of these neighborhoods are found in traditional low income/working class and minority communities, such as Chinatown in Boston, Mission in San Francisco and Bedford-Stuyvesant in New York, but can also be found in middle-class urban neighborhoods, such as the North End in Boston, Russian Hill and Potrero Hill in San Francisco, or hip, artsy, bohemian neighborhoods that are attractive to tourists, such as Venice in Los Angeles and Haight-Ashbury in San Francisco.

Wachsmuth and Weisler (2018, 10) describe "Airbnb-induced gentrification" as a new type of gentrification without redevelopment, requiring little capital, and providing a quick turnabout. Comparing the revenue flows from STRs to long-term rental revenue by neighborhood in NYC, they identify two types of neighborhoods: "post-gentrified" neighborhoods, such as centrally located Times Square, and currently gentrifying neighborhoods, such as Bedford-Stuyvesant and Bushwick, Brooklyn, areas with "cultural cachet, public transportation and amenities." The opportunity for profit is greater in the latter than the former and, as they note, "the only necessary step for converting a long-term rental to a short-term rental is to remove the existing tenant."

A case in point is Boston's Chinatown. Chinatown, which has historically served as the entry point for Chinese immigrants, is located close to downtown, in walking distance from the Financial District and Tufts University Medical Center. This densely populated area is rapidly gentrifying and has become one of the hottest real estate markets in the city for investors. In a neighborhood where 90 % of residents are renters, these trends have been accompanied by a rash of evictions. A recent study of community displacement, co-produced by the Chinese Progressive Association and MIT's Displacement Research Action Network (Main and Bell 2019), concluded that Airbnb was part of the problem. Local action groups such as Chinatown Community Association, the Chinese Progressive Association and the Chinatown Community Trust, along with local media, have identified Airbnb as a leading culprit in displacement and evictions (Hung 2018; Conti 2017; Semuels 2019).

While our focus is on cities, it is worth noting that concentration and displacement are not limited to urban areas and have afflicted small resort communities, such as ski towns in the western mountain states. In Crested Butte, Colorado, a small town (population 1,500) with working class roots, the most pressing issue is workforce housing. Neither police officers nor teachers, let alone ski-lift operators and waiters, can find housing within a commutable distance. As the number of investor-owned STRs has grown, long-term rentals have decreased from 43 % of the town's housing stock in 1997 to 24 % in 2016 (Vanderbilt 2017). In effect, the whole town has become gentrified and unaffordable to locals, and the resulting changes are undermining the very qualities that have made Crested Butte attractive in the first place.

The social fabric of cities and neighborhoods

The spatial concentration of STRs has social as well as structural consequences. As more residential housing is turned into STR and residents are replaced by visitors, neighborhoods become fractured, losing their cohesion and character.

These changes have been accompanied by a host of negative externalities for residents, generally referred to as "quality of life issues." Party atmosphere, noise pollution, crime and lessened security, the lack of parking, failure to observe garbage rules, and the presence of strangers and lock boxes have dominated media reports. These negative effects are not unique to the four cities we have examined but are part and parcel of Airbnb's "disruptive" presence in cities in the US and elsewhere. In European cities, among them Barcelona, Berlin and Amsterdam, where these challenges have been extreme, there has been a significant backlash against tourists giving rise to the term "overtourism" (Ali 2018).

First and perhaps foremost, the continual coming and going of visitors means that neighborhoods lose their most important asset, the neighbors (Barber 2016, 2). Transient visitors have different interests than long-term residents; they may use the local restaurants and amenities but they have no stake in the local community, in its schools and libraries, or in local issues. Social relations can become frayed as visitors come and go and people do not know who lives next door.

Venice Beach, Los Angeles, is a prototypic example of this process; Venice had the highest density of Airbnb listings in LA in 2014, in large part due to conversion of rent-stabilized apartments and buildings into hotels. Although Venice's several-mile-long Ocean Front Walk has long been a popular tourist attraction, the neighborhood is also a residential area. But the loss of its long-term rental housing threatens Venice with a loss of its identity as a hippie/fringe community, whose resident poets, musicians and artists populate the local coffee houses, bookstores and boardwalk. As one reporter put it: "I hate to break it to fans of Harry Perry, the turbaned roller-skating bard of Venice Beach, but the noise of rolling suitcases threatens to supplant his wailing guitar as the soundtrack of Ocean Front Walk" (Abcarian 2017). Judy Goldman, the co-founder of the LA anti-Airbnb organization Keep Neighborhoods First, notes that the area is now so full of Airbnbs that there are "housekeepers wheeling carts down the streets, ringing the doorbells at 5 a.m. saying things like 'Housekeeping'" (Barber 2016). As Samaan notes: "If we continue to lose affordable housing and move people out, you change what makes Venice, Venice" (Abcarian 2017).

These processes are particularly pronounced in cities where tourism is the major driver of the economy such as New Orleans. In New Orleans, Treme-Lafitte and several other neighborhoods around the French Quarter, distinguished by their single- and two-family dwellings, have experienced similar threats to their character as they turn into tourist zones. One issue is the new owners: residents report that, while the first gentrifiers were mostly local, they were succeeded by the non-resident investors, and increasingly, corporate owners and, with them, a professionalized short-term rental industry replete with property managers and providers of services to handle day-to-day operations from housekeeping, to concierge, to landscaping and repairs (New Orleans Planning Commission 2018).

One result is that the rhythm of a living neighborhood has changed to that of a stage set. Emptied of its low-income/middle-class mostly minority residents, the streets are even empty of tourists for half of the week before the weekenders arrive. Describing a typical scenario, a local resident said that when the tourists roll in on Thursdays and fill hundreds of units, Treme suddenly comes alive, but mostly with white college-aged kids, loud parties, overflowing garbage cans and other issues that bother the remaining residents (Perkins 2019).

In Treme, one of the oldest African American communities and a center of African American and Creole culture in a majority black city, real estate listings and tax bills show a sharp increase in house prices and taxes since 2015. This has displaced homeowners as well as resident tenants. In a city of renters, where 63 % of all renter households were cost-burdened in 2016, the greatest increase in rents is correlated with the neighborhoods – like Treme – with the highest concentration of STRs (DeDecker et al. 2018). Changes in home ownership and tenancy have changed the racial dynamics of the area. An analysis of STR permit data shows that neighborhoods with the highest concentrations of permits have gotten whiter than the rest of the city (Peck and Maldonado 2017).

Although it is generally acknowledged that gentrification and loss of affordable housing citywide have contributed to Treme's plight, the feeling about STRs is that they add "jet fuel on the fire" (DeDecker quoted in Perkins 2019, 2).[6] City policy has not helped; the city's first regulatory efforts (2017–2018) basically set no limits on STRs and were toughened somewhat beginning in 2019 (DeDecker et al. 2018). An analysis of the concentration of STR licenses by neighborhood, by *The Lens* and *HuffPost*, found that Treme-Lafitte has one of the three highest concentrations of STRs in the city, with 6 % to 8 % of residential addresses having an STR license (Peck and Maldonado 2017). One estimate is that STRs now operate on approximately 45 % of the historic Faubourg Treme District's parcels (Perkins 2019, 2) and a resident reported that on her block, 10 of the 16 homes were licensed for STRs. The New Orleans City Planning Commission's 2018 report entitled "Short Term Rentals" ranked Treme-Lafitte as sixth of the top 20 New Orleans neighborhoods in terms of number of active STR licenses and fourth highest in terms of the ratio of licenses to housing units (2018, 57), making both the loss of permanent residents and neighborhood character prominent issues.

Commenting on the neighborhood's transformation, one resident said: "Everyone I know lives next to an Airbnb" (Peck and Maldonado 2017). This has given rise to many Airbnb stories. One of the best is that of a lawyer and his family who woke up one morning to find that the STR guests next door – a bachelorette party from Texas – had taped inflatable penises to the front of the house, not bothering to think about whether neighboring residents might mind. There was, of course, a family next door. As a long-term resident put it: "Before Airbnb, you had neighbors you could depend on. They looked out for you. If you went out of town, they'd get your mail, your paper" (Peck and Maldonado 2017). With so much turnover, stability has notably decreased and trust lost.

What happens when locals can't afford to live like locals and neighbors have been replaced by a revolving cast of strangers? Although there have been no systematic studies of how residents respond to these changes, a small empirical study of a neighborhood in Oahu, Hawaii, found that residents who did not mind visitors during the day, had negative perceptions of "tourists to residential areas both overnight and for longer periods of time than a restaurant or attraction visit" (Jordan and Moore 2018). Discussing the many negative externalities inflicted upon neighbors, an Economic Policy Institute report on the costs and benefits of Airbnb notes that there are good reasons for zoning laws that ban short-term travel accommodations in residential neighborhoods and keep them from becoming like Times Square (Bivens 2019, 20).

Many find Airbnb-fueled gentrification to be far worse than the more traditional type of gentrification because the new people next door are only temporary. They come and go and their objectives are similarly short-term; on vacation they often ignore the behavioral norms that pertain in their own backyards. Writing about these neighborhood changes, Peck and Maldonado (2017) note:

> Airbnb-powered gentrification comes with all the downsides of traditional gentrification – home prices and rents are going up, lower-income residents and people of color are moving out – but with fewer upsides. Tourism and gentrification typically bring cleaner streets and less crime, but tourists don't stick around to clean up the neighborhood, vote in local elections or lobby for better schools.

Although Venice and Treme are known tourist destinations, other non-tourist, predominantly residential areas have been similarly impacted by a concentration of Airbnb listings. Hollywood Hills, Silver Lake and other sections of LA which feature mega mansion-style homes have been beset by homes rented out for large parties or events several times a month, with the attendant noise in neighborhoods zoned for privacy and the gridlock on winding roads with scenic views (Barber 2016). Moreover, investors have moved in, displacing neighbors. In Silver Lake, 39 % of the 303 properties sold in 2015 were not intended as primary residences; in

2018, the comparable figure was 60 % of 396 homes. In 2019, there were upwards of 300 STR listings for entire homes in Silver Lake posted on Airbnb alone. The head of the Silver Lake Neighborhood Council describes how the short-term renters are pushing out the stakeholders and "changing the whole feeling of the community" (Flemming 2019). As Judy Goldman of Keep Neighborhoods First points out: "When the primary resident is not there, you see a real disrespect for the common spaces in our city" (Barber 2016, 15). What used to be occasional nuisances now become the new normal.

Vertical communities. These issues occur within high-rise apartment buildings as well as within the spread-out contours of neighborhoods. And while the concentration of STR listings intensifies the negative effects for a given neighborhood, the negative effects in a densely populated vertical community are arguably more troublesome. Residents and visitors must interact within the confines of a given building, sharing hallways, elevators, exits, entries and other common spaces. The net result is that security feels compromised.

In NYC, where STR enforcement was stepped up considerably over the past few years, one of the most dramatic raids by Airbnb enforcement officials was in a 46-story mid-Manhattan condominium with 500 apartments. Responding to over 100 complaints by residents, violations were issued for 20 condo owners, including two members of the condo board. The board president – also manager of the building – was accused of organizing the illegal Airbnb racket. The residents, who formed a WhatsApp group to combat the STRs, filed a lawsuit describing "'bullying' tactics that have made life in the building 'akin to a 1920s Gulag instead of a white-glove luxury building'" (Cameron 2018). Their list of complaints included strangers coming and going at all hours; no ID checking by the doorman; mattresses, furniture and boxes of linens standing in the halls; and visitor services, such as a daily continental breakfast in the lobby. Asked why she did not enjoy the complimentary breakfast, one resident said that she did not buy her condo to live in a hotel and meet strangers in the lobby.

Writing about NYC's strong housing regulations, Ellen and O'Flaherty have emphasized its structural basis. Since NYC is the only major metro area in which a majority of housing units are located in buildings with five or more units and no other US city has half of NYC's population density, they suggest that the potential negative effects of people crowded together in a small space demands more regulation. "The development of trust and social capital among neighbors seems more critical in dense residential environments" (2013, 304). Accounts of disruption by STRs in multi-unit/high-rise buildings also raise issues of security given the frequently uncontrolled entry and exit points.

Recognizing the particular problems that STRs create in high-rise/multi-unit buildings, some start-ups have begun to offer solutions such as identifying illegal listings to building managers, owners and condo associations; they even offer to alert hosts when the noise level gets too high. One travel industry consultant phrased it this way: "Everybody is sort of trying to solve a pain point" (Gmelich

2019). See Chapter 4 on Australia for a discussion of the problems in "strata," the Australian name for high-rise apartment buildings.

Visitors in our midst: the marketing of neighborhoods

Although we have discussed neighborhoods in terms of concentration effects, Airbnb is not passive in this process. In its quest for authenticity, the platform plays a crucial role by actively marketing neighborhoods on its website. In spring 2019, New York City was listed with 60 specific neighborhoods, Los Angeles with 59, San Francisco, 39, and Boston, 28.

The potential traveler who goes onto the Airbnb website and chooses a city is asked to describe the type of neighborhood she prefers, using categories such as "cultural enclaves," "great transit," "loved by locals," "nightlife," "artsy," "touristy" or "Peace & Quiet." Each neighborhood is illustrated by a photo which aims to capture its distinctive spirit and a few descriptive words; the image then opens to a fuller paragraph-length description and a button that initiates a search for rental listings. The site visitor is made to feel as if she has entered "a cool world with interesting people" (Jones 2018). She can also press an "activities" button and find a list of "experiences" run by local guides, most also neighborhood-based. The focus on specific neighborhoods means that Airbnb plays a major role in shaping tourism destinations for millions of would-be travelers, which, in turn, affects the daily lives of residents in these same neighborhoods.

Airbnb claims that it brings economic benefits to neighborhoods beyond the central hotel/tourism district, particularly to more "diverse" neighborhoods, and its websites cite simple statistics to support these claims. An Airbnb-sponsored study by NERA Economic Consulting (2017) argues that Airbnb is responsible for a large increase in travel which, in turn, stimulates economic growth in destination cities. But these claims have been refuted by critics who point to the lack of adequate methods and data (Bivens 2019). They also suggest that Airbnb is trying to take credit for what is basically the consequence of an explosion of urban tourism – that tourists visit all corners of the city regardless of where they are staying.

Still it seems likely that if visitors are staying in neighborhoods, some of their spending will be proximate to their lodgings. In one of the few studies to take up this issue, researchers at Purdue University look at data for 42 NYC neighborhoods prior to 2015 and find a positive correlation between increased Airbnb listings, workers in neighborhood restaurants and Yelp reviews, although the increase was modest (Alyakoob and Rahman 2018). However, contrary to Airbnb's claims of fostering diversity, these findings do not hold for neighborhoods that are predominantly minority or Hispanic, even those with the same density of Airbnb listings.

More to the point, while the marketing of neighborhoods is an integral part of the platform's business model and the basis for its claim to authenticity – to "live like a local" – the reality is that Airbnb is commodifying neighborhoods by actively promoting and selling them to travelers. In the words of one urban planner and community activist: "Airbnb succeeds at the expense of neighborhoods" (Harrison 2016).

Challenges to local authority

In Chapter 2 we described how cities became a battleground as they tried to assess and regulate STRs. Examining the obstacles they faced, we focused on lack of access to data and the "black box" effect. But Airbnb has been more than a passive recipient of legal gray areas in tech policy. It has actively challenged the fiscal and regulatory authority of local governments, mobilized supporters and brought corporate actors to the local level.

Given a mandate that includes providing public goods, controlling land use and protecting health and safety as well as broader social welfare issues, such as access to affordable housing and neighborhood amenities, local authorities have a large stake in these struggles. Recognizing the difficulties they confront, ten European cities recently asked the European Union (EU) for help in regulating Airbnb, stating that "cities must protect the public interest and eliminate the adverse effects of short term holiday rentals in various ways" (Gemeente Amsterdam 2019). Taxation and zoning are prime examples.

Occupancy taxes. Occupancy or lodgings tax represents a significant revenue source for localities. Taking advantage of its "third party" legal status and expanding in an unregulated environment, Airbnb initially ignored paying occupancy tax. In fact, some have attributed Airbnb's initial success and growth to the fact that, unlike hotels, neither hosts nor guests pay taxes. To appease critics and encourage localities to legalize STRs, Airbnb began offering Voluntary Collection Agreements (VCAs) to cities in 2014.[7] These agreements allow Airbnb to collect and send taxes to a given locality; both San Francisco and LA have such agreements.

VCAs have turned out to be more problematic than anticipated for localities. First and foremost, Airbnb has demanded that details of the agreements remain secret. Dan Bucks, a former director of the Montana Department of Revenue, examined 12 publicly available VCAs and suggested that localities stop making these agreements for lack of accountability. Both payments and auditing were essentially controlled by Airbnb. Bucks also noted that, because Airbnb does not provide host information, the VCAs create a "shield of secrecy" that gives special advantages to Airbnb and is unfair to other taxpayers (2017). Although the study was sponsored by the hospitality industry, its conclusions are supported by numerous reports about specific local tax agreements as well as a 2019 review of the issue by Martineau (2019).

Although the VCAs provide some additional revenue to city coffers and level the playing field with regard to traditional types of tourist accommodations, cities must take what Airbnb gives them. Basically, the agreements suffer from the same lack of access to data that is central to Airbnb's business model. This puts cities, which are typically starved for revenue, in a bind: they are damned if they do and damned if they don't. As noted in Chapter 2, the VCA has been an important factor in LA's budget. The city controller's 2020 budget commented on a steep drop in STRs after the city's ordinance went into effect and warned of a negative impact on city revenue (Blake 2020).

Zoning for what, for whom? As we discussed previously, Airbnb grew by ignoring municipal zoning laws which most commonly restrict commercial and industrial uses in residential areas. By blurring the distinction between commercial and residential use, STRs test traditional land-use zoning, making STRs potentially illegal and putting localities on the defensive when proponents of regulation ask why their locality is not defending zoning codes.

Zoning has always been controversial. Although the given rationale for separating land uses is to promote health, safety and community stability, zoning has often been used as a political tool to protect middle-class communities from multi-family housing and low-income, minority residents. At present, zoning has become a hot political issue that makes some progressives uneasy (Badger and Bui 2019; Holder 2019). Although progressives have long called for upzoning and "Yes in my backyard" to allow denser housing in areas previously reserved for single-family homes, they are suspicious of the Trump administration's motivations in arguing that single-family residential zoning is central to making housing unaffordable and to its deregulatory attack on zoning and building restrictions. At the same time, low-income/minority communities fear that upzoning will accelerate gentrification.

The resulting quagmire opens the door to opponents of STR regulation who want to update zoning codes to legalize STRs or get rid of restrictions entirely. As Josh Bivens, director of the Economic Policy Institute and author of a January 2019 cost-benefit analysis of Airbnb, concludes: "There may be plenty wrong with the status quo in cities' zoning decisions. But the proper way to improve local zoning laws is not to simply let well-funded corporations ignore the status quo and do what they want" (Bivens 2019, 24).

This raises the question of the role of corporate interests at the local level. As a global corporation, Airbnb markets cities which are the main locus of regulatory control, but although most of the conflicts are local, all actors are not necessarily local. Known for aggressively defending as well as developing the local market for STRs in the US and abroad, Airbnb stepped up its public relations and lobbying efforts in 2016 by adding a corporate policy team headed by Chris Lehane, a former political consultant in the Clinton administration.

Recognizing the highly localized nature of regulation, Airbnb has sponsored over 400 homesharing clubs to mobilize hosts at the local level, supplying them with talking points and sending corporate spokesmen to town meetings. This strategy of "getting hosts to hearing rooms and polling booths" to testify that they use Airbnb to help pay the rent illustrates how major corporations create grassroots movements as part of their public relations activity (Steinmetz 2016; See also Walker 2014).[8] As we have seen in the previous chapter, Airbnb strategically mobilized its host community to successfully fight Proposition F in San Francisco;

when San Diego was on the brink of passing tough regulation in July 2018, Airbnb threatened to collect signatures to defeat the law at the ballot box. Fearing they would lose, the city withdrew the law.

As Airbnb has met with regulations and lawsuits, the company's strategy has changed from "the laws don't apply" to an arguably more conciliatory approach. An early example was the "One Host, One Home" policy announced in 2017 in response to its dispute with NYC. In fall 2019, in expectation of a public stock offering in 2020 and in response to negative media reports of scams and shootings in Airbnb rentals, Airbnb's CEO Brian Chesky announced a series of measures to improve the safety of hosts and guests and restore trust in the company. Airbnb plans to verify all seven million listings on the website by December 2020 "using a combination of technology and guest reports" to check the accuracy of photographs and other information and guarantees that guests will receive a 100 % refund if the unit they booked does not meet their expectations (Yaffe-Bellany 2019). It has also made conciliatory moves towards trade unions, agreeing to team up only with those developers who hire union labor (Parker 2020).

Along with Airbnb, the National Association of Realtors (NAR) supplies legal counsel to local hosts fighting regulations that limit STRs. They argue that the right to rent is "a fundamental aspect of private property ownership," and their website provides a list of ready answers under the heading "Advocacy Tips to Protect the Right to Rent." NAR representatives, presented as neutral experts, appear at local hearings where they intimidate communities by underlining the legal challenges localities will face if they attempt to regulate STRs. Some suggest that attempts to regulate Airbnb and STRs may be giving rise to a "Right to Rent" movement.

Airbnb's main corporate opponent in the US has been the American Hotel and Lodging Association (AHLA) along with the associated trade unions employing hotel workers. In addition to sponsoring research, AHLA has launched lobbyists and media campaigns at city, state and federal levels (Benner 2017). Arguing that platforms like Airbnb run a lodgings business but do not pay taxes or follow city and state safety and security regulations, AHLA has called for an "equal playing field." Both the AHLA and the hospitality workers unions, such as the Hotel Trades Council, AFL-CIO and Unite Here locals, have provided organizational and financial support to city efforts to regulate STRs, mobilizing anti-Airbnb coalitions at the national and local level. A prominent example is ShareBetter, founded in NYC in 2014. A nationwide coalition of neighbors, community activists and elected officials, ShareBetter is engaged in anti-Airbnb lobbying and works with local anti-Airbnb coalitions in their fight for regulation. A notable example is the 2019 landslide success of a referendum in Jersey City – a short subway ride from NYC – in which 70 % of voters voted in favor of stricter regulations despite the fact that Airbnb spent $ 4.2 million to fend off the new rules. Some have noted that the position of the hotel lobby may change as their interests evolve and they begin to engage in homesharing, and as Airbnb makes conciliatory approaches to the unions.

★ ★ ★

Whether or not corporate actors are directly involved, there is a ready army of proponents and opponents of regulation at the local level where a generic scenario unfolds. As STRs appear in neighborhoods, some residents object, arguing that their neighbor's commercial activity upends norms of everyday life as well as zoning codes or building regulations. Where once relative unanimity existed among householders, divisions of activity and interest now pit neighbor against neighbor. Residents who want to rent out their homes or apartments go up against residents who have chosen (and paid) to live in residentially zoned neighborhoods or condos and fear for their quality of life, their security and the value of their property. Mom-and-pop residents who want extra revenue clash with investors hosting multiple commercial listings; hosts who follow the law by registering and paying taxes spar with hosts who ignore existing regulations.

Business interests are also split between those that profit from and those which are hurt by STRs. Proponents of regulation include the hotels, motels and bed-and-breakfasts whose businesses have suffered due to "unfair competition" and want STRs to meet the same regulatory framework of taxes, insurance, and fire and sanitation codes that they must observe. Restaurants and retail may take a more favorable view because they believe visitors will eat out and shop more often.

Localities generally favor the interests of property owners and businesses, but in this case, these groups are themselves divided. And given the ubiquitous nature of the housing crisis, localities are sensitive to the demands of homeowners who want additional income as well as to local housing groups who argue that STRs undermine their efforts to protect and provide affordable housing. Moreover, as noted in Chapter 2, the conflict does not end with the passage of an ordinance. Typically, no one gets what they want and the fight goes on over regulatory enforcement as well as regulations.

Airbnb and STRs have added a new dimension to these disputes: the question of whether the needs of residents for housing and quality of life should take precedence over those of visitors. In the next two chapters, we explore how these debates have played out in cities beyond the US.

Notes

1 In these studies, "residential rentals" and "rental rates" refer to long-term rentals to residents as opposed to short-term rentals to visitors. Some localities also distinguish residential rentals on the basis of the number of days per year that the housing unit is rented.
2 Some studies exclude private room rentals or lump them with shared rooms assuming that they do not detract from housing supply. But some argue that these private room listings are a means of converting apartments and entire buildings into hotels and that they remove the option of long-term roommates (Wachsmuth et al. 2018; Lee 2016).
3 Sheppard and Udell, who look at the impact of Airbnb listings on residential properties in NYC, conclude that house prices are likely to increase "as long as the Airbnb properties themselves are not the source of extensive or concentrated negative externalities." They estimate the increase to be about 17 %, depending on location and negative externalities (2018, 41).

4 Some of the difference in these estimates can be explained by differing definitions of what constitutes a commercial operator or the time period during which the data were collected.
5 In NYC and LA, which are considerably larger geographically as well as in terms of population, the studies identified up to nine neighborhoods, compared to five to six in Boston and San Francisco.
6 A regulation passed by the New Orleans City Council in January 2019 making it illegal to convert whole-home investment properties into STRs in residential zones may help limit displacement. A similar regulation in the French Quarter in 2016 has led to some reversal in demographic trends with young families returning to the district (Perkins 2019).
7 Portland, Oregon, was the first city to make a tax agreement with Airbnb in July 2014. In 2016, an Airbnb official met with 100 mayors to push the program and by April 2016, 100 cities had signed up.
8 Edward Walker (2014) argues that much grassroots advocacy today is the work of an elite corps of consultants who "incentivize public activism as a marketable service" and who are hired by large corporations and powerful interest groups, such as Airbnb.

References

Abcarian, Robin. 2017. Venice Has Become an Epicenter of Los Angeles' Struggle Over Short-term Rentals. Call It the Airbnb Problem. *Los Angeles Times*. August 9. www.latimes.com/local/abcarian/la-me-abcarian-venice-housing-20170809-story.html

Ali, Rafat. 2018. The Genesis of Overtourism: Why We Came Up with the Term and What's Happened Since. *Skift*. August 14. https://skift.com/2018/08/14/the-genesis-of-overtourism-why-we-came-up-with-the-term-and-whats-happened-since/

Alliance of Downtown Community Organizations (ADCO). 2017. Airbnb Boston Quarterly Comparison. July 11. https://drive.google.com/file/d/0B5SuN3ZfUU7ROGs3S3k2SGI4eFE/view

Alliance of Downtown Community Organizations (ADCO). 2018. Memo. Why ADCO Supports Mayor Walsh's Revised Short-term Rental Ordinance. June1. https://drive.google.com/file/d/1dKaj4oioqIh0tqHw2GmG7eI_xKQ_mCuT/view

Alyakoob, Mohammed and Mohammad Saifu Rahman. 2018. Shared Prosperity (or Lack Thereof in the Sharing Economy. May 17. https://ssrn.com/abstract=3180278 or http://doi.org/10.2139/ssrn.3180278

Badger, Emily and Quoctrung Bui. 2019. Cities Start to Question an American Ideal: A House with a Yard on Every Lot. *The New York Times*. June 18. www.nytimes.com/interactive/2019/06/18/upshot/cities-across-america-question-single-family-zoning.html

Barber, Megan. 2016. Airbnb vs. the City. *Curbed*. November 10. www.curbed.com/2016/11/10/13582982/airbnb-laws-us-cities

Barron, Kyle, Edward Kung and Davide Proserpio. 2018. The Sharing Economy and Housing Affordability: Evidence from Airbnb. April 1. https://papers.ssrn.com/sol3/papers.cfm?abstract_id=3006832

Barron, Kyle, Edward Kung and Davide Proserpio. 2019. Research: When Airbnb Listings in a City Increase, So Do Rent Prices. April 17. https://hbr.org/2019/04/research-when-airbnb-listings-in-a-city-increase-so-do-rent-prices

Benner, Katie. 2017. Inside the Hotel Industry's Plan to Combat Airbnb. *The New York Times*. April 16. www.nytimes.com/2017/04/16/technology/inside-the-hotel-industrys-plan-to-combat-airbnb.html

Bivens, Josh. 2019. The Economic Costs and Benefits of Airbnb. *Economic Policy Institute*. January 30. www.epi.org/publication/the-economic-costs-and-benefits-of-airbnb-no-reason-for-local-policymakers-to-let-airbnb-bypass-tax-or-regulatory-obligations/

BJH Advisors. 2016. Shortchanging New York City: The Impact of Airbnb on New York City's Housing Market. www.hcc-nyc.org/documents/ShortchangingNYC2016FINAL protected_000.pdf
Blake, Matthew. 2020. L.A. Short-term Rental Inventory Has Plunged in Last Four Months. *The Real Deal*. March 02. https://therealdeal.com/la/2020/03/02/l-a-short-term-rental-inventory-has-plunged-in-last-four-months/amp/
Bredderman, Will. 2018. Hotel Industry, Activists and Comptroller Go to War with Airbnb. *Crain's New York Business*. May 8. www.crainsnewyork.com/article/20180508/REAL_ESTATE/180509894/hotel-industry-activists-and-comptroller-scott-stringer-go-to-war-with-airbnb
Bucks, Dan R. 2017. Airbnb Agreements with State and Local Tax Agencies. March. www.ahla.com/sites/default/files/Airbnb_Tax_Agreement_Report_0.pdf
Cameron, Christopher. 2018. Hell's Kitchen Condo Residents Are Rebelling Against Its "Creepy" Boss. *New York Post*. November 11. https://nypost.com/2018/11/11/hells-kitchen-condo-residents-are-rebelling-against-its-creepy-boss/
CBRE Hotels' Americas Research. 2017. Hosts with Multiple Units – A Key Driver of Airbnb Growth. March. www.ahla.com/hosts-multiple-units-key-driver-airbnb-growth
Conti, Kathleen. 2017. Activists March Against Airbnb Rentals they Say Are Squeezing Chinatown. *The Boston Globe*. October 5. www.bostonglobe.com/business/2017/10/05/housing-advocates-say-airbnb-rentals-are-replacing-chinatown-apartments/Z9KwIgppY89rHbbflvKC6H/story.html
Cox, Murray. 2016. Airbnb vs Rent: City of Los Angeles. August 30. http://insideairbnb.com/airbnb-vs-rent-city-of-la
Cox, Murray. 2017. The Face of Airbnb: New York City, Airbnb as a Racial Gentrification Tool. *InsideAirbnb*. March 1. http://insideairbnb.com/reports/the-face-of-airbnb-nyc.pdf
DeDecker, Breonne, Lydia Y. Nichols and Shanna M. Griffin. 2018. Jane Place Neighborhood Sustainability Initiative, Short-term Rentals, Long-Term Impacts: The Corrosion of Housing Access and Affordability in New Orleans. https://storage.googleapis.com/wzukusers/user-27881231/documents/5b06c0e681950W9RSePR/STR%20Long-Term%20Impacts%20JPNSI_4-6-18.pdf
Edelman, Benjamin, Michael Luca and Dan Svirsky. 2017. Racial Discrimination in the Sharing Economy: Evidence from a Field Experiment. *American Economic Journal: Applied Economics* 9(2): 1–22.
Ellen, Ingrid Gould and Brendan O'Flaherty. 2013. How New York and Lost Angeles Housing Policies Are Different – And Maybe Why. In David Halle and Andrew A. Beveridge (eds.) *New York and Los Angeles: The Uncertain Future*. New York: Oxford University Press, 286–309.
Flemming, Charles. 2019. Gentrification Hits Silver Lake. *Los Angeles Times*. October 23. www.latimes.com/opinion/story/2019-10-23/airbnb-short-term-rental-silver-lake-los-angeles-regulations
Gemeente Amsterdam. 2019. Press Release "Cities Alarmed About European Protection of Holiday Rental" [English site]. www.amsterdam.nl/bestuur-organisatie/college/wethouder/laurens-ivens/persberichten/press-release-cities-alarmed-about/
Gmelich, Krista. 2019. Airbnb Spawned an Ecosystem of Startups that Sweat the Details So Owners Don't Have To. *Bloomberg News*. May 1. www.bloomberg.com/news/articles/2019-05-01/airbnb-spawned-an-ecosystem-of-startups-that-sweat-the-details-so-owners-don-t-have-to
Gotham, Kevin Fox. 2005. Tourism Gentrification: The Case of New Orleans' Vieux Carre (French Quarter). *Urban Studies* 42(7): 1099–1112. http://citeseerx.ist.psu.edu/viewdoc/download?doi=10.1.1.616.5724&rep=rep1&type=pdf

Harrison, Pete. 2016. What I Think Every Time I See an Airbnb Renter in My Neighborhood. *Next City*. July 28. https://nextcity.org/daily/entry/airbnb-gets-housing-wrong

Holder, Sarah. 2019. Don't Call Trump's Housing Order a Yimby Plan. *CityLab*. June 26. www.citylab.com/equity/2019/06/trump-yimby-affordable-housing-reform-crisis-executive-order/592582/?utm_source=feedburner&utm_medium=feed&utm_campaign=Feed%3A+TheAtlanticCities+%28CityLab%29

Horn, Keren and Mark Merante. 2017. Is Home Sharing Driving up Rents? Evidence from Airbnb in Boston. *Journal of Housing Economics* 38: 14–24.

Hung, Melissa. 2018. Luxury Developments, Gentrification, Airbnb: The Battle for Boston's Chinatown. *Huffington Post*. January 27. www.huffpost.com/entry/bostonchinatowngentrification_n_5a6b05fae4b01fbbefb0b992

Jimenez, Sarah. 2017. The Growth of Commercial Short-term Rentals. How Boston Can Protect Affordable Housing and Quality of Life. *Community Labor United*. September. www.forworkingfamilies.org/sites/default/files/publications/images/clu_shorttermrental_report_prf7.jpg

Jones, Michael. 2018. Airbnb Goes Inhospitable. *Commonwealth Magazine*. April 18. https://commonwealthmagazine.org/economy/airbnb-goes-inhospitable-2/

Jordan, Evan J. and Jocelyn Moore. 2018. An In-depth Exploration of Residents' Perceived Impacts of Transient Vacation Rentals. www.researchgate.net/publication/316305917_An_in-depth_exploration_of_residents%27_perceived_impacts_of_transient_vacation_rentals

Kudler, Adrian. 2015. Meet LA's Most Prolific Airbnb Host with 78 Units for Rent. *Curbed LA*. March 12. https://la.curbed.com/2015/3/12/9981370/airbnb-los-angeles-most-prolific-host-ghc

Lee, Dayne. 2016. How Airbnb Short-Term Rentals Exacerbate Los Angeles's Affordable Housing Crisis: Analysis and Policy Recommendations. *Harvard Law & Policy Review* 10: 229–253. http://harvardlpr.com/wp-content/uploads/2016/02/10.1_10_Lee.pdf

Main, Kelly Leilani and Diana X Bell. 2019. Forced from Home: A Human Rights Assessment of Displacement and Eviction in Boston's Chinatown. *MIT Displacement Research and Action Network*. https://static1.squarespace.com/static/56340b91e4b017e2546998c0/t/5c7811640852290f392207ca/1551372655581

Martineau, Paris. 2019. Inside Airbnb's "Guerrilla War" Against Local Governments. *Wired*. March 20. www.wired.com/story/inside-airbnbs-guerrilla-war-against-local-governments/

NERA Economic Consulting [NERA]. 2017. Airbnb's Global Support to Local Economies: Output and Employment. *Prepared for Airbnb*. March 2017. www.nera.com/content/dam/nera/publications/2017/NERA_Airbnb_Report_2017_03_13_final_revised.pdf

New Orleans, City Planning Commission. 2018. Short Term Rental Study. September 18. http://cityofno.granicus.com/MetaViewer.php?view_id=2&event_id=21662&meta_id=422356

New York City, Office of the Comptroller, Scott Stringer [NYC Comptroller]. 2018. The Impact of Airbnb on NYC Rents. April. https://comptroller.nyc.gov/reports/the-impact-of-airbnb-on-nyc-rents/

New York Communities for Change and Real Affordability for All [NYCC and RAFA]. 2015. Airbnb in NYC: Housing Report. www.sharebetter.org/wp-content/uploads/2015/07/AirbnbNYCHousingReport1.pdf

New York State, Office of the Attorney General, Eric T. Schneiderman. (NYS AG). 2014. Airbnb in the City. https://ag.ny.gov/pdfs/AIRBNB%20REPORT.pdf

O'Neill, John W. and Yuxia Ouyang. 2016. An Analysis of the Other Side of Airbnb. September. www.ahla.com/sites/default/files/Airbnb_Analysis_September_2016_0.pdf

Parker, Will. 2020. Airbnb Looks to Boost Labor Image with Union Pact. *Wall Street Journal*. January 10. www.wsj.com/articles/airbnb-looks-to-boost-labor-image-with-union-pact-11578670200

Peck, Emily and Charles Maldonado. 2017. How Airbnb Is Pushing Locals from New Orleans' Coolest Neighborhoods: "We're Out of Here." November 4. www.theadvocate.com/new_orleans/news/article_e8e96c00-c0e9-11e7-b886-cf6fbb846[10]f57.html

Perkins, Tom. 2019. "Like a Ghost Town": How Short-term Rentals Dim New Orleans' Legacy. *The Guardian*. March13. www.theguardian.com/us-news/2019/mar/13/new-orleans-airbnb-treme-short-term-rentals

Said, Carolyn. 2018. A Leaner Vacation Rental Market. *San Francisco Chronicle*. February 16. www.sfchronicle.com/business/article/SF-short-term-rentals-transformed-as-Airbnb-12617798.php

Samaan, Roy. 2015a. Airbnb, Rising Rent, and the Housing Crisis in Los Angeles. March. www.laane.org/wp-content/uploads/2015/03/AirBnB-Final.pdf

Samaan, Roy. 2015b. Short-Term Rentals and L.A.'s Lost Housing. August 24. www.laane.org/wp-content/uploads/2015/08/Short-Term_RentalsLAs-

San Francisco, City and County, Board of Supervisors. Budget and Legislative Analyst [San Francisco Budget and legislative Analyst]. 2015. Analysis of the Impact of Short-term Rentals on Housing. May. https://sfbos.org/sites/default/files/FileCenter/Documents/52601-BLA.ShortTermRentals.051315.pdf

San Francisco, City and County, Board of Supervisors, Budget and Legislative Analyst [San Francisco Budget and Legislative Analyst]. 2016. Short Term Rentals 2016 Update. https://sfbos.org/sites/default/files/FileCenter/Documents/55575-BLA.ShortTermRentals%20040716.pdf

Semuels, Alana. 2019. The End of the American Chinatown. *The Atlantic*. February 4. www.theatlantic.com/technology/archive/2019/02/americas-chinatowns-are-disappearing/581767/

Sheppard, Stephen and Andrew Udell. 2018. Do Airbnb Properties Affect House Prices. *Working Paper, Department of Economics*, Williams College. January 1. https://econpapers.repec.org/paper/wilwileco/2016-03.htm

Steinmetz, Katy. 2016. Inside Airbnb's Plan to Build a Grassroots Political Movement. *Time*. http://time.com/4416136/airbnb-politics-sharing-economy-regulations-housing/

Vanderbilt, Tom. 2017. Did Airbnb Kill the Mountain Town? July 11. www.outsideonline.com/2198726/did-airbnb-kill-mountain-town

Wachsmuth, David, David Chaney, Danielle Kerrigan, Andrea Shillolo and Robin Basalaev-Binder. 2018. The High Cost of Short-Term Rentals in New York City. *A Report from the Urban Politics and Governance Research Group, School of Urban Planning*, McGill University. January. www.politico.com/states/f/?id=00000161-44f2-daac-a3e9-5ff3d8740001

Wachsmuth, David, Jennifer Combs and Danielle Kerrigan. 2019. The High Cost of Short-Term Rentals in New York City. *A Report from the Urban Politics and Governance Research Group*, School of Urban Planning McGill University. www.sharebetter.org/wp-content/uploads/2019/01/Impact-of-New-STR-Regs-2019.pdf

Wachsmuth, David and Alexander Weisler. 2018. Airbnb and the Rent Gap: Gentrification Through the Sharing Economy. *Environment and Planning A. Economy and Space* 50: 1147–1170. www.researchgate.net/publication/318281320_Airbnb_and_the_Rent_Gap_Gentrification_Through_the_Sharing_Economy

Walker, Edward T. 2014. *Grassroots for Hire: Public Affairs Consultants in American Democracy*. Cambridge: Cambridge University Press.

Ward, Lisa. 2017. How Airbnb Affects Home Prices and Rents. *Wall Street Journal*. October 22. www.wsj.com/articles/how-airbnb-affects-home-prices-and-rents-1508724361

Yaffe-Bellany, David. 2019. Airbnb to Verify All Listings, C.E.O. Chesky Says. *The New York Times*. November 6. www.nytimes.com/2019/11/06/business/airbnb-verify-listings.html

PART TWO
Moving beyond the US

4
AUSTRALIA, AIRBNB'S MOST PENETRATED MARKET

Given Airbnb's global reach, to what extent is its impact on housing and communities similar or different elsewhere? The following chapters look beyond the US to examine the impact of Airbnb and short-term rentals (STRs), first in Australia and then in Germany where seemingly similar consequences have been embedded in different social and political environments.

Like the US, Australia has a long history of promoting homeownership as the preferred form of housing tenure. Neoliberal policies in both countries have promoted the increasing financialization of housing. In the US, these policies provoked the 2008 financial crisis that reverberated around the world. Australia stands out among advanced industrial societies in that it avoided an economic recession and, unlike the US where house prices plummeted and were followed by widespread mortgage defaults, house prices in Australia remained high and increased steadily in the subsequent period.

In contrast to the US, where Airbnb gained traction during a financial crisis, Airbnb arrived in Australia in the midst of a housing boom. In the US, early critics of Airbnb were concerned that it was removing long-term rentals from the housing market, but Airbnb was well-received in Australia where it encountered little resistance from housing advocates and local authorities. In 2017, five years after opening its first office in Sydney, Airbnb's country manager Sam McDonagh proudly announced that Australia was Airbnb's "most penetrated market in the world" (Thomson 2017). At the same time, researchers noted that "Australian governments were treading lightly around Airbnb" (Gurran and Phibbs 2017). How do we explain these differing opening scenarios?

In discussing the Australian case, we will follow the same format as for the US. We begin by outlining the basic structure of the housing sector, describe the changes introduced by neoliberal regimes and look at the impact of the Global Financial Crisis (GFC) on housing markets. We then summarize the evidence regarding the impact of Airbnb and STRs on housing and neighborhoods in Australia's two largest cities, Melbourne and Sydney.

The housing sector and home finance

> Australians watch housing markets intensely, perhaps more so than citizens of any other country.
>
> *(Phillip Lowe, Governor, Reserve Bank of Australia 2019)*
>
> Looking at real estate is more than just research – it's an investment opportunity, a hobby and entertainment combined.
>
> *(Tyrone Hodge, Australian Property Institute, quoted in Hendy 2019)*

As these quotes illustrate, real estate in general and homeownership in particular are national obsessions. Homeownership – commonly referred to as the "Great Australian Dream" and the dominant housing tenure in Australia – has been considered part of the wage earners welfare state (Castles 1994). At its high point in 1986, 70.4 % of Australians were homeowners, a higher percentage than the high of 69.2 % in the US in 2004, before the GFC.

Despite being highly urbanized, Australia's rental sector has traditionally been relatively small, and though it includes social and private rental, the large majority of tenants rent from private landlords. According to the 2016 census, 30.3 % of Australians were renters: 25.3 % in the private sector and only 3.5 % in the social sector (AIHW 2018). Rental tenure has been considered unattractive, "a temporary short-term station," as renters do not benefit from the generous tax expenditures given to homeowners, and perhaps more importantly, because it is insecure. There is no rent control; 95 % of all leases are limited to one year and renters have little protection against eviction or rising rent prices under existing tenancy laws (Daley et al. 2018; Bate 2018).

Australia's traditional home finance system relied upon deposit-taking institutions and conservative lending standards. Although similar to the Savings & Loans (S&Ls) in the US, there were several notable differences: the most common mortgage instrument was the variable rate mortgage, larger down payments were required and borrowers had to repay the full loan even if they had negative equity. The net result was a comparatively low foreclosure rate. These characteristics also protected financial institutions, which could adjust their mortgage rates when interest rates were rising, unlike the S&Ls in the US which were stuck with long-term fixed-rate mortgages and whose demise jump-started the restructuring of the home finance system.

This changed beginning in the 1980s as neoliberal policies such as financial deregulation introduced new actors – mortgage brokers and wholesale-funded mortgage originators – new instruments such as conversion mortgages, and new flows of international capital into home finance (Murphy 2011). As Morris, among others, have observed: "Australia has been in the forefront of the financialization of housing" (2018, 64; see also Rogers and Power 2017).

Using wholesale money markets and securitization, the new lenders created a market for nonconforming mortgages, the Australian version of the subprime. From the mid-1990s, Australia developed "one of the largest ABS (asset-backed securities) markets in the world" which, in 2007, amounted to US $ 215 billion (Green and Wachter 2010, 425). This market basically reflected the growth of residential mortgage-backed securities. The result was that the mortgage market "shift[ed] from credit constrained and conservative lending regimes to more price competitive and product innovative markets" (Murphy 2011, 340). This neoliberal turn made for easier loan criteria as well as easily available money and promoted a housing boom between 2000 and 2006, much of it speculative and investor driven.

Tax policies have been crucial in promoting both homeownership and investment in housing. Owner-occupied housing has received particularly favorable treatment. It is exempt from capital gains and imputed rents as well as from a social assets test for pensions and state land tax. Investors in rental housing benefit from negative gearing, which allows an investor whose rental stream is less than her mortgage payment to deduct the loss. Investors also benefit from a 50 % discount on income from capital gains (Martin et al. 2016, 17–18; Daley et al. 2018). From a social perspective, the rationale has been to increase housing as a source of untaxed wealth and financial security for ordinary Australians as they approach retirement. The net effect has been to make investment in housing extremely attractive. Observers have noted that tax policies are responsible for the large number of vacant dwellings, particularly in capital cities, "driving a mismatch between the supply of housing and housing need" (Troy and Randolph 2016).

In 2016, investors owned an estimated 27 % of all housing stock, accounted for nearly 47 % of new mortgage originations and provided the majority (48 %) of rental housing in Australia (CoreLogic 2016, 4). Leaving aside foreign investors, who purchased an increasing share of residential real estate between 2010–2016, the typical Australian investor has traditionally been a small-scale landlord owning one to two properties.[1] Although becoming more popular with the self-managed super funds, 2016 data indicate that investing in residential property remains a small proportion of investment (4.3 %) compared to commercial non-residential (13 %).

Unlike other industrialized nations, the GFC had relatively minor consequences for the Australian housing market (Martin et al. 2016). Comparing Australia to the US and the UK, Murphy notes that the impact was "shallow" and brief with house prices declining to a much lesser extent (Murphy 2011). Although the banks faced liquidity problems due to their reliance on international capital, they were not exposed to subprime mortgages as in the US. It was the nontraditional lenders who were primarily responsible for nonconforming mortgages which crashed, but those mortgages accounted for only a small percentage of the mortgage market (Dobbie 2009).[2]

Australia's policy response also helped. Between 2008 and 2009, a government stimulus included construction of new social (rental) housing in addition to hefty support for first-time homebuyers, who accounted for 25 % of all mortgages in 2008 (Murphy 2011, 344). The net effect was a rapid recovery. House prices began to rise and, in contrast to the US, Australia's housing market entered boom conditions by early 2009.

Both Australia and the US experienced a liberalized market and a pre- GFC housing boom. In the aftermath of the GFC, there was less downturn and a rapid recovery in Australia with only minor price declines in housing. For different reasons, this set the stage for Airbnb.

Post-crisis conditions, renters and rentiers

One consequence of the long housing boom and the rising prices was that many would-be homeowners became renters. In the two decades between 1997–1998 and 2017–2018, the proportion of households renting rose from 27 % to 32 % (Letts 2019). These national figures understate what was happening in Sydney and Melbourne. In these premier cities soaring house prices turned the dream of owning a home into an illusion for many. The rising proportion of renters, particularly among younger cohorts, prompted warnings that they were destined to be "permanent renters" (Davies 2017; Daley et al. 2018; Yates 2017).

At the same time, those who could, became rentiers, parking their money in residential housing. Recent discussions of housing policy have criticized the policies and practices that prioritize housing-as-investment and argue that these trends have changed the way Australians think about their home – not as a place to live and raise a family but as a place to grow capital (Rogers and Power 2017; see also Daley et al. 2018; Alexander 2018; Ronald 2017; Bluett 2017). Some fear that "rentier driven, rather than entrepreneur-led economic growth has reduced the housing market's resilience to cyclical instability" (Maclennan 2019) and raise the specter of a bubble similar to the housing bubble in the US that set off the GFC (Bajkowski 2016; Dun 2018).

Others have focused on the social consequences of a housing haves and have-nots divide in a country where homeownership has been part of the welfare state narrative, an equalizing factor in a nation of immigrants and, more recently, a savings bank in the face of welfare state retrenchment. They argue that neo-liberal housing policies have contributed to growing inequality and polarization (Maclennan 2019; Daley et al. 2018; Rogers and Power 2017; Yates 2017). As one observer put it:

> The reason declining access to home ownership for younger people is of such concern is that housing is much more than housing. The wealth accumulated in our homes over our lifetimes has come to represent economic security and a means to live more comfortably in old age. It's seen as a buffer in times of hardship – buying a home is an implicit part of the welfare system in many contexts.
>
> *(Ronald 2017)*

A 2018 investigation into housing affordability published by the Grattan Institute captures these concerns:

Within living memory, Australia was a place where housing costs were manageable, and people of all ages and incomes had a reasonable chance to own a home with good access to jobs. But home-ownership rates are falling among all Australians younger than 65 especially those with lower incomes. Owning a home increasingly depends on who your parents are, a big change from 35 years ago when home-ownership rates were high for all levels or incomes. Those on low incomes – increasingly renters – are spending more of their income on housing.

(Daley et al. 2018, 3)

By encouraging an investor-led housing boom, Australia inadvertently facilitated what has been described as "a natural expansion" of Airbnb's market" as rentiers took advantage of the platform's new opportunities for revenue (LeMay 2012).

Airbnb arrives during the boom and is well received

In Australia, Airbnb took advantage of the existing investor-owned and mostly vacant apartments. When Airbnb opened an office in Sydney in November 2012, the platform already had 5,000 listings in Australia. Within five years, the number of listings had grown exponentially to 160,500 (InsideAirbnb data cited in Che et al. 2019).[3]

In Australia, Airbnb was embraced "by both the public and private sectors. Government organizations such as Tourism Victoria and corporate giants like Quantas forged partnerships with the platform" (Alexander 2018, 2). Quantas partnered to offer frequent-flyer miles to members who booked Airbnb accommodations through Quantas.com; Tourism Victoria, a state agency, worked with Airbnb to encourage tourism to less touristy middle and outer suburbs of Melbourne (Mannix 2015). Tourism revenue was a major incentive. Australian travelers have long been among the most enthusiastic users of Airbnb (Bogle 2016; Farnsworth 2018). According to Sam McDonagh, 30 % of Australians are Airbnb users: "Australians are relatively early adopters of technology, but we're also wonderful world travelers" (ADMA 2018).

Expanding rapidly in prime areas of inner cities and nearby beach communities, Airbnb found an easy fit in the highly financialized Australian housing market. As Leshinsky and Schatz note: "The model of capitalizing on a property asset is particularly attractive for property owners in Australia where a great deal of individual capital is tied up in property ownership, especially single lot investment apartments which are ideal for use as STRs" (2018, 418).

Cities as a locus

As has been the case elsewhere, Airbnb is found throughout Australia but has been most concentrated in metropolitan regions and resort communities. Foremost among these are Australia's two largest and most dynamic cities, Sydney and Melbourne.[4] The two cities which are home to 40 % of the population are also major tourist destinations, combining beach and city vistas along their sprawling coastlines.

Sydney, the capital of New South Wales (NSW) and headquarters for global companies in the Asia-Pacific region, is Australia's largest metropolitan region with a population of 4.6 million. Melbourne, the capital of Victoria, is Australia's second largest metropolitan region, a cultural as well as financial center, with a rapidly growing population currently at 4.15 million. They are also expensive cities where housing affordability issues are acute.[5] Both have undergone urban renewal and lost affordable housing in their inner "suburbs" as they have become increasingly gentrified hubs for professional services employment (Gurran and Phibbs 2017, 83–84). In the five-year period between 2012 and 2018, house prices rose 50 % in Melbourne and 70 % in Sydney, outpacing increases in income and making homeownership unaffordable for an increasing number of residents. Rents have also increased, although the increases are more in line with wages. Nonetheless, almost half of those in private rentals experience financial stress, paying over 30 % of their income for housing (Horne and Adamson 2016; Daley et al. 2018).

Emergence of high-rise cities. For much of the post-war period, Australia has been a suburban nation characterized by its dominant housing stock, the single-family house on a quarter acre lot.[6] Starting in the 1990s, in response to changing economic and demographic forces, metropolitan planning policies began to contain suburban sprawl and promote greater density in existing neighborhoods (Foster 2006, 178). As a result, the housing stock has become more diverse and now includes a significant number of medium and high-density dwellings (Foster 2006; Stapledon 2017; Smith 1997).[7] The turn toward medium and high-density buildings has been particularly pronounced in Sydney and Melbourne and is reflected in the transformation of their skylines.

In Greater Sydney, following a construction boom, high-rise apartments increased 33.6 %, from 155,000 to 276,000 between 2011 and 2016 (News.com.au 2017). In 2016, Greater Sydney's housing stock still consisted of 55 % single family homes, but 20.3 % were medium density and 23.5 % were high-density dwellings. The overall proportion of renters rose from 31.6 % in 2011 to 34.1 % in 2016 (Dow 2016). However, these figures were radically different in specific neighborhoods. In 40 % of Sydney neighborhoods, the majority of households are renters (Wade 2018). In the inner city of Sydney, for example, only 1.9 % of dwellings were single-family in 2016, 21.8 % were medium density and 74.6 % were high-density.

While Melbourne has historically had fewer high-rise apartments than Sydney, the city has been rapidly overtaking Sydney in terms of an apartment boom. Between 2011 and 2016, high-rise apartments in Melbourne increased by 82 % and the percentage of medium density housing stock jumped from 11.6 % to 16.8 % (News.com.au 2017). During the same period, the proportion of renters increased from 27.2 % to 30 % (Domain Reporters 2017). As in Sydney, these figures differ significantly by neighborhood, and in several neighborhoods, renters make up between 42 % to 50 % of the population (Davies 2017).

Known for a more laissez-faire approach to business and property development (Alexander 2018), Melbourne's high-rise apartment buildings in its center are four times the maximum density of Hong Kong and New York City. There are also no height limits in its central business district (CBD) which is also Australia's most densely populated area (Searle 2017). Needless to say, Melbourne's market-driven apartment building boom has been criticized for lack of planning control. In the words of one planner, the result is "vertical slums of micro-apartments under 50 square meters with windowless bedrooms" (Searle 2017). Discussing the "architectural and urban implications" of this sort of development, Alexander writes:

> In contrast to Airbnb's opportunistic use of existing housing stock in other global cities, in Melbourne, there is some evidence to suggest that the relationship between short-term rentals and the construction of new homes has been more symbiotic – perpetuating, and in some cases, even driving housing models.
>
> *(2018, 3)*

Foreign investors and vacant apartments. Foreign investment in real estate, which has stimulated much of this growth, has contributed to the affordability crisis in these cities. Investor-owned property is geographically concentrated in inner capital city apartment markets (CoreLogic 2016, 16). In Greater Sydney, investors own approximately half of the apartment stock and in Melbourne, 58 %, of which 87 % has been driven by foreign investment from China (CoreLogic 2016, 18–20).[8] Many of the high-rise units, which are often built on the sites of former affordable housing blocks, are left empty as investors have purchased these units to capitalize on the rising property market (News.com.au 2017).[9]

Although vacant apartments have been a feature of Australia's capital cities since at least the late 1990s, sales to foreign investors have increased dramatically since 2010. As affordability pressures increased, critics have blamed investors for propping up house prices, putting pressure on rents, and consuming newly built supply. A study by Cashmore (2015) found that, in 2014, a total of 82,724 properties in Melbourne – 4.8 % of its housing stock – appeared unoccupied and underutilized as measured by very low water usage during the year; 30 % of these properties recorded no water usage and were assumed to be vacant. A 2017 UBS Australia housing survey reported that "at a time when ordinary working Australians are struggling through the worst housing affordability crisis on record," Melbourne had 200,000 more empty homes than a decade ago (News.com.au 2017). Although foreign investment peaked in 2016 and has since declined in response to China's tightened control, to Australia's increased surcharge for foreign investors, and to general market conditions, there is still a large investor market in residential real estate.

In short, high-rise construction fueled by foreign investors created an open-house environment for Airbnb and STRs. Investors who might have left their apartments vacant, could now take advantage of new opportunities for revenue. Media accounts note that Airbnb management companies "are seducing landlords with promises of big bucks at seminars costing as much as $5000" (Tan 2019). According to a Melbourne real estate professional, questions about Airbnb rental ability are now part of the purchaser conversation and new investors are willing to pay up to 3 % more for a residential property with a record of "a high yielding Airbnb income stream" (Bleby 2018).

Airbnb's impact in Sydney and Melbourne

Sydney and Melbourne were "top hotspots of Airbnb activity" from the start, with Sydney ranking among Airbnb's top ten destinations world-wide and Melbourne in the top 20 (Alizadeh et al. 2018b). In Sydney, Airbnb listings rose from about 5,000 in November 2014 to 28,000 in December 2017 during peak tourism season and dropped to 20,000 in February 2018. Melbourne had a similar but less steep trajectory and without the seasonal change; Airbnb listings increased from 5,000 listings in August 2015 to 18,000 in February 2018 (AirDNA data cited in Crommelin et al. 2018b, 30).

As was the case elsewhere, the exponential growth of Airbnb and the accompanying negative externalities became the topic of local media reports before there was any official inquiry. In Australia, the concerns were primarily about quality of life and neighborhood amenities.

Not surprisingly, an early response by the state of Victoria focused on the amenity issue. In 2014, Victoria created an independent panel to look into behavioral issues related to STRs in Melbourne's CBD.[10] The panel considered various options ranging from restriction to registration (including self-regulation and amending strata rules) but could not come to a unanimous agreement. Sidestepping regulation, the panel recommended that the government consult with industry and residents (Victoria, Independent Panel 2015).

One year later, the State of NSW launched a parliamentary inquiry to determine the necessity of regulation of STRs. The inquiry, which invited public submissions from stakeholders (residents, owners corporations, local governments, Airbnb, InsideAirbnb, the hospitality industry and planners), held several hearings and published the results in a report (NSW Parliament 2016).[11] Although the report focused primarily on amenities, it did identify housing affordability and availability as a rising concern but concluded that, while the evidence seemed compelling, it was "only anecdotal" and called for "a program to collect data" (2016, 12).

The inquiry, however, served as an impetus for empirical research, mostly by planners who sought to provide data to address the existing regulatory vacuum and to examine planning policy.[12] In 2017, Gurran and Phibbs published a study, followed by two other studies published in *Urban Policy and Research* in 2018 (Alizadeh et al. 2018a; Crommelin et al. 2018a). The most comprehensive and systematic of the empirical studies was by Crommelin et al. under the auspices of the Australian Housing and Urban Research Institute (2018b).[13] Using data from InsideAirbnb and AirDNA together with socio-economic and demographic data, the study examined a broad range of issues including the impact on the housing market, patterns of geographic and socio-economic concentration, amenities, host characteristics and motivation, planning regulation and social equity.

Neighborhood amenities and concentration effects

The Victoria and NSW inquiries indicated that neighborhood amenity or quality of life was the foremost concern of Australians. As elsewhere, it was the concentration of listings that fueled much of the anti-Airbnb opposition; complaints were amplified as the number and density of listings increased. This created special problems, particularly in locations which had not previously been tourist areas.

High-rise apartments, strata. A large proportion of Airbnb listings in Sydney and Melbourne are located in high-rise apartments or strata. The Victoria Independent Panel on Short-Stay Accommodation found that more than one quarter of apartments in some buildings were STRs. According to a 2016 Grattan Institute report, 70 % of whole-premise listings in Sydney and Melbourne were apartments. The report concluded that negative externalities "seem most acute in apartment complexes, where neighbors are in close proximity and share ownership and use of common areas and facilities such as lifts, gyms and pools" (Minifie 2016, 26).

As part of their inquiry, the NSW Parliamentary Committee documented the complaints of strata residents and owners corporations. For example, the Owners Corporation Network (OCN) testified that strata living was incompatible with STRs and listed a host of issues: breaches of building security, blocked fire exits, smoking in non-smoking areas, strangers in common areas such as laundries, excessive wear and tear on common property, excessive noise, blocked garbage disposals, excessive water use, violation of visitor parking restriction, insurance risk and overcrowding (Owners Corporation Network 2017).[14] The report also discussed several cases regarding STRs in strata that went to litigation and received media coverage. Although the Committee did not favor restricting STRs in strata, it did find that, compared to detached houses, strata represented a "special case" and that owners needed more control (NSW Parliament 2016).

While the OCN preceded the advent of Airbnb, STRs have given rise to new organizations aimed at protecting and defending the quality of life of strata residents. Among the most important are Neighbors not Strangers in Sydney (founded in 2016) and We Live Here in Melbourne (founded in 2015). Both have lobbied their respective state governments to pass legislation that would regulate Airbnb and other STRs and have criticized proposed regulations as woefully inadequate.

Along with inner-city CBDs packed with apartments, inner-city beach suburbs were also hot spots for Airbnb listings and thus complaints. In Sydney's Bondi Beach in 2016, for example, 9 % of all dwellings were listed on Airbnb, compared to 5 % in other beachside suburbs (Minifie 2016, 23). The NSW report noted the existence of party houses along with parking and congestion issues in these suburban areas, but as there were relatively few complaints, it concluded that the costs to neighbors in detached dwellings was less severe.

Commercial activity and concentration effects

Compared to the US, Airbnb's impact on housing has been a secondary topic in Australia. Two academic studies have attempted to fill the data gap, Crommelin et al. (2018b) and Gurran and Phibbs (2017). Crommelin et al. examine Airbnb's impact on private housing opportunity in Sydney and Melbourne, in particular, the affordability and availability of long-term rentals in the private rental market. Using AirDNA data for March 2018, they correlate SA2s (an Australian census unit similar in size to neighborhoods) with census data and data on rental availability (rental bond lodgment data).[15]

Like other studies, they focus on commercial listings – the type most likely to displace long-term residents – and use two indicators of commercial activity: hosts with multiple listings and dwellings available more than 90 days per year. In Sydney, they find that 40 % of the listings are from hosts with multiple listings and that 29 % of the city's 23,121 listings could be categorized as commercial. Although these figures represent only a small share of the 500,000 rental units in the Greater Sydney region, the report finds that the concentration of listings at the local level could impact the supply of residential rentals in those locations. Listings cluster around the CBD, in the eastern suburbs (Bondi, Bronte and Coogee), on the northern side of the harbor and at the Northern Beaches. In areas of high concentration, such as Bondi, the ratio of commercial listings to rental housing is as high as 14.7 % of rentals and coincides with a decline in the rate of new rental bonds lodged (Crommelin et al. 2018b, 25).

Taking into account the local housing market – the substantial growth in housing supply (new construction) and the large number of vacant or unoccupied units – the authors argue that one would have expected *both* long-term rentals and owner-occupied dwellings to have increased over the 2014–2018 period. As these figures remained unchanged and the new housing stock did not contribute to long-term housing options, they cautiously suggest that "the option of STL [short-term lets] is adding to a package of incentives that are driving investment in housing" and conclude that Airbnb was one of the factors contributing to the loss of long-term rental housing stock in Sydney (Crommelin et al. 2018b, 28).

In Melbourne, commercial listings represent a larger share of all listings (44 %). As has been the case in Sydney, the report identifies areas of significant spatial concentration such as the CBD and the southern part of the city (the Port Phillip Bay side of the Mornington Peninsula), a well-known vacation spot. Looking more closely at areas with the greatest concentration of commercial listings relative to rentals, they cite central Melbourne, Docklands, Southbank, Fitzroy and St Kilda. Of the top five SA2s, Melbourne SA2 – where listings increased six-fold between August 2015 and January 2018 – is a "clear standout" Crommelin et al. 2018b, 30).

But Melbourne presented a bit of a puzzle. Aside from central Melbourne (SA2), rental bond lodgments remained stable or marginally increased in areas like Docklands and Southbank, despite a significant construction boom. A confounding factor is the large number of vacant or unoccupied dwellings, estimated to be as high as 27 % of the housing stock in Docklands. The authors note that this makes it "difficult to establish a direct impact [of Airbnb] on the supply of rental housing" (Crommelin et al. 2018b, 36). They conclude that, although Airbnb's impact in Sydney and Melbourne is "limited" at the metropolitan level, in localized areas with high concentrations of listings, the impact is potentially more significant.

Supplementing their spatial research with data on host motivation and use of property, Crommelin et al. (2018a) use an online survey and in-depth interviews with current and potential hosts. They find that one-fifth of respondents previously rented to long-term tenants, suggesting that "in the short-run, STLs platforms are disrupting parts of the private housing market in Sydney and Melbourne." However, given the complex nature of the housing market in these areas (new construction, vacant housing), they suggest that Airbnb was not the only culprit.

The 2017 Gurran and Phibbs study looks at Airbnb's impact on Sydney's housing market using a different methodology and reaches different conclusions. Following US studies such as Lee (2016), Gurran and Phibbs use rental vacancy rates as an indicator of supply pressures to understand the impact of conversion to STRs on Sydney's rental vacancy rate of 3 % and on the metropolitan area rental vacancy rate of 1.9 %. Drawing upon InsideAirbnb data on frequently available listings together with the rental vacancy rates, they estimate that the number of units removed from the permanent rental market in the region is about half of Sydney's current vacancy rate. In the five popular tourist areas and the city of Sydney where listings were concentrated, these effects are more extreme (Gurran and Phibbs 2017, 88–89).

Supporting these conclusions, Professor Phibbs refers to a 2019 report by the Reserve Bank of Australia which found that vacancy rates were the "strongest predictor" of rents (Plastow 2019). Phibbs concludes that these findings put the lie to Airbnb's claims that it does not affect the Australian housing market and proves that Airbnb is having a definite effect on rental prices (Plastow 2019).

Disadvantaged neighborhoods and Airbnb pressure

In light of the historic connection between homeownership and social equity, it is not surprising that social inequality has been an important theme in discussing Airbnb's impact in Australia. Alizadeh et al. (2018a) specifically addresses equity by estimating the pressure of Airbnb listings on rental markets in areas indexed by socio-economic advantage/disadvantage (Socio-Economic Indexes for Areas, SEIFA). Using 2016 data from InsideAirbnb, the 2011 census and rental data, they find that most listings were located in areas with high socio-economic indicators (SEIFA index 9–10) which are also attractive to tourists. Although this pattern is less pronounced in Melbourne, they find a strong "socio-economic bias" in both cities with few listings in disadvantaged areas with low SEIFA scores. They conclude that, because pressure on rentals is limited to high-end areas, it is therefore not "much of an affordability issue" although it raises future concerns regarding the supply of long-term rentals in the higher-end areas with an accompanying threat to long-term residents (Alizadeh et al. 2018a).

Crommelin et al. take up Airbnb's claim to help low and middle-income hosts "make ends meet." In their survey of hosts, the authors find that the majority of hosts are young, educated individuals whose primary motivation is to get additional income rather than help pay housing expenses. The authors suggest that by providing additional flexibility to individuals who are already property rich, Airbnb only adds "to the barriers already confronted by those seeking to enter the housing market, particularly in local areas where affordability is already an issue" (Crommelin et al. 2018b, 57).

Moving towards regulation

Unlike the US where the power to regulate STRs is located with the local authority, in Australia this power is located at the level of state planning and operationalized by local councils. Unlike the US where existing zoning laws made STRs illegal, in Australia STLs were not in outright defiance of local planning and land-use regulations. However, given the lack of clear thresholds in classifying private dwellings as opposed to guest houses or hotels in planning instruments, STLs fell into a grey area, raising the question of whether they could still be classified as a private dwelling (Daley et al. 2018, 70). Several court cases in 2013 tested but did not resolve this issue (Daley et al. 2018, 70–71; Gurran and Phibbs 2017). The disjunction between state planning authority and metropolitan and local government in the Australian case made for additional confusion regarding both regulation and the tier of government which should be in charge (Tomlinson 2017).

At the same time that American cities and cities around the world were beginning to question the legality of Airbnb and regulate the platform, Australian local authorities remained on the sidelines. As noted earlier, it was not until 2015 that the NSW government launched its inquiry to consider the pros and cons of Airbnb and explore the possibility of regulation. In February 2018, during a visit to his home country, anti-Airbnb data activist Murray Cox summed up the situation in these words: "The regulatory vacuum in Australian cities is at odds with global cities such as London which has a 39 day limit on Airbnb rentals; Paris, which has a 120 day limit and Amsterdam, a 60 day limit to be reduced to 30 days from 2019" (Han 2018). Cox suggested that state governments give local councils some control.

Given the generally conservative estimation of the impact of Airbnb and STRs on Sydney and Melbourne's housing markets, it is not surprising that regulation has been slow and minimal to date and has focused on clarifying and amending planning law.

Several academically based planners entered the debate about how best to regulate the STR platforms. Noting that the "issue of how to regulate is unsettled," Leshinsky and Schatz (2018, 320) review cases in cities in Europe and the US and conclude that the effectiveness of existing regulations varied, that more research was needed, and that meanwhile, authorities should work "collaboratively with STR companies for self-regulation or offer incentives to landlords not to cut long-term tenancies short" (2018, 426). Gurran et al. compare a traditional planning model with a private arbitration model using data from two geographic areas. Although they suggest that the private arbitration model has lower transaction costs, they conclude that it would not be effective in situations with high levels of homesharing (2018a, 414).

Although these planners were responding to planning's inability to deal with STRs under the existing state planning laws, their suggestions were notably circumspect. What, if anything, did the state governments of NSW and Victoria decide to do regarding regulation?

New South Wales and Sydney

While the 32 local government councils in NSW had the authority to set the rules for STRs within the constraints of state planning policy, given the regulatory uncertainty, their response to STRs were haphazard (InsideAirbnb.com; Australian Productivity Commission 2015). According to government sources, as of 2016 only 12 councils had regulatory rules and the rules varied greatly (Sanson 2016).

The 2016 NSW Parliamentary Inquiry concluded that there was no need for heavy regulation and proposed some possible measures: changing the planning code to allow short-term accommodations, allowing STRs in the principal place of residence and in empty properties without restriction, and establishing a short-term rental code of conduct. However, the report strongly rejected what it referred to as "business regulation through a registration model," arguing that it would be costly and outweigh any benefits (NSW Parliament 2016, 16).

It took over two years to move from the report to legislation. The New Short-term Holiday Letting Regulations, a regulatory framework designed to maximize "the economic benefits of short-term letting, while protecting neighbors from anti-social behavior," was passed on August 14, 2018 (NSW Fair Trading 2018). The regulatory "framework" applied a cap to STRs, outlined a code of conduct and amended the strata law. Hosts who are present can rent short-term for 365 days; hosts who are not present have a cap of 180 days per year in Greater Sydney and elsewhere in NSW for the full 365 days.

To address the issue of amenities and behavior, the government planned to introduce a code of conduct for hosts, guests, online platforms and rental agents with a "two strikes and you're out policy." The code of conduct reads like a wish list: strikes would be recorded on an online register and infringements punished by banning people from the platform for five years; platforms and property agents would have to check the list of those banned and failure to do so would result in significant fines; and code, enforcement and compliance would all be funded by the industry. NSW also planned to amend the Strata laws to allow strata to prohibit STRs in investor units although not in the principal place of residence.[16]

As of spring 2020, the regulatory framework remains to be implemented and conflict between proponents and opponents of regulation continues. This conflict is illustrated by a loophole proposed in August 2019 that would allow STRs for

21 days or more not to count toward the 180-day cap. Proponents of the loophole argue that those who stay longer will not be tourists and will not negatively affect amenities (Saulwick 2019; Davidson 2019). Opponents, such as the OCN director, have countered that the policy has been watered down and fear "the true extent of short-term letting can never be monitored or measured" (quoted in Razaghi 2019).

Airbnb's Chris Lehane enthusiastically welcomed the framework as "fair and forward-looking" and a "potential model for others" (Burke and Razaghi 2018). However, the framework was subject to severe criticism from anti-Airbnb Organizations, such as Neighbors not Strangers, We Live Here, Play Fair Airbnb, the NSW Tenants Union, owners corporations and local government councils. The Tenants Union pointed out that the 180-day cap would not discourage investors from listing their property on STRs. Noting that Sydney lagged behind other world cities, most critics called for a registration system similar to those in Europe and the US (Williams 2018). Neighbors not Strangers called on the government to implement legislation similar to that implemented in San Francisco (2017).

Critics and observers also questioned enforcement. Asked how the rules would be enforced, Crommelin said: "I'd like to see a lot more information on how this code of conduct will be applied and whether any responsibilities will be placed on the platforms. The onus is still on the hosts" (Burke and Razaghi June 5, 2018). However, the government has continued to resist the idea of registration, a system vehemently opposed by Airbnb, and has claimed that the two-strike rule would be a sufficient deterrent. Announcing the law in June 2018, Matt Kean, the Minister for Innovation and Better Regulation in Victoria, called the new legislation, "the toughest law in the country" (NSW Financial Services 2018).

Victoria and Melbourne

As of 2015, STRs in Melbourne were basically unregulated. Several strata owners corporations, backed by the city, had attempted to ban STRs, but the results were mixed. After a number of wild parties, including one in Melbourne's EQ Tower in which a student was killed and another in Point Cook where police broke up a gathering of 200 teenagers, the Victorian government passed the Owners Corporation Amendment Act in August 2018, effective February 2019. This law, which tried to strike a balance between the rights of owners and the rights of residents to live peacefully, built upon the 2014 Victoria inquiry (Victoria, Independent Panel 2015).

The Owners Corporation Act makes owners responsible for disruptive guests and allows owners of an apartment to file a complaint about guests in another apartment. Complaints include excessive noise, interfering with owner or guests, creating hazards to health and safety in common areas, preventing access to common areas and creating damage to any aspect of the apartment complex. Owners can submit written complaints to the owners corporation, which then decides if action is warranted. If the offending owner does not cooperate, the Victorian Civil and Administrative Tribunal (VCAT) gets involved. The VCAT can fine owners up to $1,100 and charge an amenity compensation fee to be paid to the complainant for up to $2,000 per complaint. Both the owner and the guest can be fined.

On its website, Airbnb described the new law as "tough but fair" and claimed: "It protects the right for people in owners corporations to share their homes, whilst highlighting the responsibilities of hosting and addressing isolated incidents of people doing the wrong thing" (Airbnb 2019). We Live Here, which represents apartment owners in 300 Melbourne buildings, had a different opinion and called the law, the "weakest" short-stay regulation in Australia (Schlesinger 2018).

The law, which aimed at deterring bad behavior, has had a number of critics. Strata owners argue that it does not give owners corporations the power to regulate whether or not STRs should be permitted in their buildings. It also does not help residents in detached dwellings outside the CBD who live next door to party houses.

In sum, the exceptionally lenient regulatory efforts of NSW and Victoria are noteworthy for their focus on negative amenities. Although the proposed NSW regulation puts a cap on STRs, the 21-day loophole undermines the cap, and continuing conflict has derailed any serious attempt to address housing market issues. Like Airbnb, the focus has been primarily on punishing bad actors and bad behavior.

What's missing and why?

Affordability

Although affordability has been a major issue in Sydney and Melbourne and the subject of numerous reports, none of the studies we have examined attempt to estimate the effect of STRs on house prices or rents or to quantify these effects. Overall, the affordability crisis in Australia seems to be differently perceived with much of the attention centering on the inability to buy a home. This is not only because home prices have increased more sharply than rents, but because of the economic benefits as well as the cultural bias towards homeownership. Most Australian families find that "high-rise apartments are simply unsuited to their requirements" (Birrell and Healy 2018, 13).

Despite the data which show that an increasing number of Australians are renters, most Australians do not yet consider rental status as a viable permanent tenure; the discussion about rent in Australia is not primarily about cost, but about what Ronald and others refer to as the emergence of "Generation Rent" (2017). In a system in which homeownership has been part and parcel of general economic security as well as an equalizing factor, generational inequalities generated by housing markets that price would-be homeowners out of the market and make them potentially permanent renters threaten to undermine the social contract.

In general, when rents are discussed, it is in the context of low-income and disadvantaged areas and/or households as in Alizadeh et al. (2018a). This brings up gentrification and displacement. Although gentrification has become something of a sponge word, it is interesting to note that, while it has become a theme in discussing Airbnb elsewhere, it has not been a theme in the discussion of Airbnb in Australia. Gentrification in the form of urban renewal preceded the arrival of Airbnb and STRs as it did elsewhere, but it also coincided with the rapid increase in investor-driven high-rise development, making the displacement of low-income by higher-income households a reality in both metropolitan areas.

A 2011 report by Atkinson et al. on gentrification and displacement for the Australian Housing and Urban Research Institute (AHURI), notes that while gentrification is missing from policy discussions about housing affordability, "the gentrification process is both visible and measurable in Australian cities in terms of rising house prices, higher rents, improved social and physical infrastructure and so forth" (2011, 3, 50–52). The authors, who examine neighborhood change by measuring the migration of high-income households into existing low-income neighborhoods and the displacement of low-income households in Melbourne and Sydney between 1996 and 2006, find significant evidence of gentrification-induced displacement with lower-income households pushed to the outer suburbs away from jobs, transit and services. The report, which includes extensive interviews with government officials as well as displaced residents, notes that officials do not speak about gentrification but rather about affordable housing.[17] "It has not tended to be a term with significant currency or application" (Atkinson et al. 2011, 50).

It is likely that more attention will be paid to the supply and price of long-term rentals in the near future as "generation rent" expands. Housing experts such as Yates argue that, as urbanization continues apace, more than three-quarters of the Australian population will soon be living in capital cities and the pressures on the private rental market will grow. Demand will come from higher income families who choose to rent as a matter of life-style as well as from low- and middle-income residents excluded from homeownership (Yates 2017; Troy 2016).

Looking ahead

Both housing prices and Airbnb listings may have peaked in metropolitan Sydney and Melbourne. After a long real estate boom, there have been signs since 2017 that the housing bubble might be deflating. House prices have declined particularly in Sydney and Melbourne and there is a glut of new apartments. There has also been a long-run decrease in investor lending, particularly among foreign investors. Contributing factors include stricter lending criteria, new taxes on foreign buyers, stagnant wages and rising unaffordability, and shrinking rental returns as rents have been falling (Verrender 2019).

What does this mean for Airbnb? Airbnb's exponential growth rate has shown signs of slowing down, leading some to conclude that "Sydney is close to reaching a peak Airbnb in terms of supply" (Swami 2019). Real estate analysts suggest that "the Airbnb gold rush appears to be ending with fed-up landlords returning to the long-term rental market" after complaining about "difficult and hands-on management, less-than ideal profits, and a saturated market" (Malo 2018). This is not due to a decline in tourism as tourism continued to increase in both metro areas up to the fires of December 2019. More likely, the rise in the long-term rental market is associated with the oversupply of apartments in the metropolitan housing market (Tan 2019). The lack of regulation by local and state authorities notwithstanding, a combination of market saturation and oversupply may temper the future impact of Airbnb and STRs on Australia's residential housing.

The Australian case presents an interesting comparison. Australia's housing system was as financialized as that of the US and its homeownership rate was historically higher. However, the GFC had only a mild effect on its housing market and was followed by a rapid recovery led by an investor-driven boom in apartment development. Airbnb arrived during this post-crisis boom and was embraced by both the public and private sectors as a means to maximize profit and minimize risk, particularly for owners of vacant inner-city apartments that were unattractive to families. Criticism of Airbnb and STRs has focused on quality of life issues and regulation has been mild, primarily taking the form of codes of conduct.

Notes

1 Data on foreign investors in residential real estate is relatively limited and based on the number of approvals by the Foreign Investment Real Estate Board. Basically, foreign and domestic investors purchase property in different markets; foreign investors are limited to new housing to ensure that more units are built whereas domestic investors can purchase existing as well as new housing (Commonwealth Report on Foreign Investments 2014).
2 Banks remained competitive in the mortgage market by providing additional financial products to borrowers (Dobbie 2009).
3 Although Airbnb has 70 % of the STR listings, HomeAway and Stayz are also active in the Australian STR market.
4 Coastal resorts have also registered concern. See the reports by Gurran et al. (2018b) and Che et al. (2019).
5 A 2015 survey by the Economist Intelligence Unit ranked Sidney and Melbourne the fifth and sixth most costly cities in the world (Calligeros 2015).
6 In 1991, 75 % to 77 % of the Australian housing stock consisted of single-family dwellings (Foster 2006; Baker 2017).
7 Single-family dwellings refer to detached single-family houses on a lot. Medium density dwellings refer to semi-attached, townhouses, row and terrace houses. They can be "strata" which, like condominiums, are legally divided. High-density buildings refer to apartment buildings, whether strata or rental.
8 Over the past 25 years, lending to domestic investors for residential property has risen from 15 % to peak at 45 % in May 2015, and dropped to 38 % in 2017 (KPMG 2017, 12). Domestic investors have not contributed substantially to the apartment boom as they tend to purchase established housing, not pre-built from developers.
9 About half of these units are either left vacant or used on a temporary basis according to a UBS housing survey (The Urban Developer. 2019).
10 The report did not consider the impact of STRs on housing affordability or availability.
11 The inquiry was criticized for the selective nature of the submissions.
12 There are also several reports on Airbnb and STR activity in coastal areas, such as Che et al. (2019).
13 The Australian Housing and Urban Research Institute (AHURI) comprises a network of universities and receives funding from the federal and state governments. It issues a series of peer-reviewed final reports.

14 Representing owners and residents in residential strata schemes, OCN was established in 2002 to help members with common challenges such as building defects, insurance issues and noisy neighbors.
15 The rental bond lodgment rate is used as a proxy for the number of long-term rentals since rentals require that bonds be lodged in a government agency. It is similar to the security deposit in the US but it does not go to the landlord.
16 Apparently, there has been no progress in developing the Code of Conduct despite the fact that a working group of government agencies, industry and community groups has drafted several versions (Burke and Razaghi 2018).
17 Gentrification has been part and parcel of mainstream planning and policy whether under the rubric of urban renewal, concepts such as the "compact city" or plans such as Melbourne 2030 (see among others Easthope et al. 2017; Sintusingha 2017).

References

Airbnb. 2019. Victorian Government Home Sharing Law Now in Effect: Owners Corporation Amendment (Short-stay Accommodation) Act 2018. February 1. https://press.airbnb.com/en-au/victorian-government-home-sharing-law-now-in-effect-owners-corporation-amendment-short-stay-accommodation-act-2018/

Alexander, Jacqui. 2018. Domesticity On-Demand: The Architectural and Urban Implications of Airbnb in Melbourne, Australia. *Urban Science*. September 12. www.researchgate.net/publication/327613688_Domesticity_On-Demand_The_Architectural_and_Urban_Implications_of_Airbnb_in_Melbourne_Australia

Alizadeh, Tooran, Reza Farid and Somwrita Sakur. 2018a. Towards Understanding the Socio-Economic patterns of Sharing Economy in Australia: An Investigation of Airbnb Listings in Sydney and Melbourne Metropolitan Regions. *Urban Policy and Research* 36(4): 445–463. https://doi.org/10.1080/08111146.2018.1460269

Alizadeh, Tooran, Reza Farid and Somwrita Sakur. 2018b. Airbnb: Who's in, Who's Out, and what This Tells Us about Rental Impacts in Sydney and Melbourne. *The Conversation*. May 20. http://theconversation.com/airbnb-whos-in-whos-out-and-what-this-tells-us-about-rental-impacts-in-sydney-and-melbourne-95865

Association for Data-Driven Marketing and Advertising [ADMA]. 2018. Are Digital Marketplaces the Future of Travel? August 5. www.adma.com.au/resources/are-digital-marketplaces-the-future-of-travel

Atkinson, Rowland, Maryann Wulff, Margaret Reynolds and Angela Spinney. 2011. Gentrification and Displacement: The Household Impacts of Neighbourhood Change. *Australian Housing and Urban Research Institute (AHURI)*. Final Report No 160. January. www.ahuri.edu.au/__data/assets/pdf_file/0007/2122/AHURI_Final_Report_No160_Gentrification_and_displacement_the_household_impacts_of_neighbourhood_change.pdf

Australian Government, Australian Institute of Health and Welfare [AIHW]. 2018. Housing Assistance in Australia 2018. June 28. www.aihw.gov.au/reports/housing-assistance/housing-assistance-in-australia-2018/contents/housing-in-australia

Australian Government Productivity Commission [Australian Productivity Commission]. 2015. Australia's International Tourist Industry. *Productivity Commission Research Paper*. February. www.pc.gov.au/research/completed/international-tourism/international-tourism.pdf

Bajkowski, Julian. 2016. Is Airbnb Fueling an Australian Apartment Bubble? March 1. www.governmentnews.com.au/is-airbnb-fuelling-an-australian-apartment-bubble/

Baker, Emma. 2017. Australia's Demand for Housing, in CEDA Housing Australia 2017, pp. 67–78. www.ceda.com.au/CEDA/media/General/Publication/PDFs/Housing AustraliaFinal_Flipsnack.pdf

Bate, Bronwyn. 2018. Ideas of Home Ownership in Australia Might Explain the Neglect of Renters' Rights. November 1. https://theconversation.com/ideas-of-home-and-ownership-in-australia-might-explain-the-neglect-of-renters-rights-104849

Birrell, Bob and Ernest Healy. 2018. Immigration and the Housing Affordability Crisis in Melbourne and Sydney. *The Australian Population Research Institute*. July. https://tapri.org.au/wp-content/uploads/2016/04/immigration-and-housing-affordability-crisis-july-2018.pdf

Bleby, Michael. 2018. Airbnb Premium: Investors Will Pay '2–3pc More' for Short-term Rental Properties. *Financial Review*. March 13. www.afr.com/property/airbnb-premium-investors-will-pay-23pc-more-for-shortterm-rental-properties-20180312-h0xdlo

Bluett, Ros. 2017. Australia's Home Ownership Obsession: A Brief History of How It Came to Be. *ABC News*. August 22. www.abc.net.au/news/2017-08-23/why-australians-are-obsessed-with-owning-property/8830976

Bogle, Ariel. 2016. How Airbnb Is Glad-handing Its Way to Legality in Australia. *Mashable*. August 29. https://mashable.com/2016/08/29/airbnb-lobbying-australia/

Burke, Kate and Tawar Razaghi. 2018. "Look to the Future": Airbnb Welcomes NSW Government's Announcement on Short-term Letting. *Domain*. June 5. www.domain.com.au/news/looks-to-the-future-airbnb-welcomes-nsw-governments-announcement-on-shortterm-letting-20180605-h10zii/

Calligeros, Marissa. 2015. Melbourne: The World's Sixth Most Expensive City. March 4. www.theage.com.au/national/victoria/melbourne-the-worlds-sixth-most-expensive-city-20150304-13uilq.html

Cashmore, Catherine. 2015. Speculative Vacancies 8: The Empty Properties Ignored by Statistics. *Prosper Australia*. www.prosper.org.au/wp-content/uploads/2015/12/11Final_Speculative-Vacancies-2015-1.pdf

Castles, Francis. 1994. The Wage Earners' Welfare State Revisited: Refurbishing the Established Model of Australian Social Protection, 1983–93. *Australian Journal of Social Issues* 29(2): 120–145.

Che, Deborah, Sabine Muschter, Tania von der Heidt and Rodney Caldicott. 2019. Airbnb in the Byron Shire – Bane or Blessing? An Investigation into the Nature and Range of Impacts of Airbnb on a Local Community. March 20. www.scu.edu.au/media/scueduau/news/images/Airbnb_Byron_Community_Report-March-2019.pdf

Commonwealth of Australia, House of Representatives, Standing Committee on Economics [Commonwealth Report on Foreign Investments]. 2014. Report on Foreign Investment in Residential Real Estate. November. www.aph.gov.au/Parliamentary_Business/Committees/House/Economics/Foreign_investment_in_real_estate/Tabled_Reports

CoreLogic. 2016. Profile of the Australian Residential Property Investor. June. www.corelogic.com.au/resources/pdf/reports/CoreLogic%20Investor%20Report_June%202016.pdf

Crommelin, Laura, Laurence Troy, Chris Martin and Chris Pettit. 2018a. Is Airbnb a Sharing Economy Superstar? Evidence from Five Global Cities. *Urban Policy and Research* 36(4): 429–444. https://doi.org/10.1080/08111146.2018.1460722

Crommelin, Laura, Laurence Troy, Chris Martin and Sharon Parkinson. 2018b. Technological Disruption in Private Housing Markets: The Case of Airbnb. *Australian Housing and Urban Research Institute (AHURI)*. October. www.ahuri.edu.au/__data/assets/pdf_file/0022/28615/AHURI-Final-Report-305-Technological-disruption-in-private-housing-the-case-of-airbnb.pdf

Daley, John, Brendon Coates and Trent Wiltshire. 2018. Housing Affordability: Re-imagining the Australian Dream. *Grattan Institute*. March 18. https://grattan.edu.au/wp-content/uploads/2018/03/901-Housing-affordability.pdf

Davidson, John. 2019. Airbnb's Days Really Are Numbered. *Financial Review.* August 20. www.afr.com/technology/irbnb-by-the-numbers-20190815-p52hlk

Davies, Anne. 2017. More Australians Are Renting – And Their Voice Is Getting Louder. *The Guardian.* November 16. www.theguardian.com/australia-news/2017/nov/17/more-australians-are-renting-and-their-voice-is-getting-louder

Dobbie, Phil. 2009. How Australia Ducked the Crisis. October 26. www.cbsnews.com/news/how-australia-ducked-the-crisis/

Domain Reporters. 2017. Census 2016: The Australian Cities Where Home Ownership Declined the Most. *Domain.* June 27. www.domain.com.awww.domain.com.au/news/census-2016-the-australian-cities-where-home-ownership-declined-the-most-20170627-gwz85x/u/news/census-2016-the-australian-cities-where-home-ownership-declined-the-most-20170627-gwz85x/

Dow, Aisha. 2016. Melbourne's Skyline to Become Tallest in the Nation. *The Age.* February 12. www.theage.com.au/national/victoria/melbournes-skyline-to-become-tallest-in-the-nation-20160212-gmstuj.html

Dun, Friedrich. 2018. Financialization of Housing. July 17. https://medium.com/@friedrichdundee/financialization-of-housing-53fdb3b04b6d

Easthope, Hazel, Laura Crommelin and Laurence Troy. 2017. This Is Why Apartment Living Is Different for the Poor. August 20. https://theconversation.com/this-is-why-apartment-living-is-different-for-the-poor-82069

Farnsworth, Sarah. 2018. Airbnb in Australia: Entire Homes, Commercial Listings "Surge" Amid Growing Concerns. *ABC News.* February 23. www.abc.net.au/news/2018-02-23/entire-homes-commercial-listings-have-surged-on-airbnb/9473368

Foster, Clive. 2006. The Challenge of Change: Australian Cities and Urban Planning in the New Millennium. *Geographical Research* 44(2): 173–183.

Green, Richard and Susan Wachter. 2010. The Housing Finance Revolution. In S. Smith and B. Searle (eds.) *The Blackwell Companion, the Economics of Housing: The Housing Wealth of Nations.* Oxford: Wiley-Blackwell, 414–445.

Gurran, Nicole and Peter Phibbs. 2017. When Tourists Move In: How Should Urban Planners Respond to Airbnb? *Journal of the American Planning Association* 83(1): 90–92. www.tandfonline.com/doi/full/10.1080/01944363.2016.1249011

Gurran, Nicole, Glen Searle and Peter Phibbs. 2018a. Urban Planning in the Age of Airbnb: Coase, Property Rights and Spatial Regulation. *Urban Policy and Research* 36(4): 399–416. www.tandfonline.com/doi/abs/10.1080/08111146.2018.1460268

Gurran, Nicole, Yuting Zhang, Pranita Shrestha and Catherine Gilbert. 2018b. Planning Responses to Online Short-term Holiday Rental Platforms. *Research Report for the Australian Coastal Councils Association*, The University of Sydney. https://stokes2013.files.wordpress.com/2018/09/acca-online-str-research-project-report-final-24-09-2018.pdf

Han, Misa. 2018. Murray Cox, the Australian "Data Activist" Taking on Airbnb. March 2. www.afr.com/property/residential/murray-cox-the-australian-data-activist-taking-on-airbnb-20180226-h0wn4g

Hendy, Nina. 2019. Australians Exposed as Property Obsessed. May 8. www.smh.com.au/money/investing/australians-exposed-as-property-obsessed-20190506-p51keg.html

Horne, Ralph and David Adamson. 2016. Our Cities Will Stop Working Without a Decent National Housing Policy. *The Conversation.* June 14. https://theconversation.com/our-cities-will-stop-working-without-a-decent-national-housing-policy-60537

InsideAirbnb.com. Adding Data to the Debate. Accessed 9/24/2019.

KPMG Economics. 2017. Housing Affordability: What Is Driving House Prices in Sydney and Melbourne. June. https://assets.kpmg/content/dam/kpmg/au/pdf/2017/housing-affordability-sydney-melbourne-june-2017.pdf

Lee, Dayne. 2016. How Airbnb Short-Term Rentals Exacerbate Los Angeles's Affordable Housing Crisis: Analysis and Policy Recommendations. *Harvard Law & Policy Review* 10: 229–253. http://harvardlpr.com/wp-content/uploads/2016/02/10.1_10_Lee.pdf

LeMay, Renai. 2012. Airbnb Officially Launches in Australia. *Delimiter*. May 11. https://delimiter.com.au/2012/11/05/airbnb-officially-launches-in-australia/

Leshinsky, Rebecca and Laura Schatz. 2018. "I Don't Think My Landlord Will Find Out": Airbnb and the Challenges of Enforcement. *Urban Policy and Research* 36(4J, 417–428. https://doi.org/10.1080/08111146.2018.1429260

Letts, Stephen. 2019. Home Ownership Continues to Fall as the Great Australian Dream Gets More Distant for Many. *ABC News*. July 17. www.abc.net.au/news/2019-07-17/home-ownership-falling-while-more-people-are-renting-abs-study/11318070

Lowe, Phillip. 2019. The Housing Market and the Economy. March 6. www.rba.gov.au/speeches/2019/sp-gov-2019-03-06.html

Maclennan, Duncan. 2019. Housing Policy Reset Is Overdue, and Not Only in Australia. *The Conversation*. March 14. http://theconversation.com/housing-policy-reset-is-overdue-and-not-only-in-australia-112835

Malo, Jim. 2018. Melbourne Landlords Return to Long-term Rentals as Airbnb Loses Its Shine. *Domain*. June 1. www.domain.com.au/news/melbourne-landlords-return-to-longterm-rentals-as-airbnb-loses-its-shine-20180601-h10t5p/

Mannix, Liam. 2015. While Uber Is Illegal, Airbnb Gets Government Help. *The Age*. December 7. www.theage.com.au/national/victoria/while-uber-is-illegal-airbnb-gets-government-help-20151206-glgm6j.html

Martin, Chris, Hal Pawson and Tyan van den Nouwelant. 2016. Housing Policy and the Housing System in Australia: An Overview. *City Futures Research Centre*, University of NSW. June. https://shapingfutures.gla.ac.uk/wp-content/uploads/2016/09/Shaping-Housing-Futures-Australia-background-paper.pdf

Minifie, Jim. 2016. Peer-to-Peer Pressure: Policy for the Sharing Economy. *The Grattan Institute*. April. https://grattan.edu.au/report/peer-to-peer/

Morris, Alan. 2018. The Financialisation of Housing and the Housing Crisis in Sydney. *Housing Finance International*. Summer. www.researchgate.net/publication/326299566_The_financialisation_of_housing_and_the_housing_crisis_in_Sydney

Murphy, Lawrence. 2011. The Global Financial Crisis and the Australian and New Zealand Housing Markets. *Journal of Housing and the Built Environment* 26(3): 335–351. www.jstor.org/stable/41261691?socuuid=3626a501-7cbc-484b-85ed-38a87d2cca0b&socplat=email&seq=1#page_scan_tab_contents

Neighbors Not Strangers. 2017. Short-term Letting in NSW. *Option Paper*. 2018 https://docs.wixstatic.com/ugd/5a8126_d2d87d24845d44c68203544f0d171570.pdf

NewsComAu. 2017. High Rise Development Is Taking Over Our Cities. October 23. www.news.com.au/news/high-rise-development-is-taking-over-our-cities/news-story/00e8fc57d3a2d12ef899ecc0d991a30f

New South Wales, Financial Services and Innovation. 2018. www.finance.nsw.gov.au/about-us/media-releases/short-term-holiday-letting-plan-win-win

New South Wales Government Fair Trading [NSW Fair Trading]. 2018. New Short-term Holiday Letting Regulations. August 15. www.fairtrading.nsw.gov.au/news-and-updates/news/new-short-term-holiday-letting-regulations

New South Wales Legislative Assembly, Committee on Environment and Planning [NSW Parliament]. 2016. Adequacy of the Regulation of Short-term Holiday Letting in New South Wales. Sydney. October. Report 1/56. www.parliament.nsw.gov.au/ladocs/inquiries/1956/Final%20Report%20-%20Adequacy%20of%20the%20Regulation%20of%20Short-Term%20Holiday%20Letting%20in%20New%20South%20Wales.pdf

Owners Corporation Network. 2017. Our Strata Community Our Choice. *Submission to the NSW Government's Short-term Holiday Letting Options Paper.* October. www.ocn.org.au/sites/ocn.org.au/files/OCN-Final-Submission-Final.pdf

Plastow, Killian. 2019. How Airbnb Is Putting Pressure on Rent Prices. *The New Daily.* March 11. https://thenewdaily.com.au/money/property/2019/03/11/airbnb-rent-affordability/

Razaghi, Tawar. 2019. NSW Still Without Airbnb Rules, One Year After Plan Was Announced. *Domain.* June 4. www.domain.com.au/news/nsw-without-airbnb-rules-one-year-after-plan-was-announced-845152/

Rogers, Dallas and Emma Power. 2017. Explainer: The Financialisation of Housing and What Can Be Done About It. *The Conversation.* March 22. https://theconversation.com/explainer-the-financialisation-of-housing-and-what-can-be-done-about-it-73767

Ronald, Richard. 2017. Moving on from Home Ownership for "Generation Rent." *The Conversation.* February 15. https://theconversation.com/moving-on-from-home-ownership-for-generation-rent-71628

Sanson, Marie. 2016. Airbnb: What NSW Councils Need to Know. *Government News.* October 21. www.governmentnews.com.au/airbnb-local-councils-need-know/

Saulwick, Jacob. 2019. Fears Raised about Loopholes to Sydney Airbnb Limits. *The Sydney Morning Herald.* September 16. www.smh.com.au/national/nsw/fears-raised-about-loopholes-to-sydney-airbnb-limits-20190916-p52rw7.html

Schlesinger, Larry. 2018. "Weakest" Airbnb Rules Imposed in Victoria. *Australian Financial Review.* August 9. www.afr.com/property/commercial/weakest-airbnb-regulations-imposed-in-victoria-20180809-h13quu

Searle, Glen. 2017. City Planning Suffers Growth Pains of Australia's Population Boom. *The Conversation.* July 5. https://theconversation.com/city-planning-suffers-growth-pains-of-australias-population-boom-75930

Sintusingha, Sidh. 2017. When a Suburb's Turn for Gentrification Comes . . . *The Conversation.* May 4. https://theconversation.com/when-a-suburbs-turn-for-gentrification-comes-75609

Smith, Stewart. 1997. Urban Consolidation: Current Developments. *Briefing Paper No. 23/97.* NSW Parliamentary Library Research Service. November. www.wyongratepayers.org.au/TEPCP/TEPPS%20RESEARCH%20PAPERS/Urban%20Consolidation%20Current%20Developments%2023-97.pdf

Stapledon, Nigel. 2017. Is the Current Period of Price Movement Unusual. In *CEDA, Housing Australia 2017,* pp. 35–50. www.ceda.com.au/CEDA/media/General/Publication/PDFs/HousingAustraliaFinal_Flipsnack.pdf

Swami, Aditya. 2019. Airbnb in Sydney: An Exploratory Data Analysis with Python. April 14. https://towardsdatascience.com/airbnb-in-sydney-an-exploratory-data-analysis-ec91334e4780

Sydney, City of. Community Profile. *Dwelling Type.* https://profile.id.com.au/sydney/dwellings

Tan, Su-Lin. 2019. Traditional Rentals Are Winning Against Airbnb. May 3. http://reia.asn.au/wp-content/uploads/2019/05/6-May-2019-Traditional-rentals-are-winning-against-Airbnb.pdf

Thomson, Jimmy. 2017. Aussie's Global Website Skewers "Sinister" Airbnb. *Domain.* January 20. www.domain.com.au/news/aussies-global-website-skewers-sinister-airbnb-20170118-gtttm0/

Tomlinson, Richard. 2017. Airbnb and Empty Houses: Who's Responsible for Managing the Impacts on Our Cities? *The Conversation.* September 18. https://theconversation.com/airbnb-and-empty-houses-whos-responsible-for-managing-the-impacts-on-our-cities-83959

Troy, Laurence. 2016. Apartment Construction Boom: Is This the End of the Dream? http://blogs.unsw.edu.au/cityfutures/blog/2016/07/apartment-construction-boom-is-this-the-end-of-the-dream/

Troy, Laurence and Bill Randolph. 2016. Negative Gearing Has Created Empty Houses and Artificial Scarcity. March 24. www.smh.com.au/opinion/negative-gearing-has-created-empty-houses-and-artificial-scarcity-20160324-gnqoeb.html

Verrender, Ian. 2019. The Housing Bust and Why It's Likely to Continue. *ABC News*. April 14. www.abc.net.au/news/2019-04-15/why-the-housing-bust-is-likely-to-continue/11002296

Victoria. 2015. Independent Panel on Short-stay Accommodation in CBD Apartment Buildings. *Final Report*. June 6. www.consumer.vic.gov.au

The Urban Developer. 2019. Chinese Buyers "Increasingly Sensitive to Upfront Costs." *UBS*. March 15. https://theurbandeveloper.com/articles/chinese-buyers-increasingly-sensitive-to-upfront-costs-ubs

Wade, Matt. 2018. Renters Now in the Majority in Over 40 Percent of Sydney: Report. *The Sydney Morning Herald*. November 5. www.smh.com.au/business/the-economy/renters-now-in-the-

Williams, Sue. 2018. Councils Call for Compulsory NSW Registration System for Short-term Rental Properties. *Domain*. December 2. www.domain.com.au/news/councils-call-for-compulsory-registration-system-for-short-term-rental-properties-789001/

Yates, Judith. 2017. Housing Australia, in CEDA Housing Australia, August 2017. www.ceda.com.au/CEDA/media/General/Publication/PDFs/HousingAustraliaFinal_Flipsnack.pdf

5
GERMANY, ONE OF AIRBNB'S LEAST PENETRATED MARKETS

Germany presents an interesting counterpoint to Australia. Although Western Europe is Airbnb's biggest market and Germany is Western Europe's most populous and one of its richest countries, Germany lags behind in Airbnb listings. This is particularly true for major German cities which have been magnets for tourists in recent years and where Airbnb listings tend to be concentrated. Here too, the number of Airbnb listings is comparatively small. Berlin, the city with the most Airbnb listings in Germany, had only 22,500 listings in 2018, ranking fifth after London with 77,000 listings, Paris with 59,800, Rome with 29,400 and Copenhagen with 26,000 (Luty 2019).

Although tourism *per se* may account for some of this discrepancy, it does not fully explain the relatively low number of listings in German cities. In this sense, Germany represents one of the least penetrated markets for Airbnb in Western Europe, raising the question: what accounts for this seeming incongruity?

Several factors stand out. Germany, in sharp contrast to the US and Australia, is a nation of renters. Among the wealthy, industrialized countries, its homeownership rate has been notably low. In 2018, almost half (48.1 %) of German households were renters, a figure which was considerably higher for large cities where it ranged from 75 % to 88 % (Statistica 2019). Also in contrast to the US and Australia, the German housing system has been described as "corporatist, non-financialized and somewhat 'boring'" (Wijburg and Aalbers 2017, 1). To the extent that financialization occurred, it took place primarily in the large rental market, not in the home mortgage market as in the US and Australia (Wijburg and Aalbers 2017). These features contributed to the comparatively modest impact of the Global Financial Crisis (GFC) on the German housing market.

Nonetheless, Germany today confronts an acute housing crisis characterized by "skyrocketing" rents and significant housing shortages (Henger and Voigtländer 2019). In this context, and given the historical, cultural and political importance of rental tenure, we will argue that Airbnb and short-term rentals (STRs) have met with a degree of skepticism and resistance that may well outweigh their actual contribution to the housing crisis in German cities.

In discussing the German case, we will follow the same format as with the US and Australia. We will first describe the structure of the housing sector, look at the impact of the GFC on the German housing markets; and last, examine the impact of Airbnb and STRs on housing and neighborhoods with a focus on two of Germany's largest cities, Berlin and Munich.

The housing sector and housing tenure

Making a nation of renters

The roots of Germany's housing system go back to the end of the Second World War when Germany confronted a major housing crisis: 20 % of its housing stock was destroyed and another 20 % was badly damaged (Voigtländer 2009, 357). Moreover, the lack of supply was exacerbated by the arrival of over 12 million refugees, expellees and displaced persons. The 1946 Census showed that some 5.5 million housing units were needed in what would become the Federal Republic of Germany (West Germany) in 1949.[1]

In the absence of capital and private assets, the Federal Republic of Germany passed its first housing law. Based on the principle of the "common interest" (*Wohngemeinnützigkeit*), the government subsidized construction by providing interest-free loans to building associations to be paid back within a 30- to 35-year period. Investors were required to rent to households with incomes below specific thresholds, and rents were determined by the costs incurred by owners (*Kostenmiete*). This system, which represented a compromise between state-owned and market-oriented housing, cut housing shortages in half by 1956. By 1980, one-fourth of all rental units in the Federal Republic of Germany were in the hands of these publicly subsidized housing companies (*Gemeinnützigen*).

Although Germany recovered from the war to become an economic powerhouse beginning with the *Wirtschaftswunder* in the 1950s, Germans have remained a nation of renters.[2] This seeming contradiction has intrigued students of comparative housing policy and raised the question: why a nation of renters in a wealthy country? Among the explanatory factors are the strong legal protection for tenants, tax incentives to produce and maintain quality rental housing, and the relative lack of advantage of homeownership.

German housing laws, which predate World War I and are highly complex and codified in civil law, protect housing in general and renters in particular (Discher 2018). The tenancy law, which strongly favors renters over landlords, makes for "some of the toughest rent control laws in Europe" (Streit 2018). Observers have also noted that the inclusion of private developers in the social housing sector made for a supply of well-built as well as moderate rental alternatives, contributing to the "deep-rooted rental culture" (BPD 2016). Unlike the US and Australia where rental is typically viewed as a temporary way station to homeownership, renting in Germany is for the long term and people "regard their rental property as their home" (BPD 2016). Renters are also political stakeholders. In addition to legal protection, the interests of tenants are represented by the *Deutsche Mieterbund* (tenants associations) at federal, state and local levels. With three million members, the *Mieterbund* represent an important political voice in Germany's semi-corporatist model and advocate for tenants on a number of fronts.[3]

Homeownership, in comparison, has its difficulties. Despite recent policies to increase homeownership, the conservative home finance system does little to facilitate the purchase of a home. German banks tend to be risk averse, and mortgages are far more difficult to get than in the US and Australia. Banks require large down payments of 30 % to 40 % and mandate pre-payment penalties which challenge many would-be homeowners. In contrast to the US and Australia, the tax system does not favor homeownership. Mortgage interest is not tax deductible and homebuyers must pay a state tax that varies between 3.5 % and 6.5 % (Voigtländer 2009; Boehm and Schlottmann 2014; Kaas et al. 2017; Reisenbichler 2016). In Germany, the benefits of owning and renting have historically favored renting over owning for large segments of the population.

Like the Second World War, the 1989 reunification of Germany was a major historic event that affected housing markets as well as the macroeconomic environment. In the early 1980s, the center-right government began to retreat from promoting social housing in accordance with the prevailing neoliberal *Zeitgeist*. This trend accelerated after reunification and, according to Nolte, the transformation of German Democratic Republic (GDR) after reunification "elevated the neoliberal agenda to a new level" (2019).

One of the first acts of the unified Germany was the reform of the tax law (1990) which eliminated the *Wohnungsgemeinnützigkeit*. This ended rent control for 3.4 million rental units and made it possible to privatize the subsidized housing stock. In 2006, the government shifted responsibility for subsidized housing from federal to state and local governments. While the federal government tried to stimulate the housing sector by encouraging homeownership and promoting new construction, particularly in the former GDR including East Berlin. Given the precarity of a large segment of the population in those parts of the country, the policies were not successful.

The net result was that, from the mid-1990s to the early-2000s, home ownership increased only slightly with home prices remaining relatively stable. Rents did not increase significantly and rentals remained the dominant housing tenure. Investors were not attracted to the German housing market which leading economists described as "boring." This meant that at a time when the housing markets of most Western European countries "thrived on mortgage credit and increasing homeownership rates . . . mortgaged home ownership in reunified Germany did not increase" (Wijburg and Aalbers 2017, 977). The low homeownership rate and the conservative home finance system made for the relatively mild impact of the 2008 GFC on the German housing market (Kofner 2014a). As one observer noted, "given the economic spasms suffered in house crazy economies . . . the German approach to housing looks pretty good right now" (Phillips 2014). In short, Germany did not experience a housing boom and, hence, there was no housing crash.

The privatization and financialization of rental housing

The rental market, however, has had a different trajectory. It began to change in the early 2000s when the technological ease of global capital flows enabled investors to enter the large German rental housing market. Internally stressed by the costs of reunification, some local authorities – particularly in the former GDR, the North-Rhine Westphalia region and previously divided Berlin – began to sell off the heavily indebted non-profit housing associations "en bloc" to US hedge funds and private equity. The result was what Wijburg and Aalbers refer to as an alternate model of housing financialization, the "financialized privatization" of a significant share of Germany's subsidized housing (2017, 970). During the three-year period 2004–2007, over 250,000 units per year were sold (Savills 2015). These investments did not bring as fast a return as initially expected and were eventually resold to new commercial real estate companies listed on the stock exchange. The two largest of these companies are Vonovia with 400,000 units and Deutsche Wohnen (DW) with 163,000 units in Germany.

Germany's housing boom occurred after the GFC. In the uncertain financial environment that followed the GFC, the very characteristics that had made the German market boring became attractive for domestic as well as foreign investors seeking a safe haven. Housing investment was further fueled by historically low and even negative interest rates and real estate became known as *Betongold* (concrete gold). In addition to the large-scale privatization of the non-profit rental sector, banks also expanded their mortgage lending activities and homeownership increased to 51 % by 2017.[4] The net effect was that house and rent prices began to rise, leading some observers to speak of a housing bubble and marking the start of today's "Housing Crisis" (*Wohungsnot*) (Colombo 2012; Richter 2012).

Most housing analysts agree that the greater integration of German housing into international real estate markets has contributed to rising rents and prices, creating greater volatility in the housing sector and less security for tenants.

Housing angst and housing crisis

As a nation of renters, the German housing crisis is, first and foremost, a crisis of the rental market. Today, half of the country's 42 million housing units are rental units (21.1 million). Eighty percent of all rentals are defined as "private rentals," owned either by individuals or real estate companies, such as Vonovia and DW, which are listed on the stock exchange. The remaining 20 % is social housing. In the German context, social housing must be defined "functionally" as "rental dwellings currently subsidized in a social housing programme comprising special subsidies, rent ceilings and occupancy commitment" (Kofner 2017). This includes municipal housing associations and cooperatives (*Genossenschaften*). Social housing has been a declining share of the rental market due to the time-limited nature of the subsidies and the lack of adequate construction.

In this context, rent control has been an important social and political issue. German rent laws are notoriously complex with rents controlled differently in different segments of the market. In the social housing sector, which includes municipal as well as non-profit housing organizations, rents are controlled as long as the housing remains subsidized (*Kostenmiete*). In the private sector, rents are determined by the *Mietspiegel* (average area rent) set by the local authority in collaboration with the relevant stakeholders. More recently, the government introduced additional regulations to control rent, such as the *Mietpreisbremse* (a rent cap) which allows local authorities to limit rent increases to 10 % for new rentals in designated areas.

After a long period of relative stability and despite government efforts to control rent increases, both rent and house prices increased rapidly between 2009 and 2018. This was particularly the case in major cities where house prices rose almost 70 % (DPA the Local 2019a). Rent prices rose even more rapidly between 2009 and 2018, ranging from a 104 % increase in Berlin to a relative low of 21 % in Essen.[5] There were also large increases in Munich (61 %), Hamburg (49 %) Nürnberg (54 %), Hanover (52 %) and Frankfurt (42 %) (Immowelt.de 2018).

According to policy analysts, several factors have contributed to the housing crisis. In a much quoted and discussed 2019 report, the German Economic Institute (Institut der Deutschen Wirtschaft, IW) emphasized the lack of housing supply and cited demographic trends such as migration (internal migration to big cities, Eurozone migration, immigration), land and construction costs, and planning and land use approvals. It concluded that Germany needed to produce 341,700 new dwellings over the next two years (Henger and Voigtländer 2019).

But, while there is general agreement on the need for additional housing construction, the question is not just how much housing, but what kind of housing? Critics note that the IW report did not address affordability and downplayed other factors that contributed to the current housing crisis such as government policy, in particular the withdrawal of the federal government from social housing, cut-backs in subsidies for new social housing and the entry of corporate real estate companies whose primary objective is profit.

Since the federal government turned the responsibility for constructing social housing to the states in 2007, construction of new social housing has varied by state. Overall social housing has decreased significantly in the two decades between 1990 and 2018 from 2.87 million units in 1990 to 1.15 million in 2018 and is projected to fall to 1.07 million units in 2020 (Janson 2018). In one year alone (2017–2018), Germany lost 42,500 social housing units as subsidized units returned to the market and fewer new units were built (DPA/The local 2019b). Although some newer programs have built social housing, they have not been able to keep up with the loss, let alone with new demands due to population increases. A 2018 study commissioned by the Hans Böckler Foundation examined the need for affordable housing in large cities and estimated that Germany needed to build 1.9 million affordable units to meet the demand for low- and middle-income housing (Holm et al. 2018).

Another issue has been the impact of corporate ownership of large blocs of rental housing on the housing crisis. Although these holdings are not evenly distributed throughout the country, their operations have been sharply criticized in areas of concentration such as the former GDR, parts of North-Rhine Westphalia and Berlin. As publicly listed companies whose primary objective is profit, a common tactic is the use of modernization to circumvent the rent laws and legally increase rents. Surveys by tenant associations have revealed that tenant relations are strained and conflictual with many disputes about operating costs.

Critics also suggest that government tax policies, such as deducting the costs of modernization, have contributed to speculation and "in some locations unnecessary gentrification pressure" and should be revised (Kofner 2014b, 9). Some demand fairer taxation of capital gains. Another issue is more equitable access to acquiring land for construction. Municipalities are criticized for holding up building permits and, more generally, for the way that land and property are administered (Fuchs 2018).

The "housing summit." The federal government responded to the widespread protest and pressure directed at the housing crisis. Acknowledging the historic role of housing in German society, it convened a "housing summit" in Berlin in September 2018 and attended by representatives of the government, housing associations, trade unions and tenants associations (*Mieterbund*). The preamble to the final report states that "the housing question is a central social question of our time" and proposes several measures to alleviate the housing shortage, including providing monies to the states for social housing and giving tax advantages to developers and investors to incentivize the construction of rental housing (Federal Republic of Germany, Bundeskanzleramt 2018).

These proposals have been criticized from the right and the left. The *Deutsche Mieterbund* (the tenants' association) said that the plan to incentivize new construction needed a "give-back" such as rent caps or the new housing would be too expensive for ordinary tenants. The problem, according to Ulrich Ropertz of the *Deutsche Mieterbund*, was that the federal government had failed to recognize the need for more social housing (Oberhäuser 2018a). The German Homeowners Association, on the other hand, found the construction cost limit too low, wanted cities to relax building codes and wanted funding to go to deluxe projects inside cities such as loft conversions and rooftops (Oberhäuser 2018b). Skeptics noted that existing policies aimed at controlling large rent increases and protecting renters, such as the *Mietspiegel* and the *Mietpreisbremse*, had failed to stem the rapidly rising rents.

The power balance has been shifting from tenant to landlord due to the shortage of housing in German cities. Recent data from Berlin, Munich and Hamburg indicate that many landlords simply ignore the *Mietpreisbremse*. Although tenants could go to court, in the words of Anja Franz from the *Mieterverein* Munich, "most are happy if they can find an apartment" and do not want to aggravate their landlord. A study by the research institute RegioKontext, commissioned by the Berlin *Mieterverein*, showed that rent prices in the capital were 31 % above the legal rent (RegioKontext 2016). Surveys of rents in Hamburg and Munich found similar results. According to the *Deutsche Mieterbund*, more than half of the rents were above the legal limit. One problem is the lack of sanctions for landlords and little to no enforcement (Ludwig and Bielicki 2016). The net effect is that 16 % of Germans are rent burdened, spending more than 40 % of their income on housing and making "Germany one of Europe's worst offenders for housing cost overburden," the fourth highest in the European Union (Jackson 2019).

Although rising rents and tenant insecurities have made homeownership a potentially more attractive alternative to rentals, house prices have also increased and, together with Germany's stringent mortgage requirements, price first-time buyers out of what has become a dynamic international real estate market (Jackson 2019).[6]

Rental insanity and rental angst have in effect mobilized large sectors of the urban population to demonstrate for more affordable housing. Most recently in April 2019, thousands took to the streets in Munich, Cologne, Stuttgart, Leipzig and Dresden demanding government action. In Berlin, protesters have collected signatures for an initiative to buy back previously sold public housing and have demanded that no company should own more than 3,000 apartment units.

In this context, it is not surprising that Airbnb and STRs have been implicated in the German housing crisis.

Airbnb and German cities

Airbnb officially entered the German market by purchasing a small German competitor (Accoleo) in June 2011 and opening an office in Hamburg with 30 employees (Bradshaw 2011). This marked the homesharing platform's first foray into Europe. In 2013, Airbnb opened its European headquarters in Dublin to take advantage of Ireland's low corporate tax and lax regulation, and today, Dublin is its second largest office worldwide after San Francisco (Worstall 2013). The platform grew slowly at first in Germany with 26,000 listings in 2014 and 38,000 in 2015. Between 2015 and 2017, Airbnb more than doubled to 100,000 listings for the country as a whole, and by 2018, it had 160,000 listings. As elsewhere, listings have been highly concentrated in major cities such as Berlin, Cologne, Hamburg, Munich and Leipzig.

At the start, Airbnb was not illegal in Germany. The typical rental contract allows tenants to sublease with the permission of the landlord, but since landlords could only refuse permission for "important reasons," permissions were generally granted. Some landlords avoided the strict tenancy laws by renting out for short periods rather than to long-term residents.

Although urban tourism had increased significantly before the arrival of Airbnb, Airbnb's brand of less expensive and more "authentic" travel made city tourism even more attractive, particularly for young visitors (Brauckmann 2017).[7] New opportunities to rent out dwellings short-term to tourists not only attracted residents looking to supplement their incomes, but as elsewhere, attracted investors who turned entire apartments and even buildings into STRs. This was particularly true in Berlin where housing was still comparatively inexpensive.

A debate about Airbnb began to kick off in Germany as early as 2011 with residents, city officials, the media and renters associations concerned that Airbnb and STRs were making the housing shortage worse. In contrast to Australia where Airbnb was received with open arms, Airbnb met with skepticism and apprehension in Germany, particularly in large cities with stressed (*angespannt*) housing markets. Another factor was the increasing number of visitors in previously residential neighborhoods, particularly in Berlin where "touristification," or overtourism as it was later labeled, became early targets.[8] STRs quickly became the focus of a heated discussion about whether "Airbnb was good or bad for cities" (Skowronnek quoted in Brzoska 2018).

Was Airbnb good or bad for cities?

Several widely cited multi-city studies which tried to address the question found that STRs had a negative effect on the residential housing market.[9] *Capital*, a business magazine, published an article in 2012 entitled *"Gewinnen statt Teilen"* (winning instead of sharing) based on webscraped data for entire dwellings in four cities (Berlin, Hamburg, Munich and Cologne). It identified an "explosive number of Airbnb listings, ranging from 6,000 in Berlin to 1,133 in Hamburg," and concluded that the sharing economy was big business (*Capital-Redaktion* 2014).

A 2016 study for GBI, a real estate development company, examined the impact of Airbnb listings for entire dwellings on residential housing and the hospitality industry in 179 German cities (*GBI Presse* 2016; Müller 2016). This study identified 46,000 listings concentrated in large cities and concluded that these STRs exacerbated the already strained residential housing market. In Berlin alone, there were 14,000 dwellings permanently rented short-term and most of these were small apartments in inner-city locations in demand by young people and students. By taking such "in-demand" dwellings off the tight housing market, STRs created an extreme bottleneck.[10] In 2017, the *Süddeutsche Zeitung* examined Airbnb listings in the ten largest German cities and found that 58 % of the total listings were for entire apartments, 18 % of hosts listed at least one additional apartment and 34 hosts listed ten or more apartments (Brunner and Endt 2017).

To hone in on Airbnb's impact on German cities and the response, we will take a closer look at Berlin and Munich. While Berlin differs from other German cities because of its recent history as a divided city and the resultant demographic and socio-political consequences, Berlin is a natural choice because of the way in which tourism and housing interact. As a major tourist mecca, ranking third among European cities after London and Paris, Berlin is also the *Hochburg* of Airbnb in Germany with as many Airbnb listings as the next three cities combined. The city has a high proportion of renters (86 %) and a severe housing crisis as rents have increased more rapidly in Berlin than in any other German city. Berliners, known for their left-wing political culture, have protested both Airbnb and the lack of affordable housing and were the first to demand action and put restrictions into effect.

Munich, in some respects, will act as a check on Berlin's uniqueness. The city ranks second as a tourist destination as well as in terms of Airbnb listings. Munich is well known as Germany's most expensive city and its dynamic economy has been compared to that of San Francisco's Bay Area. Munich also has fewer renters (75 %) than Berlin, the structure of its rental sector differs and its political culture has tended to be more conservative.

Berlin, from *"arm aber sexy"* to cool and gentrified

> Berlin holds a unique position because its situation is quite unlike that of any other city within the Federal Republic of Germany.
>
> (Häussermann and Kapphan 2004)

Over the past two decades, Berlin's image and status among European cities has been transformed from a backwater, surrounded by the GDR and propped up by government subsidies and tax relief, to the capital of a united Germany, an economic, political and cultural center that has attracted new businesses, among them, high tech and creative industries. The city's labor market, cultural scene and universities have drawn newcomers, Germans as well as citizens of the Euro-zone (and elsewhere) and immigrants. Between 2000 and 2018, the city's population increased by almost one-half million, from 3,382,169 to 3,748,000 and is expected to reach four million by 2025 (Schliess 2017; Berlin, Senatsverwaltung für Stadtentwicklung und Wohnen 2017). Along with the many newcomers who have settled more or less permanently, Berlin is also a tourist hotspot.[11]

In 2015, Berlin's major daily paper, *Der Tagesspiegel*, published a three-part investigative report entitled "*Häusserkampf*" (which translates as "the battle over housing") linking investors and STRs to Berlin's housing crisis, focusing on trendy inner-city neighborhoods. The team of reporters noted that, as early as 2007, "real estate sharks who buy apartment blocks to turn them into condos" showed up in Berlin, one of the best places in Europe, to buy, sell and manage STR property for investors (*Der Tagesspiegel* 2015, 2). The reporters described the impact on gentrifying neighborhoods: tenants in buildings undergoing renovation were harassed, long-term tenants were displaced and rents rose astronomically as the new owners could pass on the costs of renovation to tenants. Traditional neighborhood stores and services gave way to a more touristic and upscale retail environment.

To understand the *Häusserkampf* and the Berlin case, we have to examine the coming together of Berlin's particular housing market and the city's promotion of tourism as a development strategy.

Berlin's housing market and the Häusserkampf

Reunification was quite literal in Berlin. A wall came down and the divided city attempted to unite eastern and western sectors with their differing economies, politics and cultures. Housing is a case in point. The two sectors had very different housing policies, and the resultant tenure and settlement patterns reflected these differences. In East Berlin, the inner-city was devalued along ideological lines, and new slab housing was built at the periphery. This meant that at reunification, parts of Berlin's historic center – Mitte, Prenzlauerberg and Freidrichshain – which lay in the eastern zone, were for the most part neglected and vacant.

West Berlin, which had begun large-scale urban renewal to demolish the nineteenth century buildings in inner-city districts such as Wedding, Neukölln and Kreuzberg in the 1960s, shifted its approach when it faced stiff resistance from a squatters movement in the late 1970s/early 1980s and the loss of public funding. Planners turned to "cautious urban renewal" featuring renovation and preservation of the social milieu. In Kreuzberg, this meant that, at the moment of reunification, there were still cheap rental apartments in what was a working-class minority neighborhood with a counter-cultural mix of artists and students (Siemer and Matthews-Hunter 2017).[12]

When Berlin was designated the national capital of a united Germany in 1990, hopes were high for a quick turnabout. However, this did not materialize. From the mid-1990s to the early 2000s, Berlin's economy faltered; there were massive job losses, high unemployment and the city lost population (Krätke [2004] 2013). At the same time, the city confronted an enormous debt due to its absorption of East Berlin as well as its own speculative real estate projects (see Bernt et al. 2013, 127–129). Even as late as 2004, Berlin's unemployment rate stood at 18 % and the city confronted a debt of € 64 billion (Burgess 2004).

In the prevailing neoliberal climate of the early 2000s, the city turned toward privatization to offset its budgetary crisis, selling off a significant share of its large social housing stock. This ultimately amounted to 220,000 units or about one fourth of the 1990 housing stock (Egner et al. 2018).[13] According to Uffer, this represented a "radical change in housing provision," from small private landlords and non-profit housing companies to for-profit corporate ownership (2013, 155–156). Today, for example, DW owns some 111,000 rental units in the city, the vast majority of which (95,000) were once owned by the state. These large-scale selloffs are the focus of much of the current protest, as many observers feel that the city jump-started the present housing crisis by selling off large blocks of city housing at bargain prices. In retrospect, both city and state have regretted these sales and began to buy back some of these properties as early as 2011 (Hunziker 2013; Göbel and Gringmuth-Dallmer 2019; Kusiak 2019).

After reunification in 1989, Berlin was known as an inexpensive place to live. There was a surplus of apartments and the rental vacancy rate was as high as 8 % (Fields and Uffer 2016). Prices for the dilapidated inner-city buildings were much lower than in London or Paris. Not only was Berlin's real estate relatively cheap, after the GFC it was viewed as a safe investment.

The Urban Land Institute referred to Berlin as "one of Europe's most highly rated residential markets for residential investment" (quoted in Füller and Michel 2014, 1311). Attracting small as well as large investors, many Germans as well as other Europeans purchased a second home in Berlin. As Füller and Michel note, many of these investor-owned apartments were used for STRs.

As investment increased rents skyrocketed, rising 104 % between 2008 and 2018, twice the percentage of Munich's rent increase (Immowelt 2018). The citywide vacancy rate dropped to between 0.9 % and 2.1 % depending on the neighborhood (Investitionsbank Berlin 2018). As wages did not keep up with rent increases, by 2017, 44 % of residents paid more than 30 % of their income in rent (Egner et al. 2018). The net effect is Berlin's current housing crisis and *Häusserkampf*, characterized by rising rents and the gentrification of inner-city neighborhoods with the accompanying displacement of long-term residents. To the extent that Berlin's housing crisis has coincided with the exponential growth of tourism to the city, Airbnb has created a potentially toxic mix in the city.

Tourism as an urban development strategy: success and backlash

Tourism, which was negligible before reunification, grew rapidly after 1989 and seemed a ready answer to Berlin's economic problems. Taking an entrepreneurial approach, the city seized on tourism, an increasingly popular urban development strategy (Hoffman et al. 2003), and delegated management to a quasi-public coalition. A tourism development strategy would serve multiple functions: it would attract investment and business as well as visitors, provide jobs for residents and change Berlin's then negative image. In 1993, Berlin created the first public-private partnership to market the city to tourists. Originally called Berlin Tourism Marketing, and later renamed VisitBerlin, the company together with another marketing organization, Partner für Berlin, was composed of members of the tourism and business community. Although partially funded by the public sector, the private sector had the leading role (Häussermann and Colomb 2003; Novy 2017).

The tourism marketing campaign proved to be successful in terms of both revenue and the number of visitors. Overnight stays rose from 6 million in 1989 to 33 million in 2018. Tourism also proved successful as a cash cow, generating a gross revenue of € 2 billion in 2017 and creating more than 235,000 jobs.[14] In the words of Willy Weiland, president of the Berlin Hotel and Restaurant Association, "tourism is a Berlin success story" (*Der Tagesspiegel* 2017).

However, tourists did not only visit traditional sites such as museums, the Brandenburg Gate or Check-Point Charlie. Many headed to the newly trendy neighborhoods in the city center promoted by tourism marketing campaigns, such as Friedrichshain-Kreuzberg, Neukölln, Mitte and Prenzlauer Berg, districts which previously had not been tourist attractions.[15] Even before the arrival of Airbnb, many locals in these neighborhoods were becoming disaffected with the large numbers of tourists in their bars (*Kneipen*) and the congestion, noise and drunkenness in the streets. Given the lack of accommodations, visitors were essentially day trippers in the neighborhoods. By offering online booking, relatively inexpensive lodging and an "authentic" Berlin experience, Airbnb became an immediate success. It also became an easy target for local residents as it combined their concerns about the loss of the neighborhood milieu and rising rents.

Not surprisingly, Berlin became an early hotspot for discussion, debate and protest. In 2011, responding to rising concerns that tourism and STRs were changing neighborhoods, the Green Party organized a well-publicized meeting, "Help! The Tourists are Coming," in Kreuzberg. The meeting was attended by 200 residents who voiced their frustration about the "touristification" that was destroying their neighborhoods and demanded action (Gennies 2011; Reimann 2011; Novy 2013). As Novy notes, while the creation of public-private partnerships in the 1990s had effectively "depoliticized" tourism development and the question of to whom the benefits accrued, this early wave of protest "re-politicized" tourism (2017, 68). Drawing attention to gentrification pressures and rising rents, it marked a new political arena, the intersection of tourism and housing, which in turn led to the Senate's regulation of STRs in 2014.

Moving towards regulation

Although the debate in Berlin was heated, there were no systematic data. Several early studies attempted to address this gap. In 2011 the Berlin association of tenants – the Berlin *MieterGemeinschaft* (BMG) – conducted an online survey of holiday flats near members' houses. Adding listings from Airbnb and two other platforms and mapping the listings in Berlin, they estimated that there were 12,000 listings in 2011. Although this number represented only 0.7 % of total housing units in Berlin, they found that the listings were heavily concentrated in several districts, in particular Mitte and Friedrichshain-Kreuzberg (Berner and Wickert 2011).

Under increasing pressure to act, the Berlin Senate commissioned a study in 2012 from GEWOS, a Berlin research institute, to determine whether the lack of "sufficient appropriate" housing at the neighborhood level necessitated new regulatory legislation. The study, which identified 8,918 entire "vacation flats" (STRs) and 12 negatively impacted districts, provided the impetus for drafting a law directed at regulating STRs in impacted districts (GEWOS 2012). The resultant legislation, the *Zweckentfremdungsverbot-Gesetz* (the misuse of living space law), abbreviated as ZwVbG, was passed in 2013 and went into effect in 2014.[16]

Additional support for regulation was provided by a study published online by students at Potsdam University. Using scraped data for 2015, they identified 7,714 entire flats listed as STRs. While this amounted to only 0.4 % of all flats in Berlin, the listings were highly concentrated in trendy inner-city neighborhoods, like Friedrichshain-Kreuzberg, Neukölln and Prenzlauer Berg, locations where housing was "cheap to buy." The study also documented professional or commercial usage finding that 10 % of hosts had more than one listing and the top ten hosts listed 20 to 44 units (Parnow et al. 2015). The media coverage was intense; within an 18-month period, there were 100 articles on STRs and the problems with misuse of housing in Berlin (Holm 2016).

Berlin's ZwVbG law

Like NYC, Berlin had the advantage of having a pre-existing legal framework that could be used to regulate STRs, the 1971 federal ZwVbG (misappropriation of living space law). Berlin's first ZwVbG law did not make STRs illegal, it placed limits on hosting. Residents could rent out 49 % or less of their entire living space. Those who wished to list their whole unit for STR or business had to apply for a permit at the local district office. Permits were seldom granted. The law also addressed speculation by making it illegal to keep an apartment vacant for more than six months. Violators could be fined up to € 100,000 and city district offices were put in charge of enforcement. Although, legally challenged by several property managers as well as by the platforms, the courts dismissed the challenges and the law, which had a phase-in period, went into full effect in May 2016. At its passage, Berlin's regulatory law was cited as one of the toughest in the world (O'Sullivan 2016; Beck 2018).

Expectations were high regarding the effectiveness of the law. An AirDNA report on its impact found some evidence that "stiff fines seem to be particularly effective in rooting out professional hosts as the number of monthly listings by hosts with more than one property fell by 60 %." Moreover, listings for entire apartments also decreased from a high of 10,000 in December 2015 to a low of 6,000 in June 2016, a month after the full law went into effect, but increased again to 7,000 in January 2017 (Hsi 2017).

But as has been the case elsewhere, enforcement proved to be a difficult and even impossible task. Although most districts hired inspectors and asked residents to report illegal listings online, in the absence of user-specific data from the platforms, it was costly, time-consuming and ultimately ineffective. Even in cases where officials were able to identify illegal listings, the legal process could itself take up to two years. Nonetheless, these efforts met with modest success. In the two-year period from 2014 to 2016, the city was able to return 1,518 short-term rental units to the regular rental market, including 526 units in Friedrichshain-Kreuzberg. These meager results convinced the Senate to toughen the 2014 law (Sethmann 2017).

Meanwhile, Airbnb continued to lobby against the law and, as elsewhere, organized homesharing clubs and encouraged hosts to make their voices heard at district meetings. To add empirical support to their claims, Airbnb commissioned a study from GEWOS in 2016. Comparing the number of Airbnb listings for entire apartments to the total number of apartments in Berlin, the study concluded that, since the listings represented less than 1 % of Berlin's housing stock, Airbnb's impact on the long-term rental market was inconsequential. The study noted that since 90 % of hosts had only one listing, the data supported their claim that the vast majority of hosts were not commercial users and argued that visitors contributed positively to the social mix of the neighborhoods (GEWOS 2016).[17]

The report, which received considerable press coverage, also met with considerable skepticism. *Der Tagesspiegel* pointed out that, in failing to consider the effect of listings at smaller geographic scales such as the neighborhood level, the study ignored the well-known effect of spatial concentration (Schönball 2016). Furthermore, the conclusion that only 10 % of hosts were commercial was misleading because it failed to compare the relative share of listings and revenue of the commercial to the individual hosts. Elsewhere, such figures showed that a disproportionate share of rental activity and income accrued to commercial hosts.

In March 2018, the Berlin legislature voted to revise the initial law. The new law, which was both liberalized and toughened, went into effect in May 2018. While it made STRs of entire primary dwellings legal for an unlimited time period, it also put into place a permit and registration system that requires hosts to register, pay a permit fee of € 225 and display their registration number on the listing. Second homes, which must also be registered, are capped at 90 days per year. So-called homesharers, individuals who rent out 49 % or less of their home, must also register but do not need a permit. Previous limits on vacancy were reduced from six to three months to prevent speculation and non-compliant property could be put into trusteeship. To toughen the law and deter potential offenders, the revised law radically increased penalties from a maximum of € 100,000 to a maximum of € 500,000. The head of Airbnb in Germany welcomed the revised law, saying: "Normal people who want to share their home with visitors will profit" (*Der Tagesspiegel* 2018). After all, Airbnb was not held accountable.

Estimating the effect of the ZwVbG law

It is difficult to assess the effectiveness of Berlin's revised ZwVbG law. One year after passage of the 2018 law, the Berlin senator responsible for city development reported some success in that 9,300 apartments that had been vacant or illegally used between 2014 and 2018 had been returned to the long-term rental market (Jürgens 2019). Other reports were less sanguine. The radio station Rundfunk Berlin-Brandenburg used InsideAirbnb data to report that only one-fourth of the listings on Airbnb's website for Berlin in March 2019 had been registered. This indicated that hosts were willing to risk the exceedingly high fines. Even when authorities were able to identify illegal listings, hosts could contest the fines and enter into a lengthy legal process. Although more than € 4 million in fines have been imposed since 2014, the city has only been able to collect € 400,000 (Gabriel 2019).

Several empirical studies which examine the impact of Airbnb listings on housing shed light on the effectiveness of both the 2014 and 2018 laws and illustrate the methodological challenges. Two studies, which use data for the time period before and after the first ZwVbG law went into effect, find large numbers of illegal dwellings concentrated in specific inner-city neighborhoods (Schäfer and Braun 2016; Mindl 2019). Using data based on visitor reviews on the Airbnb website, Mindl finds that Airbnb listings continued to increase steadily between 2010 and 2018.

However, he did not distinguish types of listings (rooms, entire dwellings, etc.). Economists Duso el al. (2019) also find that listings increased after each law, but after the 2018 law, the increase was primarily due to an increase in the number of private rooms listed. They suggest that the high fines imposed in the 2018 law may have discouraged multiple listings and commercial usage.

Although Berlin was the first German city to pass a ZwVbG law, other cities, such as Munich (2014) and Hamburg (2017), quickly followed. The laws differ in terms of specific requirements and the role, if any, played by platforms. Although local authorities elsewhere in Germany have tried to make Airbnb responsible for enforcement by either providing host data for illegal hosts and/or removing unregistered hosts from their website, the Berlin law has no such requirement, and attempts by the city to force Airbnb to supply user data to support enforcement have been unsuccessful.[18]

STRs at the intersection of tourism and housing

In view of the political debate and conflict accompanying Airbnb and STRs, it is surprising that there have been relatively few systematic studies that bring empirical evidence to bear on the issue. In an early study on the backlash against tourism in Kreuzberg, Füller and Michel (2014) call attention to vacation rentals or STRs. Based on interviews conducted by Kritische Geographie Berlin in 2011 to 2012 and the Berliner MieterGemeinschaft (BMG) data mentioned earlier, Füller and Michel argue that anti-tourism activity should be placed in the context of housing market dynamics, specifically the investor-driven purchase of apartments for STRs. Since BMG data estimate that only 2 % of all housing units in eastern Kreuzberg were listed as STRs in 2011, they conclude that STRs "added only slightly to the tightening of the housing market" (Füller and Michel 2014, 1304). Given that STRs grew rapidly after 2012, this conclusion now seems premature. Later studies, discussed next, suggest more significant effects.

Schäfer and Braun (2016) are the first to explicitly examine the relationship between Airbnb listings and rents in Berlin. Comparing scraped Airbnb data with rents for all 89 Berlin districts during a two-month period after the ZwVbG law went into effect (December 2014 to January 2015), they identify a considerable number of "misused" flats and hosts with multiple listings. Similar to other studies, listings are concentrated in a few inner-city districts. Classifying the districts by the density of listings, they find that the greatest rent increases were in districts with the highest density of listings and conclude that STRs probably exacerbate "the already tight situation with additional pricing pressure" (Schäfer and Braun 2016, 305).

Starting from the well-established fact that Airbnb listings tend to be concentrated in certain neighborhoods where they have the greatest impact, Mindl (2019) disaggregates even further. Looking within districts at the relationship between listings, rental prices and availability of long-term rentals between 2013 and 2015, Mindl shows the extreme concentration of listings at the smallest planning level, the 66 *Planungsräume* (PLRs) in Mitte and Kreuzberg. For every ten advertised long-term rentals, he finds 2.2 "professional" Airbnb listings.[19] These figures are considerably higher in locations such as Oranienplatz in Kreuzberg with 46 Airbnb listings and only six long-term rentals. Using an econometric model, he estimates that Airbnb was responsible for 16.8 % of the increases in rent for small apartments in these central districts between 2013 and 2015.

Economists Duso et al. (2019) make use of "policy interventions" – the ZwVbG law – as a control for exogenous variation in the number of Airbnb listings. Using data from InsideAirbnb.com and rent data and controlling for neighborhood characteristics, they find that the rent for dwellings within 250 meters of an entire home listed on Airbnb increased by 5 % after the first law went into full effect (2014) and by 9 % after the 2018 law. Compared to average rents, they estimate that this represents an increase of about 0.5 % to 0.8 %. Since Airbnb listings tend to cluster, they suggest "these estimates imply an economically significant impact of Airbnb on rents" (Duso et al. 2019, 18).

Airbnb and Berlin's housing crisis

Meanwhile rising rents are linked to gentrification and displacement, giving rise to protests and demands by tenant activists.[20] In April 2019, some 40,000 people demonstrated for "affordable housing and against displacement through rising rents." Demonstrators led by the grassroots organization, Expropriate Deutsche Wohnen and Co., collected signatures for a referendum calling for the government to buy back some hundreds of thousands of apartments owned by private companies and demanding that no landlord should own more than 3,000 units (Wildon 2019; Schultheis 2019). These radical demands, which made headlines around the world, may be feasible under the German constitution.[21]

While some observers, such as housing analyst Andrej Holm, hope that the current movement in Berlin may "reverse the radical market orientation of 25 years of neoliberalism" (Hermsmeier 2019, 8), rating services such as Moody's threaten to downgrade Berlin's rating should the referendum pass, and economists argue that the referendum as well as the *Mietendeckel* will stifle investment and worsen the housing shortage (Blackman 2019).

Protests against Airbnb continue in the inner-city neighborhoods where Airbnb is concentrated. In October 2019, people demonstrated in front of the headquarters of the lobby "Homesharing Berlin" and the home of a superhost, carrying signs such as "this is our neighborhood (*Kiez*)," "more holiday flats, more rent, more profits" (Berliner Mieterverein 2019). Responding to political pressure, Berlin authorities have bought back buildings and passed a new and controversial law, the *Mietendeckel* (rental price cap), effective as of January 1, 2020. It freezes rents for five years and mandates substantial fines as high as € 500,000. The city has also started to build more housing.

Given the paucity of systematic data and the highly politicized environment, it is difficult to distinguish symptom from cause. Some emphasize the broader demographic context of housing supply and demand, population growth and the lack of adequate new construction (Kirschbaum 2019, 4). But most believe that the housing crisis is rooted in previous neoliberal policies and that Berlin's response has been inadequate. They argue that Berlin has lagged behind other major cities in new construction, while trying to control the problem with stringent rent controls. This raises a question posed by Stors and Kagermeier, among others: whether Airbnb "became a scapegoat for the complex and expensive challenge to provide enough affordable housing for the city's rising number of inhabitants" (2017, 5).

In Berlin as elsewhere, Airbnb and STRs have been spatially concentrated in inner-city neighborhoods. Many of these areas, neglected under state socialism and restored to their former status as Berlin's historic city center after reunification, had lost a significant share of their social housing and had attracted investors in residential real estate. This set the stage for Airbnb. While residents initially focused upon the tourism that was disrupting their way of life and displacing local residents and businesses, the debate quickly turned to housing issues as evidence suggested that Airbnb in particular and STRs in general were removing housing from the long-term market and contributing to rising rents. Although Berlin's housing crisis has deeper roots, the concentration of STRs in these popular central areas has made regulating STRs a popular political decision.

Munich, Germany's own Bay Area

Germany's third largest city and the capital of Bavaria, Munich is Germany's economic powerhouse. Like most large German cities, Munich was heavily bombed during the Second World War. Half of the city, including most of the historic center, was destroyed and the population reduced by half. In the early 1950s when Berlin was still struggling to rebuild, Munich had already restored its historic center and, in contrast to Berlin which lost population, Munich's population increased to almost one million by 1952. In 2019, the city's population stood at 1.5 million and is expected to reach 1.85 million by 2035.

When Berlin became a divided city surrounded by the GDR, Munich's economy flourished as major German companies, such as Siemens and Allianz, relocated their headquarters to the city. Today, Munich is home to six of the largest German companies and a major center for tech companies and digital start-ups. Munich is a rich city; it's GDP per capita is twice that of Berlin's (Rickens 2017) and the city's unemployment rate, at 3.5 % in 2018, is the lowest in Germany (Munich, Referat für Arbeit und Wirtschaft 2019a).[22] As Germany's undisputed boom metropolis, the city has been compared to San Francisco (Rickens 2017).

Like Berlin, Munich is also a popular tourist destination. Tourism to the city almost doubled between 2008 and 2018 (from 9.5 million to 17.1 million) and brings in € 7.65 billion in revenue (Munich, Referat für Arbeit und Wirtschaft 2019b). The type of tourism, however, differs. Munich is known for its beer gardens, Oktoberfest and world-class soccer team, the Bayern München. Munich has also been a destination for medical tourism, primarily from the Gulf states, Russia and former Soviet states. While the relative proportion of tourists is the same as in

Berlin, tourists to Munich tend to come in waves, attracted by festivals and sports events as well as seasonal shopping, and tend to concentrate in the same inner-city areas where the hotels are located (Namberger et al. 2019; Joebges 2018).

Munich's housing crisis

One of the downsides of Munich's boom economy has been the city's extremely expensive housing market, both for houses and in rents. The city's vacancy rate is the lowest in Germany – 0.7 % in 2018 – thus availability is an issue. The average house price per square meter is twice that of Berlin and rents are also double with households spending between 35 % and 40 % of their income on housing (Rickens 2017; Egner et al. 2018).[23] A high and rising real estate market has recently led analysts to refer to Munich as "the biggest bubble risk in Europe" (Roberts 2019).

As in other large German cities, the majority of Munich's residents are renters, although the proportion of renters (75 %) is lower than in Berlin. Although Munich did not sell off its social housing – the city has been committed to keeping its share of social housing at 11 % of housing stock – social housing has declined over time, as has been the case throughout Germany.

The ownership of rental housing stock also differs. Unlike Berlin, most of the city's housing stock is still owned by *Genossenschaften* (non-profit housing societies), private individuals and condominium societies. The large private housing companies like DW and Vonovia, which have been the focus of housing angst and protest in Berlin where they own 20 % of the housing stock, own only 4 % of Munich's housing stock. A 2019 report by Savills, a property investment consultancy, concludes that unlike Berlin, Munich is not an attractive place for international investments. In addition to high prices, Savills cites the relatively high rate of homeownership compared to Berlin and the fact that 60 % of rentals are owned by cooperatives compared to 12 % in Berlin. The large-scale blocs of housing that attracted private corporate buyers to Berlin have not been available in Munich (Savills 2019).

The city has tried to address its housing crisis with a number of programs directed at rents as well as construction (Egner et al. 2018; Stroh 2018). These efforts have not been able to stem the rise in prices or keep up with demand. Policy discussion about the housing crisis in Munich tends to stress the unavailability and high cost of land (60 % of housing costs), the lack of enough new construction in the face of a large increase in population and changes in household composition – mostly one-person households (55 % of all households) (Baléo 2019). Given the cost of land, a proposal to increase density by constructing high-rises has met with strong opposition from Munich residents who want to keep their historic city image with no buildings higher than the Frauenkirche (Dürr 2019).

Given the tight housing market, housing-based protest has been an ongoing reality that predated Airbnb and STRs. Protest has been directed at rising prices, real estate speculation and general uncertainty about the security of rental tenure and has taken the form of demonstrations as well as grassroots organizing in individual buildings – the so-called *Mieterstammtische* (regular tables for renters) where people get together to exchange "tips" concerning displacement and luxury renovations.

The *Mieterstammtische*, together with 90 organizations including political parties and unions, was instrumental in organizing a demonstration under the motto #*ausspekuliert* (end speculation) in September 2018. This was the "largest tenant demonstration ever seen in Munich" (Britzelmeier 2018) with 10,000 to 11,000 people of all ages demonstrating for affordable living space and against "rental sharks and speculators" (Menrad 2018). In the following year (September 2019), the Munich *Mieterverein* and a coalition of trade unions and political parties organized a "festival for fair rents" to put an initiative on the ballot – to which the Lord Mayor gave his official support – for a six-year rent brake with fines for violators (*Abendzeitung* 2019).

In contrast to Berlin where the movement to expropriate has gained momentum, expropriation is not part of the agenda in Munich. Private real estate companies, such as Vonovia and DW, own only a small percentage of the housing stock in Munich; additionally, most political parties in the Bavarian state legislature agree that such an approach is not acceptable in Bavaria (Heintze 2019). Berlin, as both a state and a city, has more political autonomy compared to Munich which must deal with a far more conservative state legislature. Unlike Berlin, which has a long history of left-wing politics and protest, Munich is a liberal city located in the conservative state of Bavaria, the home of the right of center CSU sister party of the CDU.

In Munich, most protests have centered on real estate speculation associated with renovations and displacement. Given the high cost of real estate, investors have used renovations to get around rent control and increase rents. In a city where many rental units are owned by private individuals, there is a wide-spread fear that as owners die their heirs will use renovation to raise the rent or sell the building to new owners who will raise the rent (Steinburg 2018; Stroh 2018). Although Munich residents have voiced the usual complaints about Airbnb, such as congestion, trash and noise pollution, unlike Berlin there have been no organized protests against STRs in Munich. To the extent that one hears about STRs, it is primarily in respect to medical tourism and ads featuring STRs close to medical clinics.

In contrast to Berlin, tourism in Munich has not been a source of mobilization and protest. As Munich's tourism director noted: "Overtourism is currently not an issue in Munich." On the contrary, Munich's goal is a "Welcome Culture" (Buchwald 2019) and unlike Berlin, which advertises itself as edgy and "cool," Munich's message is *Gemütlichkeit* and *Herz*. The geography of tourism may also play a role in the relative tolerance of tourists. A district like Kreuzberg, for example, was not a historic destination for tourists, and thus, tourism was viewed as invasive, whereas in Munich, residential and tourist areas such as Schwabing have traditionally been more mixed and there has been more of an overlap between tourist accommodations and residential housing.[24]

Regulation and a data war

Unlike Berlin, demonstrations in Munich did not specifically target Airbnb. Nonetheless, the extremely critical housing situation in Munich provoked the city was to act (*Herausforderung*). In concert with the *Mieterverein*, which lobbied for regulation, the city council decided that every single housing unit counted and that the city needed to use every possible legal means to keep its housing for residents. This meant the city needed to do something about Airbnb (Süddeutsche Zeitung 2016). As a city official pointed out, "It is not acceptable when needed living space is rented to tourists" (quoted in Die Welt 2018).

Like Berlin, Munich expanded the ZwVbG (misuse of living space law) to apply to STRs. Munich's law, which passed the same year as Berlin's, also added the misuse of dwellings for tourist accommodations. Misuse was indicated when more than 50 % of a dwelling was listed as an STR; whole dwellings were misused if they were available for more than eight weeks per year, and the initial fine for illegal rentals was € 50,000.

In 2017, the Bavarian State Assembly gave local authorities additional power to increase the fine up to € 500,000 and to remove violators (Bayrisches Staatsministerium 2017). The City of Munich promptly followed suit by increasing its fine to a maximum of € 500,000 and, to enable enforcement, demanded that Airbnb disclose host data for listings that exceeded the yearly cap between January 2017 and 2018 (Munich Rathaus Umschau 2019). To enforce the regulation, the city created a special unit to detect illegal uses of dwellings in 2015 and, in 2016, added a website for reporting illegal rentals. Although the number of inspectors was increased, enforcement, as elsewhere, has been difficult and time-consuming. In addition to identifying illegal listings, inspectors need proof and owners have legal recourse. Although this is an ongoing process, to date the city has been able to win most court cases and has collected € 1.6 million in fines. It has also been able to return several hundred "misused dwellings" (vacancies, offices as well as STRs) to the long-term rental market.

Without specific transaction data from Airbnb, however, these efforts could only meet with modest results. When Airbnb refused to provide the requested data, the city went to court. Airbnb argued that since their headquarters was located in Ireland, they need not comply with German law. The Bavarian Administrative Court decided in favor of the city (December 2018) finding that, since Airbnb was operating in Germany, it had to comply with German law.

Airbnb immediately appealed the decision, and the court allowed the appeal; Munich was required to specify individual listings rather than request information on all listings in a given time period. As in NYC, the court did not permit a fishing expedition based on "mere abstract suspicion" (*Süddeutsche Zeitung* 2019).[25]

Airbnb's impact on housing and neighborhoods

Although we do not have much empirical data on the impact of STRs in Berlin, the data for Munich is even more limited. We have been able to locate only one study by the city's statistical office in 2018, several years after the misappropriation of living space law, *Zweckentfremdungssatzung* (ZeS) was passed. Taking its title – "Cozy room in the heart of Munich" – from an online listing, the study uses scraped data from Airbnb listings for one week in April 2018 to examine the numbers and types of listings (Joebges 2018). Eliminating listings that appeared to be outside city limits, the study identifies 7,154 listings offered by 6,401 hosts. More than half the listings (3,854) are whole dwellings and only 2.2 % are shared rooms. While the majority of hosts list one dwelling, 6.2 % offer two dwellings and 119 hosts list more than three dwellings suggesting they were commercial actors. The top ten hosts list 97 dwellings, and the largest host has 14 listings.[26]

The listings are highly concentrated in the inner-city with few listings outside the city center. The Munich statistical office's study, which also compares Airbnb beds to beds in traditional accommodations, finds that the spatial distribution of Airbnb follows the distribution of traditional tourist hotels. For example, Ludwigvorstadt-Isarvorstadt, which has the largest number of Airbnb listings, also has the largest number of traditional accommodations and beds in the city. As noted earlier, the overlap between STRs and traditional tourism accommodations was not as obvious as in Berlin where previous working-class hot spots, such as Kreuzberg, lacked traditional accommodations.

Airbnb responds to regulation and criticism

While Berlin and Munich were among the first to regulate the platforms, other cities have followed in their path. In response, Airbnb seized the initiative to change the narrative. It commissioned a multi-city study of Berlin, Hamburg, Munich and Dortmund in 2019 from Empirica, a Berlin-based research institute, with the goal of providing "objective" data to debunk the prevailing view that Airbnb promoted a housing crisis in German cities.

Claiming to be the first study to use data provided directly by Airbnb, Empirica argued that the results would be more accurate than studies which relied on third-party or scraped data. In Berlin, the study identifies 26,500 listings, half of which are whole dwellings, with half of these listed for fewer than 30 days (only rented occasionally). The study only considered the 11 % of whole dwellings listed for at least 138 days as "income generating," i.e., commercial. Comparing the 2,600 "commercial" dwellings to the number of housing units built in Berlin between 2007 and 2017, it concludes that Airbnb's impact on the Berlin housing market is inconsequential because the 2,600 commercial units represent only 2.3 % of the 114,799 new units.

In Munich, Empirica identifies 11,000 listings of which half are whole dwellings with 500–600 of these rented for more than 138 days. Comparing the number of commercial listings to the total number of new dwellings built between 2007 and 2017, the study concludes that the impact is minimal since the listings represent only 2.1 % of dwellings in Munich. There are similar findings for Hamburg and Dortmund.

To further minimize the contribution of Airbnb and STRs to the housing crisis, the study refers to other factors such as migration in major cities and the lack of new construction. It even finds a silver lining to the presence of Airbnb, arguing that since STRs decrease the demand for traditional accommodations, instead of building additional hotels, more land "could be used for housing and thus decrease the burden on the housing market" (Empirica 2019, 32). Although the Empirica study did not examine the spatial distribution of listings – the concentration effects – or test for a relationship between increasing rents and Airbnb listings, the research director categorically stated that "there is no recognizable relationship between increasing rents and Airbnb listings in cities" (quoted in Schlautmann 2019).

As might be expected, the study received considerable media attention and engendered critical responses from local authorities and tenants' associations. Helmut Dedy from the Deutsche Städtetag (Association of German Cities) took issue with the report's general conclusion of an "inconsequential" impact and noted that "the effects of the listings must be investigated in small spatial areas" and not for the city as a whole (quoted in *Der Spiegel* 2019). Ulrich Ropertz from the *Deutsche Mieterbund* noted: "the number of whole dwellings rented on the platform in the four cities they studied equals the yearly production of social housing in all of Germany" (quoted in Wurzbacher 2019). The Berlin *Mieterverein* referred to the study as a "whitewash" and noted that it did not consider the impact of Airbnb on inner-city neighborhoods (Sethmann 2019). In Munich, Dorothee Schiwy, the head of the social services department reacted by demanding that Airbnb end its lawsuit against the city and begin to cooperate to stop illegal renting to tourists. She said, "In a stressed housing market such as in Munich, every additional removal contributes to increased prices. We do not need studies for that. It is a question of supply and demand" (Munich Rathaus Umschau 2019).

The politics of Airbnb in Germany

Although we have focused on Berlin and Munich, by 2018 all large German cities have regulated STRs and have been engaged, to a greater or lesser extent, in legal struggles with the platform. In fact, regulating Airbnb has been part of the overall strategy for combatting the housing crises in these cities (Anzlinger and Wittland 2019), and with the exception of Berlin, tourism has not been a primary driver of anti-Airbnb legislation.

How do we explain the generally skeptical stance and strong legal response to this issue in Germany, which was certainly not propelled by data? By way of explanation, we need to return to the distinctive features of Germany's housing system and its place in German society. First and foremost, Germany remains a nation of renters. This means that for most Germans, the home is rented, not owned, and enjoys a protected legal status. Moreover, renters are well organized and well represented in the political arena.

Taken together, these factors make the question of ownership of rental property particularly salient. As the proportion of social housing has declined over the past two decades and the corporatization and financialization of rental housing has increased, the balance between providing affordable housing and profit-making has been changing. One consequence is housing *Angst* – the widespread fear of displacement due to rising rents and neighborhood gentrification. A 2018 survey found that three out of four respondents feared that rising rents would cause them to lose their homes. The vast majority (93 %) believed that housing was a human right (Caritas 2018).

Enter Airbnb. While housing has always been an important political issue in Germany, developments over the past two decades have made housing "the social question of our time" and a "social time bomb" (Rossmann 2018). Cities and politicians, already struggling with housing issues and housing *Angst*, have identified Airbnb as a contributing factor. The cultural embeddedness of housing symbolized by the prior existence of a federal law about the misuse of living space – *Zweckentfremdungsverbot-Gesetz* – has made for a broad front against Airbnb that has helped to fuel protest and pressure city response. It also helps explain the lack of an organized and vocal pro-Airbnb user community. In this sense, Airbnb has been an easy target for German cities and politicians confronting the housing issue.

Although both Berlin and Munich regulated Airbnb at about the same time, their trajectory differed. In Berlin, anti-tourism and housing issues converged and the original impetus came from residents in inner-city districts heavily frequented by visitors. In the face of the city's historic sell-off of large blocs of social housing and the corporate ownership of large blocs of rental stock, left-leaning Berliners have demanded the expropriation of large landlords. In Munich, where housing *Angst* was the predominant factor and tourism was not an issue *per se*, the push for regulation came primarily from the *Mieterverein* and the city, and the focus has been on the policies that allow landlords to use renovation to increase rents.

The German case illustrates the limitations of the Airbnb model as originally conceived and shows how a traditionally strong rental culture and existing laws that protect housing stock from misuse could rein in the global behemoth. The effects of the GFC on the housing market were negligible, and the housing market, which had been considered "boring" before the GFC, became a safe haven for international capital. Although Airbnb seemed a logical strategy for real estate investors and struggling renters, it encountered skepticism and mounting resistance from local authorities and organized renters, leading to a tough regulatory stance. In a nation of renters facing a severe housing crisis, Airbnb and STRs have been perceived as extremely threatening because "every unit counts."

Notes

1 As part of the state socialist system, the housing system in the GDR radically differed from that of the FRG.
2 The large proportion of renters ranges from 88 % in Leipzig to 86 % in Berlin to 75 % in Munich.
3 The *Deutsche Mieterbund* goes back to the second half of the nineteenth century when working class tenants organized to fight for better housing conditions.

4   This percentage refers to the number of households who own homes as compared to the total number of households (*Wohneigentumsquote*). The Federal Statistic office, however, uses a different figure that refers only to homes occupied by the owners (*Eigentümerquote*). This figure was 42.1 % in 2017.
5   Despite Berlin's steep rent increase, the city ranks only eighth in a listing of expensive cities, the most expensive being Munich.
6   While homeownership did increase somewhat in cities with populations over 500,000, ownership remained below 30 % in the country as a whole and under 20 % in Berlin (Kohl et al. 2019).
7   Overnight stays in cities over 500,000 rose by 180 % and the market share of urban tourism increased from 11.4 % to 20.8 % from 1996 to 2015 (Merkur.de 2016).
8   The term was coined by Rafat Ali in June 2016, writing for *Skift*, an online news and analysis site covering the global tourism industry (Ali 2018).
9   The German studies refer to STRs as either vacation rentals or holiday flats. We consider these terms interchangeable and will use them as appropriate.
10 The journalist who reported this study noted, by way of comparison, that only 12,000 new apartments were built in Berlin each year (Müller 2016).
11 Berlin is one of three city-states (along with Hamburg and Bremen) among the 16 states that make up the Federal Republic of Germany. Since policy-making strategies are more easily formulated at the state level, and local authorities' policy making is constrained by state laws, Berlin has an easier time formulating policies than a non-state city such as Munich. Given the overlap between city and state, we have chosen to refer to Berlin as the city.
12 Students in Germany are not typically housed in dorms and thus compete with other residents for affordable housing.
13 In the early 1990s, Berlin had 480,000 city-owned dwelling units and an additional 360,000 dwelling units for a total of 840,000 units (Egner et al. 2018). At that time, the city was losing population and there was a high vacancy rate.
14 In its 2015 yearly report, VisitBerlin boasted that Berlin was now in the same league as New York, Hong Kong, Dubai and Singapore as a major tourist metropolis (VisitBerlin Jahresbericht 2015).
15 One factor cited in explaining the strong neighborhood reaction has been the popularity of party-tourism sponsored by low-cost carriers.
16 In Germany, *Zweckentfremdungsverbot* laws are based on a 1971 federal law which allows municipalities to pass laws to protect their residential housing.
17 Commenting on why so much protest and criticism was directed at Airbnb in Berlin, Daniel Hofmann, the head of GEWOS said: "Holiday rentals are like burkas, there are a few and they are not particularly dangerous, but many feel more secure if they are outlawed" (Schönball 2016).
18 Following the Bavarian administrative court's decision (December 2018) that Airbnb must provide requested data to Munich, several Berlin districts attempted to get Airbnb to divulge data on illegal listings to support enforcement.
19 Mindl has a particularly broad definition of professional hosts that includes hosts offering rooms as well as entire apartments.
20 In October 2018, when Deutsche Wohnen announced the purchase of 800 residential and commercial units in Karl-Marx-Allee, residents immediately organized a protest that resulted in the city's attempt to block the sale. After a legal battle between the city and Deutsche Wohnen, the city was able to purchase 670 residential units in July 2017 (Berliner Morgenpost 2019). The governing mayor of Berlin stated that this represented a first step towards the city's purchasing additional buildings.
21 Proponents refer to Article 15 of the constitution, which allows state or local governments to nationalize under certain conditions, namely, the "misuse of economic power against society."
22 Munich's economy attracts an international workforce as well as immigrants. Munich's foreign population (28.1 % in 2018) is considerably higher than Berlin's at 17.3 %.
23 An additional indicator of Munich's housing burden is that 50 % of residents are entitled to *Wohngeld*, a federal program based on the relative costs of housing and family size.

24 Munich's historical center is a mix of old and rebuilt buildings typically four to six stories, in the classic block formation. Surrounded by residential neighborhoods from the late nineteenth to early twentieth century, such as Schwabing, Ludwigvorstadt and Maxvorstadt, much of the area was gentrified in the 1970s/1980s. These central areas have attracted young professionals and are now among the most expensive parts of the city.
25 Other cities, including Berlin, are awaiting the court's decision as it has important implications for all German cities.
26 The study could not determine whether listings were available occasionally or permanently nor could it determine whether the listings were legal (maximum of eight weeks).

References

Abendzeitung. 2019. Volksbegehren Mietenstopp: Mieterinitiativen feiern- und fördern. October 13. Abendzeitung-muenchen.de/inhalt.fest-im-werksviertel-volksbegehren-mietenstopp-mieterinitiativen-feiern-und-fordern.24a9c10f-5d30-4f42-ba4e-540ffeb6bfcd.html

Ali, Rafat. 2018. The Genesis of Overtourism: Why We Came Up with the Term and What's Happened Since. *Skift*. August 14. https://skift.com/2018/08/14/the-genesis-of-overtourism-why-we-came-up-with-the-term-and-whats-happened-since/

Anzlinger, Jana and Lukas Wittland. 2019. Was Kommunen gegen den Mietwahnsinn unternehmen. *Süddeutsche Zeitung*. October 22. www.sueddeutsche.de/politik/mieten deckel-alternativen-kommunen-staedtetag-1.4651740

Baléo, Marie. 2019. Munich/Affordable Housing: The Future May Be Polycentric. *La Fabrique de la Cité*. June 6. www.lafabriquedelacite.com/en/publications/munich-affordable-housing-the-future-may-be-polycentric/

Bayrisches Staatsministerium des Inneren, für Sport und Integration. 2017. Eck: Verschärfung des Zweckentfremdungsgesetzes. May 30. www.stmi.bayern.de/med/pressemitteilungen/pressearchiv/2017/189/index.php

Beck, Luisa. 2018. Berlin Had Some of the World's Most Restrictive Rules for Airbnb Rentals. Now It's Loosening Up. *The Washington Post*. March 28. www.washingtonpost.com/world/europe/berlin-had-some-of-the-worlds-most-restrictive-rules-for-airbnb-rentals-now-its-loosening-up/2018/03/27/e3acda90-2603-11e8-a227-fd2b009466bc_story.html

Berlin. 2015. Senatsverwaltung für Stadtentwicklung und Umwelt. 2015. A Good and Secure Home: Social Housing Policy and Affordable Rent. March. www.stadtentwicklung.berlin.de/wohnen/wohnungsbau/download/mietenbuendnis/pro_mietenbuendnis_en.pdf

Berlin, Senatsverwaltung für Stadtentwicklung und Wohnen. 2017. Evaluation der Bevölkerungsprognose Berlin 2015–2030. June. www.stadtentwicklung.berlin.de/planen/bevoelkerungsprognose/download/2015-2030/eva_bevprog_2015_2030.pdf

Berliner Mieterverein. 2019. Mehr Profit Statt Wohnraum. *MieterMagazin*. November. www.berliner-mieterverein.de/magazin/online/mm1119/demo-gegen-airbnb-this-is-our-kiez-111907b.htm

Berliner Morgenpost. 2019. Berlin kauft 670 Wohungen an der Karl-Marx-Allee. July 16. www.morgenpost.de/berlin/article226491839/Berlin-kauft-670-Wohnungen-in-Karl-Marx-Allee.html

Berner, Laura and Julian Wickert. 2011. Keine Gespensterdebatte. Die Zweckentfremdung durch Ferienwohnungsnutzung nimmt weiter zu – Studie zeigt Umfang und Verteilung von Ferienwohnungen in Berlin. Berliner Mietergemeinschaft. *MieterEcho* 35. October. www.bmgev.de/mieterecho/archiv/2011/me-single/article/keine-gespensterdebatte.html

Bernt, Matthias, Britta Grell and Andrej Holm. 2013. Berlin for Sale. In Matthias Bernt, Britta Grell and Andrej Holm (eds.) *The Berlin Reader: A Compendium on Urban Change and Activism*. Bielefeld: Verlag Bielefeld, 127–129.
Blackman, Andrew. 2019. Berlin Housing Backlash Spurs Drive to Nationalize Real Estate. *Bloomberg News*. April 13. www.bloomberg.com/news/articles/2019-04-13/berlin-housing-backlash-spurs-drive-to-nationalize-real-estate
Boehm, Thomas and Alan Schlottmann. 2014. The Dynamics of Housing Tenure Choice: Lessons from Germany and the United States. *Journal of Housing Economics* 25(C): 1–19. https://doi.org/10.1016/j.jhe.2014.01.006
BPD. 2016. Germany, France, the Netherlands. Housing Markets in Perspective. *Survey Report*. September. www.bpdeurope.com/media/107467/q540_bpd_dunefra-2016_engels-lr-web.pdf
Bradshaw, Tim. 2011. Airbnb Moves "Aggressively" into Europe. *The Financial Times*. May 31. www.ft.com/content/9051978c-8baf-11e0-a725-00144feab49a
Brauckmann, Stefan. 2017. City Tourism and the Sharing Economy-potential Effects of Online Peer-to-peer Marketplaces on Urban Property Markets. *Journal of Tourism Futures* 3(2): 114–126. www.emerald.com/insight/content/doi/10.1108/JTF-05-2017-0027/full/html
Britzelmeier, Elisa. 2018. Die Grösste Mieterdemo, die München je gesehen hat. *Süddeutsche Zeitung*. September 15. www.sueddeutsche.de/muenchen/ausspekuliert-demo-die-groesste-mieterdemo-die-muenchen-je-gesehen-hat-1.4131464
Brunner, Katharina and Christian Endt. 2017. Airbnb wird von Profis überrannt. *Süddeutsche Zeitung*. August 4. sueddeutsche.de/wirtschaft/uebernachtungs-plattform-airbnb-wird-von-profi-vermietern-ueberrannt-1.3615029
Brzoska, Maike. 2018. Airbnb – A Blessing or a Curse? *The Goethe Institute*. April. www.goethe.de/en/kul/mol/dos/liv/21251332.html
Buchwald, Sabine. 2019. Der Tourismus in München boomt – aber noch nicht wie in Barcelona. *Süddeutsche Zeitung*. April 13. www.sueddeutsche.de/muenchen/tourismus-muenchen-boom-overtourism-1.4408215
Burgess, John. 2004. A Renaissance of Counterculture. *The Washington Post*. March 9. www.washingtonpost.com/archive/politics/2004/03/09/a-renaissance-of-counterculture/b7287447-d362-4a2a-8c79-d7d23fd45084/
Capital-Redaktion. 2014. Gewinnen statt teilen. *Capital*. July 25. https://www.capital.de/wirtschaft-politik/gewinnen-statt-teilen
Caritas. 2018. Menschenrecht auf wohnen. Studie zur Caritaskampagne. "Jeder Mensch braucht ein Zuhause." *Präsentation der Ergebnisse Pressekonferenz*. January 10. www.zuhause-fuer-jeden.de/caritas_studie_wohnen/
Colombo, Jesse. 2012. The Post-2009 Northern and Western Europe Housing Bubble. www.thebubblebubble.com/european-housing-bubble/
Discher, Konrad. 2018. Zweckentfremdungsverbot. Arbeitsgemeinschaft Mietrecht und Immobilien. *Karlsruher Immobilienrechtstag*. April 20. www.mietrecht-dav.de/dateien/Discher-Skript.pdf
DPA/The Local. 2019a. The Places in Germany Where Rents Are Rising Rapidly. *The Local*. February 20. www.thelocal.de/20190220/where-in-germany-rents-are-rising-rapidly-report
DPA/The Local. 2019b. Number of Social Housing Units Drops by 42,000 in Germany. *The Local*. August 14. www.thelocal.de/20190814/number-of-social-housing-units-drops-by-42000-in-germany
Dürr, Alfred. 2019. Die Hochhaus-Pläne auf dem Areal der Paketpost provozieren leidenschaftliche Reaktionen: Die Mitglieder der Stadtgestaltungskommission sind agentan,

Traditionalisten aber schäumen. *Süddeutsche Zeitung*. July 25. www.sueddeutsche.de/muenchen/muenchen-hochhaeuser-paketpost-neuhausen-1.4537802

Duso, Tomaso, Claus Michelsen, Maximilian Schäfer and Kevin Tran. 2019. Airbnb and Rents: Evidence from Berlin. November 1. https://editorialexpress.com/cgi-bin/conference/download.cgi?db_name=IIOC2019&paper_id=352

Egner, Bjorn, Max Kayser, Heike Böhler and Katharina Grabitz. 2018. Lokale Wohungspolitik in Deutschland. *Working Paper Forschungsförderung*. Hans Böckler Stiftung. Nr. 100. October. www.boeckler.de/pdf/p_fofoe_WP_100_2018.pdf

Empirica. 2019. Airbnb im Kontext (Airbnb in Context: Central Quantitative Factors Influencing Regional Housing Markets). July 29. www.empirica.com/about/the-company/

Federal Republic of Germany, Bundeskanzleramt. 2018. Gemeinsame Wohungsoffensive von Bund, Ländern und Kommunen. Ergebnisse des Wohngipfels. September 21. www.bmi.bund.de/SharedDocs/downloads/DE/veroeffentlichungen/2018/ergebnisse-wohngipfel.pdf?__blob=publicationFile&v=6

Fields, Desiree and Sabina Uffer. 2016. The Financialization of Rental Housing: A Comparative Analysis of New York City and Berlin. *Urban Studies* 53(7): 1486–1502. https://doi.org/10.1177/0042098014543704

Fuchs, Richard. 2018. Wie bezahlbarer Wohnraum entstehen konnte. *Deutschlandfunk Kultur*. Zeitfragen/Archiv. March 27. www.deutschlandfunkkultur.de/mittel-gegen-explodierende-grundstueckspreise-wie.976.de.html?dram:article_id=414075

Füller, Henning and Boris Michel. 2014. "Stop Being a Tourist?" New Dynamics of Urban Tourism in Berlin-Kreuzberg. *International Journal of Urban and Regional Research* 38(4), July: 1304–1318.

Gabriel, Thorsten. 2019. Viele Ferienwohnungen immer noch nicht registriert. *Rbb24*. April 30. bb24.de/politik/beitrag/2019/04/berlin-airbnb-zweckentfremdung-verbot-ein-jahr.html

GBI Presse. 2016. Etwa jeder elfte Städtereisende in Deutschland schläft bei Airbnb & Co. April 4. www.gbi.ag/detailansicht/news/etwa-jeder-elfte-staedtereisende-in-deutschland-schlaeft-bei-airbnb-co/

Gennies, Sidney. 2011. Kreuzberg Will seine Ruhe haben. *Der Tagesspiegel*. March 1. www.tagesspiegel.de/berlin/anwohnerwut-auf-touristen-kreuzberg-will-seine-ruhe-haben/3898110.html

GEWOS Institut für Stadt-, Regional- und Wohnforschung GmbH. [GEWOS]. 2012. Indikatorensystem zur kleinräumigen Wohnungsmarktanalyse. *Bericht*. Berlin April. http://berlinappell.blogsport.de/images/GewosGutachtenWeb.pdf

GEWOS Institut für Stadt-, Regional- und Wohnforschung GmbH. [GEWOS]. 2016. Airbnb und der Berliner Wohnungsmarkt 2016. Auswirkungen des Airbnb Angebots auf die Berliner Wohnungsversorgung. October 12. www.airbnbcitizen.com/wp-content/uploads/sites/59/2016/12/Okt.2016-Studie-GEWOS-Studie-Airbnb-und-Wohnungsmarkt-Berlin.pdf

Göbel, Jana and Götz Gringmuth-Dallmer. 2019. Die Deutsche Wohnen in Zahlen. *Rbb24*. February 12. www.rbb24.de/wirtschaft/beitrag/2019/02/deutsche-wohnen-mieten-berlin-miete-macht-rendite.html

Häussermann, Hartmut and Claire Colomb. 2003. The New Berlin: Marketing the City of Dreams. In L. Hoffman, S. Fainstein and D. Judd (eds.) *Cities and Visitors: Regulating People, Markets, and City Space*. Malden, MA: Blackwell, 200–218.

Häussermann, Hartmut and Andreas Kapphan. 2004. Berlin: From Divided into Fragmented City. *The Greek Review of Social Research* 113: 25–61. https://ejournals.epublishing.ekt.gr/index.php/ekke/article/viewFile/9216/9435

Heintze, Alexander. 2019. In München gibt es kaum etwas zu Enteignen. *Immobilien-Zeitung*. March 21. www.immobilien-zeitung.de/150593/in-muenchen-gibt-kaum-etwas-zum-enteignen

Henger, Ralph and Michael Voigtländer. 2019. Ist der Wohungsbau auf dem richtigen Weg? *Aktuelle Ergebnisse des IW-Wohungsbedarfsmodell*. IW-Report 28/2019. www.iwkoeln.de/fileadmin/user_upload/Studien/Report/PDF/2019/IW-Report_2019_Wohnungsbaubedarfmodell.pdf

Hermsmeier, Lukas. 2019. Berlin's Radical Housing Activists Aren't Afraid of Expropriations. *The Nation*. March 27. www.thenation.com/article/berlin-housing-gentrification-referendum/

Hoffman, Lily M., Susan S. Fainstein and Dennis R. Judd. 2003. *Cities and Visitors: Regulating People, Markets, and City Space*. Malden, MA: Backwell.

Holm, Andrej. 2016. Berlin: Wie verändert Airbnb den Wohnungsmarkt? Eine Politische Ökonomie der Ferienwohngen. https://gentrificationblog.wordpress.com/2016/07/05/berliin-wie-veraendertairbnb-den-wohnungsmarkt-eine-politische-oekonomie-der-ferienwohnungen/

Holm, Andrej, Henrik Lebuhn, Stephan Junker and Kevin Neitzel. 2018. Wie viele und welche Wohnungen fehlen in deutschen Grossstädten. Die soziale Versorgungslücke nach Einkommen und Wohnungsgrösse. *Hans Böckler Stiftung*. Working Paper Forschungsfoerdrung. No.063. April. www.boeckler.de/pdf/p_fofoe_WP_063_2018.pdf

Hsi, Helen. 2017. Impacts of Airbnb Regulation in Berlin, Barcelona, San Francisco and Santa Monica. https://london.wtm.com/__novadocuments/391267?v=636415031341730000

Hunziker, Christian. 2013. Alles auf Anfang. *Der Tagesspiegel*. June 15. www.tagesspiegel.de/wirtschaft/immobilien/berlin-kauft-wieder-wohnungen-alles-auf-anfang/8348724.html

Immowelt.de. 2018. 10-Jahresvergleich: Mieten in deutschen Grossstädten explodieren. August 23. https://news.immowelt.de/n/3618-10-jahresvergleich-mieten-in-deutschen-grossstaedten-explodieren.html

Investitionsbank Berlin. 2018. IBB Wohungsmarktbbericht. www.ibb.de/media/dokumente/publikationen/berliner-wohnungsmarkt/wohnungsmarktbericht/ibb_wohnungsmarktbericht_2018.pdf

Jackson, James. 2019. First-time Buyers Crowded Out of Booming German Housing Market. *DW*. April 19. www.dw.com/en/first-time-buyers-crowded-out-of-booming-german-housing-market/a-48387287

Janson, Matthias. 2018. Immer weniger Sozialwohnungen in Deutschland. *Statistica*. January 10. https://de.statista.com/infografik/12473/immer-weniger-sozialwohnungen-in-deutschland/

Joebges, Silke. 2018. "Cozy Room in the Heart of Munich" – Home-sharing Angebote über Airbnb in München. *Münchner Statis^{h}k*. 3rd quarter.

Jürgens, Isabell. 2019. Zweckentremdung ade: 9300 Wohnungen wider vermietet. *Berliner Morgenpost*. May 9. www.morgenpost.de/berlin/article217164243/Zweckentfremdung-ade-9300-Wohnungen-wieder-vermietet.html

Kaas, Leo, Georgi Kocharkov, Edgar Preugschat and Nawid Suassi. 2017. Low Homeownership in Germany – A Quantitative Exploration. September. http://jsiassi.de/nsiassi/Homeownership.pdf

Kirschbaum, Eric. 2019. Gentrification Is Changing Berlin. Officials Are Banning Rent Hikes for 5 Years. *Los Angeles Times*. June 20. www.latimes.com/world/europe/la-fg-germany-berlin-rent-increases-outlawed-20190620-story.html

Kofner, Stefan. 2014a. The German Housing System: Fundamentally Resilient? *Journal of Housing and the Built Environment* 29(2): 255–275. https://doi.org/10.1007/s10901-013-9383-0

Kofner, Stefan. 2014b. The Private Rental Sector in Germany. *OECD Consultancy Report*. Middletown, DE. December 1.
Kofner, Stefan. 2017. Social Housing in Germany: An Inevitably Shrinking Sector? *Critical Housing Analysis* 4(1): 61–71. www.housing-critical.com/home-page-1/social-housing-in-germany-an-inevitably-shrinkig
Kohl, Sebastian, Pekka Sagner and Michael Voigtlander. 2019. Mangelware Wohnraum: Ökonomische Folgen des Mietpreisbooms in deutschen Grossstädten. *FGW-Impuls*. Integrierende Stadtentwicklung 18. Heike Herrmann and Jan Üblacker (eds). www.fgw-nrw.de/fileadmin/user_upload/Impuls-ISE-18-Kohl2019_08_19-op-web.pdf
Krätke, Stefan. 2013. City of Talents? Berlin's Regional Economy, Socio-spatial Fabric and "Worst Practice" Urban Governance. In Bernt, Grell and Holm 2013, 131–154. First published in *International Journal of Urban and Regional Research 2004* 28(3).
Kusiak, Joanna. 2019. Berlin's Grass Roots Plan to Renationalize up to 200,000 Ex-council Homes from Corporate Landlords. *The Conversation*. March 5. https://theconversation.com/berlins-grassroots-plan-to-renationalise-up-to-200-000-ex-council-homes-from-corporate-landlords-112884
Ludwig, Kristiana and Jan Bielicki. 2016. Warum die Mietpreisbremse nicht funkioniert. *Süddeutsche Zeitung*. May 17. www.sueddeutsche.de/wirtschaft/mietpreisbremse-warum-die-mietpreisbremse-nicht-funktioniert-1.2995244
Luty, Jennifer. 2019. Number of Airbnb Listings in European Cities 2019. *Statista*. www.statista.com/statistics/815145/airbnb-listings-in-europe-by-city/
Menrad, Jasmin. 2018. #Ausspekuliert:Grösster Mieter-Protest aller Zeiten. *Abendzeitung*. September 16. Abendzeitung-muenchen.de/inhalt.grossdemonstration-in-muenchen-ausspekuliert-groesster-mieter-protest-aller-zeiten.201dc84b-3309–4b2f-a8eb-491a93cc01c2.html
Merkur.de. Airbnb & Co. 2016. In München über 4300 Wohungen im Angebot. *Merkur*. April 19. www.merkur.de/leben/wohnen/airbnb-muenchen-ueber-4300-wohnungen-angebot-fehlen-wohnungsmarkt-meta-6324660.html
Mindl, Felix. 2019. Home-sharing, ein Geschäftsmodell mit lokalen Nebenwirkungen- Erkenntnisse am Beispiel von Airbnb in Berlin. *Kölner Impulse zur Wirtschaftspolitik*. Nr.4. July 2. https://iwp.uni-koeln.de/sites/iwp/Dokumente/04_Publikationen/Koelner_Impulse_zur_Wirtschaftspolitik/Koelner_Impulse_zur_Wirtschaftspolitik_2019_04.pdf
Müller, Benedikt. 2016. Zu viele Feirenwohnungen, kein Platz für Mieter. *Süddeutsche Zeitung*. April 18. www.sueddeutsche.de/wirtschaft/airbnb-in-staedten-vermietung-von-ferienwohnungen-laeuft-aus-dem-ruder-1.2954475
Munich. 2019a. Referat für Arbeit und Wirtschaft. München der Wirtschaftsstandort. *Fakten und Zahlen*. March. www.wirtschaft-muenchen.de/publikationen/pdfs/de_factsandfigures_2019.pdf
Munich. 2019b. Referat fur Arbeit und Wirtschaft. *Gäste und übernachtungen in München*. www.muenchen.de/rathaus/Stadtverwaltung/Referat-fuer-Arbeit-und-Wirtschaft.html
Munich Rathaus Umschau. 2019. Airbnb-Studie- Sozialreferat fordert Airbnb zur Kooperation auf. 149. August 7. https://ru.muenchen.de/2019/149/Airbnb-Studie-Sozialreferat-fordert-Airbnb-zur-Kooperation-auf-86330
Namberger, Phillipp, Sascha Jackisch, Jurgen Schmude and Marion Karl. 2019. Overcrowding, Overtourism and Local Level Disturbance: How Much Can Munich Handle? *Tourism Planning and Development* 16(4): 452–472. https://doi.org/10.1080/21568316.2019.1595706
Nolte, Paul. 2019. A Different Sort of Neoliberalism? Making Sense of German History Since the 1970s. *Bulletin of the German Historical Institute* 64: 9–29.

Novy, Johannes. 2013. Berlin Does Not Love You. In M. Bernt, B. Grell and A. Holm (eds.) *The Berlin Reader: A Compendium on Urban Change and Activism*. Bielefeld: Verlag Bielefeld, 223–237.

Novy, Johannes. 2017. The Selling (Out) of Berlin and the De- and Re-politicization of Urban Tourism in Europe's "Capital of Cool." In C. Colomb and J. Novy (eds.) *Protest and Resistance in the Tourist City*. New York: Routledge.

Oberhäuser, Notke. 2018a. Viele Ideen für bezahlbare Wohnungen. *DW*. September 20. www.dw.com/de/viele-ideen-f%C3%BCr-bezahlbare-wohnungen/a-45546548

Oberhäuser, Notke. 2018b. Germany's Soaring Housing Prices Spark Calls for Reform. *DW*. September 21. www.dw.com/en/germanys-soaring-housing-prices-spark-calls-for-reform/a-45595777

O'Sullivan, Feargus. 2016. The City with the World's Toughest Anti-Airbnb Laws. *Citylab*. December 1. www.citylab.com/equity/2016/12/berlin-has-the-worlds-toughest-anti-airbnb-laws-are-they-working/509024/

Parnow, Jonas, Lucas Vogel, Alsino Skowronnek, Jan-Erik Stange and Michael Hörz. 2015. Airbnb vs. Berlin. https://uclab.fh-potsdam.de/projects/airbnb-vs-berlin/

Phillips, Matt. 2014. Most Germans Don't Buy Their Homes, They Rent. Here's Why. *Quartz*. January 23. https://qz.com/167887/germany-has-one-of-the-worlds-lowest-homeownership-rates/

RegioKontext. 2016. Wiedervermietungsmieten und Mietpreisbremse in Berlin. May 27. www.berliner-mieterverein.de/uploads/2016/05/pm1616-Anl1-RegioKontext-Kurzanalyse-Mietpreisbremse.pdf

Reimann, Anna. 2011. Kult-Stadtteil Berlin-Kreuzberg. Kampf den Touristen. *Spiegel Online*. www.spiegel.de/reise/aktuell/kult-stadtteil-berlin-kreuzberg-kampf-den-touristen-a-748878-2.html

Reisenbichler, Alexander. 2016. A Failed Nation of Homeowners. Why Germany Eliminated Large-scale Subsidies for Homeowners. *American Institute for Contemporary Germany Studies*. April 18. www.aicgs.org/publication/a-failed-nation-of-homeowners

Richter, Wolf. 2012. Now There Is a Housing Bubble in Germany. *Business Insider*. February 22. www.businessinsider.com/now-a-housing-bubble-in-germany-2012-2

Rickens, Christian. 2017. Germany's Own Bay Area. *Handelsblatt*. April 28. www.handelsblatt.com/today/companies/bavarian-titan-germanys-own-bay-area/23569304.html?ticket=ST-90438877-RHNBGhhwDBsSmhKQtUhU-ap1

Roberts, Hannah. 2019. Munich Property "Biggest Bubble Risk in Europe." Experts Saystandfirst: Prices in the Bavarian City Have Doubled in a Decade Making It the Most Expensive Place to Buy a Home in Germany. *The Financial Times*. April 25.

Rossmann, Robert. 2018. Wir msüsen den explosionsartigen Anstieg der Mieten aufhalten. Interview with Minister of Justice Katarian Barley. *Süddeutsche Zeitung*. July 16.

Savills. 2015. Residential Markets in Germany. *Savills*. https://pdf.euro.savills.co.uk/germany-research/ger-ger-2015/savills-research-residential-market-report.pdf

Savills. 2019. Wem die Mietwohnungen in Deutschland gehören. Eigentümerstruktur am Wohnungsmarkt. *Spotlight Savills Research*. March. https://pdf.euro.savills.co.uk/germany-research/ger-2019/spotlight-eigentumerstruktur-am-wohnungsmarkt.pdf

Schäfer, Philipp and Nicole Braun. 2016. Misuse Through Short-term Rentals on the Berlin Housing Market. *International Journal of Housing Markets and Analysis* 9(2): 287–311.

Schlautmann, Christoph. 2019. Airbnb versucht die Flucht nach vorne. *Handelsblatt*. August 6. www.msn.com/de-de/finanzen/top-stories/privatwohnungsvermittler-airbnb-versucht-die-flucht-nach-vorn/ar-AAFnGQg?li=BBqg6Q9&fdhead=CS-INT-EXP-C

Schliess, Gero. 2017. Berlin 24/7: Germany's Capital Is Growing at an Alarming Speed. *DW*. January 1. www.dw.com/en/berlin-24-7-germanys-capital-is-growing-at-an-alarming-speed/a-37105320

Schönball, Ralf. 2016. Airbnb wehrt sich im Streit um Ferienwohnungen. *Der Tagesspiegel*. October 6. www.tagesspiegel.de/berlin/studie-in-berlin-vorgestellt-airbnb-wehrt-sich-im-streit-um-ferienwohnungen/14650230.html

Schultheis, Emily. 2019. The Radical Way Berlin Plans to Solve Its Housing Crisis. *Huffington Post*. April 12. www.huffpost.com/entry/berlin-housing-crisis-gentrification_n_5caf1d7de4b0308735d59712

Sethmann, Jens. 2017. Verbot soll kommerziellen Anbietern die Zähne zeigen. *Mieter Magazin*. December. www.berliner-mieterverein.de/magazin/online/mm1217/zweckentfremdung-verbot-soll-kommerziellen-anbietern-die-zaehne-zeigen-121711a.htm?hilite=%27Zweckentfremdung%27

Sethmann, Jens. 2019. Airbnb Will Sich Weisswaschen. *Berliner Mieterverein*. October 2. www.berliner-mieterverein.de/magazin/online/mm1019/studie-zu-ferienwohnungen-airbnb-will-sich-weisswaschen-101910a.htm

Siemer, Julia and Keir Matthews-Hunter. 2017. The Spatial Pattern of Gentrification in Berlin. *Prairie Perspectives: Geographical Essays*: 49–50. https://pcag.uwinnipeg.ca/Prairie-Perspectives/PP-Vol19/Siemer-MatthewsHunter.pdf

Der Spiegel. 2019. So kämpft Airbnb gegen seinen Ruf als Mietentreiber an. *Spiegel Online*. August 8. www.spiegel.de/wirtschaft/unternehmen/airbnb-so-kaempft-das-wohnungsportal-gegen-den-ruf-als-mietentreiber-a-1280665.html

Statistica. 2019. Home Ownership in Selected European Countries 2018. www.statista.com/statistics/246355/home-ownership-rate-in-europe/

Steinburg, Eva von. 2018. In der Au: Mieter fürchten nach Verkauf Vertreibung. *Abendzeitung*. October 4. www.abendzeitung-muenchen.de/inhalt.paulanergelaende-in-der-au-mieter-fuerchten-nach-verkauf-vertreibung.979ee897-ad17-4d60-9c15-0af1c1d26962.html

Stors, Natalie and Andreas Kagermeier. 2017. The Sharing Economy and Its Role in Metropolitan Tourism. In Maria Barbas and Sandra Guiand (eds.) *Tourism and Gentrification in Contemporary Metropolises*. London: Routledge.

Streit, Matthias. 2018. Germany Tightens Rent Controls Amid Housing Shortage. *Handelsblatt*. September 14. www.handelsblatt.com/today/finance/tenants-rights-germany-tightens-rent-controls-amid-housing-shortage/23583338.html?ticket=ST-4733230-rrnGpuJpJgLs1KORdeDV-ap6

Stroh, Kassian. 2018. Die Münchner bangen um ihre Wohnungen. *Süddeutsche Zeitung*. April 3. www.sueddeutsche.de/muenchen/mietpreise-die-muenchner-bangen-um-ihre-wohnungen-1.3922092

Süddeutsche Zeitung. 2016. Eine Herausforderung für die Landeshaptstadt. April 15. www.sueddeutsche.de/muenchen/zweckentfremdung-warum-illegale-vermietungen-ueber-airbnb-so-schwer-zu-unterbinden-sind-1.2944876-2

Süddeutsche Zeitung. 2019. München gegen Airbnb: Streit geht in die nächste Runde. August 28. www.sueddeutsche.de/muenchen/muenchen-airbnb-wohnen-rechtsstreit-stadt-klage-1.4579506

Der Tagesspiegel. 2015. Häuserkampf. http://haeuserkampf.tagesspiegel.de

Der Tagesspiegel. 2017. Der Tourismus ist die Erfolgsstory von Berlin. August 18. https://causa.tagesspiegel.de/gesellschaft/wie-viel-tourismus-vertraegt-berlin/der-tourismus-ist-die-erfolgsstory-von-berlin.html

Der Tagesspiegel. 2018. Neue Regeln für private Ferienwohnungen. March 22. www.tagesspiegel.de/berlin/zweckentfremdungsverbot-gesetz-neue-regeln-fuer-private-ferienwohnungen/21104800.html

Uffer, Sabine. 2013. The Uneven Development of Berlin's Housing Provision: Institutional Investment and Its Consequences on the City and Its Tenants. In M. Bernt, B. Grell and A. Holm (eds.) *The Berlin Reader: A Compendium on Urban Change and Activism*. Berlin: Verlag Bielefeld, 154–170.

VisitBerlin. Jahresbericht. Zahlen und Fakten. 2015. about.visitberlin.de/sites/default/files/MAM//asset/2017-05/Geschäftsbericht%202015.pdf

Voigtländer, Michael. 2009. Why Is the German Homeownership Rate So Low? *Journal of Housing Studies* 24(3): 355–372. https://doi.org/10.1080/02673030902875011

Die Welt. 2018. München Will Stärker Gegen Airbnb Vorgehen. June 25. www.welt.de/regionales/bayern/article178175280/Wohnungsnot-Muenchen-will-staerker-gegen-Airbnb-vorgehen.html

Wijburg, Gertjan and Manuel Aalbers. 2017. The Alternative Financialization of the German Housing Market. *Housing Studies* 32(7): 968–989.

Wildon, Jordan. 2019. Protesters Rally Against "Rental Insanity" in Large German Cities. *DW*. April 6. www.dw.com/en/protesters-rally-against-rental-insanity-in-large-german-cities/a-48235915

Worstall, Tim. 2013. What a Surprise, Airbnb Chooses Dublin as European Headquarters, Here Comes the 2% Tax Rate. *Forbes*. September 13. www.forbes.com/sites/timworstall/2013/09/13/what-a-surprise-airbnb-chooses-dublin-as-european-headqaurters-here-comes-the-2-tax-rate/#40af30742a55

Wurzbacher, Ralf. 2019. Verdeckter Wohungsklau. Airbnb vermittelt allein in Berlin 26.000 Unterkünfte. Sozialforscher halten das für völlig vernachlassungswert. *Junge Welt*. August 8. www.jungewelt.de/loginFailed.php?ref=/artikel/360380.zweckentfremdung-verdeckter-wohnungsklau.html

CONCLUSION

Repositioning short-term rentals in the housing market

In this book we present two narratives. The first describes how Airbnb's model of homesharing has had a disruptive impact on housing and neighborhoods, particularly in cities where tourism intersects with stressed housing markets. What started out as a platform for individuals quickly became a platform dominated by commercial actors and real estate investors.

Airbnb's impact – despite media reports and scattered empirical studies – had not received a comprehensive review and analysis. Synthesizing the available empirical literature and focusing on major cities in the US, Australia and Germany, we found similar patterns:

- Commercial and professional hosts dominate listings and revenue
- Listings concentrate in inner-city, trendy and gentrifying neighborhoods
- Spatial concentration of listings is associated with rising rents, house prices and lack of availability
- Residential areas with concentrated listings become tourist milieus, displacing local residents and businesses

Sooner or later, most cities tried to assess Airbnb's impact and protect their housing and neighborhoods with regulatory legislation but their attempts to get transaction data met with resistance and led to city data wars. Our case studies of cities document the struggles to maintain or regain control over governance as localities become battlegrounds for opponents and proponents of Airbnb. Although many of the effects are similar, there are considerable differences between countries and cities within countries in terms of the way these issues played out, including the response of local authorities.

Our second narrative follows the evolution of Airbnb. Having institutionalized short-term rentals (STRs), Airbnb jump-started a growing real estate sector which has been transformed by new players and new models. While still in its infancy, we suggest that this multibillion-dollar sector foreshadows more stress on already stressed urban housing markets, increasing housing inequality and undermining housing security.

The short-term rental sector – new players, new models

> It has become widely apparent that the short-term rentals segment (outside of traditional hotels) is a massive category and part of a bigger paradigm shift in the way that housing and accommodations are managed more generally.
>
> *(Bujarski 2019)*

What is Airbnb today? We have described how Airbnb, a moving target from the start, has morphed from a homesharing platform offering alternative accommodations to travelers into a platform dominated by professional operators (both individuals and corporations) that offers a wide variety of accommodations and services, much like an online travel agency. At the same time, the hospitality industry has also converged with Airbnb by offering its own brand of STRs. Marriott is a prime example. It has expanded its homesharing offshoot – Marriott Homes and Villas – to over 100 global markets where its well-known brand, safety standards and business traveler constituency present a challenge to Airbnb (Sperance 2019). Other hotel brands are also expected to diversify to offer all types of accommodations.

More dramatic and transformative than the entry of hotel chains into the STR market is the synergy between residential and tourism markets as a widespread paradigm for the real estate industry. We have discussed the incentives Airbnb created for investors in STR properties, both buy-to-rent and rent-to-rent options and the growing number of rentiers. We have also described how Airbnb has reached out to partner with real estate developers working directly with landlords who are converting or developing new buildings with units designed to be listed on Airbnb. However, this is increasingly a two-way street as the multifamily rental sector is eager to capitalize on STRs and move into this lucrative market. Real estate publications acknowledge that "the platform has attracted large property owners and investors" including companies with hundreds of units (Sisson 2018), and that "what started with peer-to-peer rentals and private owners has quickly evolved, with new operating models and partnerships stretching from corporate real estate to nationwide multifamily housing builders" (Bujarski 2019).

At a time when Airbnb has met with increasing regulatory constraint and is planning a public stock offering, real estate – a $ 27 trillion industry in the US – is diversifying the STR sector by introducing models that help circumvent existing regulations. Its presence may also provide additional political clout.

It was not always evident that a convergence would occur: "Property owners once saw short-term rental listing sites like Airbnb Inc. as a threat. Now, some are embracing them" (Putzier 2019; see also Yale 2018). For the most part, the multifamily industry has been wary of STRs due to concerns about building security and the fear of complaints from long-term residents. There is also the regulatory issue. Before a synergy between residential and tourism markets can become a more widespread model, there are a host of legal matters to be resolved, such as local laws prohibiting STRs in residential buildings, conflict between apartment owners and tenants about STRs, and conflict among all parties over the control of and profit from STRs. That said, the growth of the STR market coupled with the ease of platform technology has made for greater acceptance of hybrids, including a "flexible" rental model which would allow landlords "to cushion against the peaks and troughs in the housing market" by using STRs to bridge the leasing gap (Karr 2019).

Indeed, two leading multifamily interest groups – the National Multifamily Housing Council (NMHC) and the National Apartment Association (NAA) – have officially endorsed STRs. Referring to the booming STR sector, their online fact sheet supports the right of multifamily companies and property owners to participate in the sharing economy with the proviso that "it is done in full compliance with existing law and regulation" (NMHC n.d.).

The real estate industry, meanwhile, has been experimenting with a variety of models which permit STRs while taking local regulatory frameworks into account, among them, branded STR apartments, apartment communities, and pop-up hotels (CBRE 2020; Shaw 2018). Some involve partnering with Airbnb or other platforms. Airbnb's partnership with Newgard Development Corporation, noted in Chapter 1, is one example; its "Natiivo" model of a condo/hotel, which explicitly allows STRs and avoids local regulation, will be built in several locations.

More threatening to renters are the developers and property managers who have leased partial or entire buildings to companies such as Sonder Corp, Stay Alfred and Lyric Hospitality Inc. Pop-up hotel models, like WhyHotel and Stay Alfred, furnish and rent unleased apartments thus minimizing leasing risk. Models like Yotelpad proactively address the regulatory issue by making STRs legal for their condo owners. Backed by venture capital, these startups use master leases to convert the units into STRs which they furnish. Airbnb has also continued to actively pursue multifamily real estate. A good example is its entry into Greystar Real Estate, a leader in rental housing and owner and manager of hundreds of thousands of apartments. To gain direct access to Greystar and expand its presence in corporate travel, Airbnb acquired the start-up Urbandoor in 2019. While real estate/sharing economy joint ventures may be most visible in the US, they can be found in all the advanced economies and are multiplying globally.

As with the prototypic Airbnb model, the application of sophisticated digital technology is central to these developments and reflects similar trends in the real estate industry at large. Referred to as proptech (property technology) in the industry, these platforms are described by Shaw who draws on Srnicek's concept of platform capitalism (2017) as "platform real estate." Shaw notes that digital technology brings together clusters of interacting users around investment, residential and commercial markets and building management on a global basis (2018). In an emerging literature on platform real estate, Fields argues that digital technology facilitated the creation of single-family rentals as an asset class in the US after the Global Financial Crisis (GFC) (Fields 2018; Fields 2019).

It is difficult to assess the size of this rapidly growing market. Available data on STRs from the tourism sector are likely to overestimate size as they does not correct for dual listings; on the other hand, tourism sector data do not include the newer real estate platforms. Examining global room sales by lodging categories 2012–2017, Euromonitor International found that STRs grew from $ 45.6 billion in 2012 to $ 82.9 in 2017 (Bremner 2017). At a "first" conference on the short-term rental sector organized by *Skift*, a travel industry news and research organization, *Skift* reported that the total consumer market for STRs was $ 107 billion in 2018, approximately one-sixth of the entire $ 600 billion travel accommodations industry. It grew 7 % to $ 115 billion in 2019 (Geerts 2020).

In short, the interest and participation of the real estate industry has been part and parcel of the growth and diversification of this dynamic sector. Although there has been relatively little attention paid to the introduction of these platforms or the resulting globalized STR market, these digitally driven systems may be as radical an innovation as financial engineering was a few decades ago and may have similarly negative consequences for housing and cities. Looking ahead, we suggest that ongoing developments, such as the shift to more flexible modes of rental tenure, have the potential to further disrupt residential housing by increasing housing inequality, undermining tenure security and further commodifying housing.

Implications for housing inequality and insecurity

According to economists, housing plays a central role in the dynamics of wealth inequality. Disparities in housing wealth – including payments to owners of real property (rent) – have grown exponentially over the past few decades and, today, are the main source of wealth inequality (Rognlie 2015; Albouy and Zabek 2016; Bivens 2019; Standing 2017).[1] Although the decline in homeownership and the rise in the proportion of households which rent have contributed to housing inequality, at the heart of this phenomenon is the exponential rise in house prices and rents.

While Airbnb is hardly the main culprit, the empirical evidence in Chapter 3 shows that the concentration of listings contributes to noticeably localized effects, raising house prices and rents in popular metropolitan neighborhoods, and that these same areas attract investors, further driving up house prices and rents. Rising house prices and rents benefit existing property owners and investors, but rising house prices and the competition for single-family houses with institutional investors who buy-to-rent present barriers for first-time homeowners. This further contributes to the concentration of housing wealth and the polarization of housing between housing haves and have-nots. Rising rents contribute to the growing number of cost-burdened renters who may face eviction and possibly, homelessness. Although both home buyers and renters are threatened by the growth of the STR sector, the primary threat is to renters.

In a financialized rental market characterized by corporate owners who maximize short-term profits, the ability of landlords to pick and choose between tenure options (short-term versus long-term rentals or rent-to-rent) adds to the already existing tenure insecurity of cost-burdened tenants. This means that, as landlords have more options, tenants have fewer options and takes us back, full circle, to the concerns raised about Airbnb in the cities we studied: that landlords were evicting long-term tenants to shift to more profitable STRs. Given the potential for greater flexibility in the use of housing stock, local laws would have to adjust to protect tenants as was the case during the condominium conversion craze in the 1980s and 1990s. The lack of adequate resources for enforcement, however, suggests that evictions and homelessness may increase with the increasing scale of this sector.

Loftium is an illustrative example of the new disruptors in this hybrid sector. A Seattle, Washington, start-up, Loftium started in 2017 by offering to help homebuyers with a down payment in exchange for hosting part of their house continuously on Airbnb for one to three years (Siegel Bernard 2017). In 2018, Loftium switched to a more profitable rent-to-rent business model. Leasing rental units directly from owners, the company then re-leases them to customers with the proviso that they host (sub-sub-let) on Airbnb. Backed by venture capital, Loftium expanded aggressively and, by 2019, operated in 11 major US cities, including Atlanta, Chicago and Houston.

What does Loftium offer the potential renter? The website states that Loftium provides "a cost-effective solution to outrageous rent prices and puts you in a home in the city you love." The renter receives a discounted rent, Loftium gets the rent plus a cut of the STR revenue and Airbnb gets its usual fee. The Loftium renter signs two related contracts: a sub-lease and a service agreement for a "hosting gig." The sub-lease resembles a typical lease, requiring security deposit and credit checks and sets a stipulated rent. The service agreement stipulates host responsibilities in exchange for a discounted rent. The discount is determined by Loftium.

The Loftium tenant/host essentially becomes the "manager of an on-site Airbnb unit" but without the ability to set the price or control the date or duration of the stay. She also has a prescribed list of responsibilities that range from setting up the Airbnb space, communicating with guests before, during and after their stay, recommending local activities, taking care of the day-to-day administration, managing the cleaning between guests and so forth. In addition, the tenant/host still has to deal with the owner/landlord regarding issues such as plumbing, electricity and general maintenance. Online reviews point out that Loftium is really a full-time job and that, for many, the savings are not worth it.

Whether or not Loftium succeeds in the long run, its business model takes commodification a step further, extracting profit from hosting as well as from the rented home. The Loftium tenant/host, for example, does not receive the full earnings for her labor, which is physical, clerical and emotional. In terms of its impact on rental housing, Loftium is standardizing the sub-sub-lease in cities across the country. This model thus depends upon removing centrally located rental housing from the direct rental market and requires the renter – now a sublessee – to sign a hosting contract. Subletting through Loftium thus further removes the renter from control of her rent, her space and her labor and makes her a combination Airbnb manager and housemaid. This comes at a high price for the sublessee/host but also for the tight long-term rental market.

Together with rising cost and lack of availability, changes in housing tenure and security promise to further destabilize our housing system. Thus, it is not surprising that housing has become a hot political issue.[2] When renting was primarily the tenure of low-income households and/or a temporary way station for future homeowners, tenants had little political clout. But as renters are increasingly middle-class residents who face costly and tight housing markets, political mobilization for legislative remedies has increased, and protection for renters is back on the political agenda in the US for the first time in decades.[3]

Listing the tenants' rights movement among the key movements of the past decade, Peter Dreier has suggested that "tenants may be the sleeping giant of American politics" (2020). Rising tenant power, however, may have a perverse effect on residential rental housing. Together with protective legislation, it may give the real estate industry an additional incentive to turn to more flexible models of housing tenure and thus set the stage for a new round of regulatory battles with cities.

Implications for cities

There are several reasons why the ongoing changes in the real estate industry should be carefully monitored for their impact on cities. From its conception, Airbnb was essentially an urban phenomenon, shifting sought-after residential space in popular metropolitan neighborhoods to visitors. This has posed a particular danger in that cities are hubs for economic activity and employment, and as the studies show, the lack of affordable housing threatens the ability of job seekers to live where the jobs are located (Albouy and Zabek 2016; Florida 2018).

Moreover, urban space is limited, making competition between residents and visitors a zero-sum game and raising the question of whether the needs of residents for housing and quality of life should take preference over the needs of visitors. Indeed, as the empirical evidence has shown, STRs have introduced new conflicts that pit residents against residents and residents against visitors and challenge the social and legal structure of communities. Evaluating the relative costs and benefits of Airbnb to cities, a report from the Economic Policy Institute concludes that "costs to renters and local jurisdictions exceed the benefits to travelers and property owners" (Bivens 2019, 2).

The need to weigh the costs and benefits of STRs has been of particular concern for cities in Europe given the economic importance of tourism. In the face of hitherto successful lobbying of the EU by Airbnb, twenty-two cities appealed to the European Commission in 2019 for help in dealing with Airbnb's impact, in particular, the growing pressure on real estate prices and affordable housing (Spinks 2019).[4] The cities called for a uniform legal framework that requires platforms to transmit data to local authorities to help them enforce regulations, publish registration numbers on listings and take responsibility for non-compliance with regulations.

As a conciliatory step, Airbnb and several other platforms signed an agreement in March 2020 with the European Commission for data exchange with Eurostat, the statistical office of the European Commission. The platforms will provide information on number of guests and number of overnight stays, aggregated at the city level on a quarterly basis. The rationale is to provide reliable data to inform policy making (European Commission 2020). However, the agreement, which protects the privacy of guests and hosts, does not provide the identity of individuals or property owners needed for local enforcement.

The lack of access to data is not the only source of tension for cities. Cities are vulnerable to biases inherent in the tech platforms. As empirical studies of Airbnb have shown in particular, and as Shaw (2018) notes in general, platform algorithms and norms have the power to discriminate along racial, gender and other dimensions and need oversight. Smart Cities ideology notwithstanding, it remains to be seen whether and to what extent local authorities are able to rein in the tech giants.

Meanwhile, the question of the tech industry's responsibility for what is on their platform has become a major political issue. As legal and regulatory challenges have made some inroads on tech's immunity, the platforms have made attempts at conciliation. Airbnb is a case in point. In addition to providing limited transaction data to a few localities, Airbnb has responded to long-standing complaints about safety issues and fraudulent listings. Following several shootings in party houses, the platform has begun to implement measures to protect hosts, guests and communities. Observers suggest that the likelihood of an impending stock offering in 2020 has made Airbnb more conciliatory.

Housing and social stability

There are broader concerns about the implications of a growing short-term rental sector for society at large. In both policy circles and the academic literature, there is general agreement that a well-functioning housing system is important for social and political stability. While housing systems in Western capitalist societies have taken different paths – depending on history and ideology – and each combines various forms of tenure, for the sake of simplicity, we can identify two basic models: ownership and rental, with the rental sector including private and publicly subsidized rental housing. The US and Australia are prime examples of homeownership societies where homeownership is commonly referred to as the "American Dream" and the "Australian Dream," whereas Germany and Switzerland are examples of renter nations.

In homeownership societies, government policy and ideology have promoted the advantages of homeownership as a source of societal as well as personal stability. However, as most households do not own their homes outright, homeownership is tied to getting a mortgage and being able to pay the monthly mortgage bill. This makes homeownership subject to insecurity as illustrated in the US by the Savings

& Loan (S&L) crisis in the 1980s and, more recently, by the housing bubble and the GFC.

In the aftermath of this crisis, both homeownership and rental models have come under scrutiny, raising questions as to their future viability. Regarding homeownership, there has been a shift in neoliberal thinking. In a special issue in January 2020 entitled "The Horrible Housing Blunder," the weekly news magazine *The Economist* addresses "why the obsession with home ownership is so harmful." The report cites Germany as a model of a society where renting is a secure form of housing tenure (2020). Leaving aside the fact that Germany is confronting its own housing crisis as its rental market has become increasingly financialized (see Chapter 5), this about-face is likely motivated, in part, by the desire to extract additional profit from housing and, as we have shown, affects rental housing as well as homeownership.

This is where Airbnb enters the picture, legitimating and institutionalizing the STR. By treating residential space as an "underutilized asset" and marketing the STR to potential hosts as well as tourists, Airbnb has propelled the growth of a highly commercialized short-term rental sector that attracts investors, professional operators and large-scale multifamily real estate in ever more financialized ventures. Although it claims to offer a solution to the affordability issue by helping some individuals, Airbnb is hardly a societal solution. Indeed, we have described a feedback cycle in which STRs contribute to our housing crises, thus fueling the need to further monetize and commodify housing in order to afford either purchase or rent.

It remains to be seen whether STRs and the homesharing ideology can or will provide the financial stability and social support needed by renters and would-be-owners at a time when residential real estate is increasingly controlled by institutional owners, rents are out of reach and homeownership is not attainable by many.

Notes

1 According to Zillow, housing wealth was at an all-time high in 2018 (Lloyd 2019).
2 A February 2020 poll by the University of Southern California found that nearly 23 % of respondents listed homelessness or housing as their top political issue in the upcoming Democratic primaries (CBS 2020).
3 Several states with Democratic majorities passed laws to protect tenants. In 2019, Oregon became the first state to impose state-wide rent controls. The 2020 California Tenant Protection Act restricts rent increases and includes a "just cause" provision requiring landlords to give a legitimate reason for eviction. New York State passed landmark legislation protecting tenants and strengthening rent regulations in 2019, and in Massachusetts, there is a movement to bring back rent control.
4 Paris, Barcelona, Amsterdam, Berlin and Munich, among others.

References

Albouy, David and Mike Zabek. 2016. Housing Inequality. *NBER Working Paper No. 21916*. January. www.nber.org/papers/w21916#fromrss

Bivens, Josh. 2019. The Economic Costs and Benefits of Airbnb. *Economic Policy Institute*. January 30. Washington, DC.

Bremner, Caroline. 2017. What the Data Tell Us About Travel and Tourism in 2018. *Euromonitor International*. September 2017. https://blog.euromonitor.com/travel-2018-data-tells-us/

Bujarski, Luke. 2019. From Traveltech to Proptech. *Luft*. October 24. https://luft.net/insights/from-traveltech-to-proptech-three-reasons-why-the-short-term-rental-discussion-is-shifting-towards-real-estate

CBRE Group. 2020. Short-term Rentals: A Maturing U.S. Market & Its Impact on Traditional Hotels. cbre.us/research-and-reports/Short-Term-Rentals-A-Maturing-US-Market-Its-Impact-on-Traditional-Hotels-January-2020

Dreier, Peter. 2020. The Decade in 11 Movements. *The American Prospect*. January 8. https://prospect.org/civil-rights/the-decade-in-11-movements/

European Commission. 2020. Commission Reaches Agreement with Collaborative Economy Platforms to Publish Key Data on Tourism Accommodation. *Press Release*. March 20. https://ec.europa.eu/commission/presscorner/detail/en/ip_20_194

Fields, Desiree. 2018. Constructing a New Asset Class: Property-led Financial Accumulation after the Crisis. *Economic Geography* 94(2), 118–140. http://unequalcities.org/wp-content/uploads/sites/17/2019/01/Fields-Desiree-Constructing-a-new-asset-class-final.pdf

Fields, Desiree. 2019. Automated Landlord: Digital Technologies and Post-crisis Financial Accumulation. *Economy and Space*. https://journals.sagepub.com/doi/pdf/10.1177/0308518X19846514

Florida, Richard. 2018. Is Housing Inequality the Main Driver of Economic Inequality? *CityLab*. April 13. www.citylab.com/equity/2018/04/is-housing-inequality-the-main-driver-of-economic-inequality/557984/

Geerts, Wouter. 2020. Travel Megatrends 2020: Short-Term Rental Winners Emerge. *Skift*. February 24. https://skift.com/2020/02/24/travel-megatrends-2020-short-term-rental-winners-emerge/

Karr, Merilee. 2019. STAA. The Short-term Rental Ecosystem Is Rapidly Changing; and It's Only Just Getting Started. August 9. www.ukstaa.org/staa-blog/2019/8/9/the-short-term-rental-ecosystem

Lloyd, Alcynna. 2019. U.S. Housing Market Value Climbs to $33.3 Trillion in 2018. *HousingWire*. January 4. www.housingwire.com/articles/47847-us-housing-market-value-climbs-to-333-trillion-in-2018/

The National Multifamily Housing Council [NMHC]. n.d. Short-Term Rental Services, Fact Sheet. www.nmhc.org/advocacy/issue-fact-sheet/home-sharing-fact-sheet/

Putzier, Konrad. 2019. In the Airbnb Era, Apartment Landlords Are the New Hoteliers. *The Wall Street Journal*. December 10. www.wsj.com/articles/in-the-airbnb-era-apartment-landlords-are-the-new-hoteliers-11575979200

Rognlie, Matthew. 2015. Deciphering the Fall and Rise in the Net Capital Share. *Brookings Papers on Economic Activity*. March.

Shaw, Joe. 2018. Platform Real Estate: Theory and Practice of New Urban Real Estate Markets. *Urban Geography*. www.tandfonline.com/doi/abs/10.1080/02723638.2018.1524653

Siegel Bernard, Tara. 2017. A Down Payment with a Catch: You Must Be an Airbnb Host. *The New York Times*. September 18. www.nytimes.com/2017/09/18/your-money/mortgages/loftium-airbnb-down-payment.html

Sisson, Patrick. 2018. Airbnbusiness: As Professionals Find Success on the Platform, Is There Still Room for Sharers? *Curbed*. February 21. www.curbed.com/2018/2/21/17032100/airbnb-business-profit-hotel-property-management

Sperance, Cameron. 2019. Marriott's Short-term Rental Plan Shows Airbnb Is a Hospitality Force to Be Reckoned With. *Bisnow Boston*. May 1. www.bisnow.com/national/news/hotel/marriotts-short-term-rental-rollout-brings-omnichannel-to-hotel-industry-98766

Spinks, Rosie. 2019. European Cities Turn to EU for Help in Battle Against Airbnb. *Skift*. June 20. https://skift.com/2019/06/20/european-cities-turn-to-eu-for-help-in-battle-against-airbnb/

Srnicek, Nick. 2017. *Platform Capitalism*. Malden, MA: Polity Press.

Standing, Guy. 2017. *The Corruption of Capitalism: Why Rentiers Thrive and Work Does Not Pay*. London: Biteback Publishing Ltd.

Yale, Aly J. 2018. 10 Years after Airbnb, Real Estate Developers See the Money in Home-sharing. *Forbes*. October 17. www.forbes.com/sites/alyyale/2018/10/17/multi-family-developers-are-leveraging-the-short-term-rental-fad-heres-how/#4285388538e0

INDEX

Aalbers, Manuel 15, 18; *see also* Wijburg, Gertjan and Manuel Aalbers
AHURI (Australian Housing and Urban Research Institute) 96, 97n13; *see also* Crommelin, Laura et al.
Airbnb: business model 12–14; commercialization 13, 60–61; concentration effects 61–63, 136, 139; convergence with hotels 137; convergence with real estate 137; data access 23–48; data wars 23–48; digital technology 2, 138; ecosystem 13, 18, 19; impact on house prices 59, 139; impact on housing 56–61, 136; impact on long-term rentals 58–59, 136; impact on neighborhoods 61–63, 136; institutionalization of short-term rentals 12, 18, 136; legitimation of homesharing 11; lobbying activities 71–72; marketing of neighborhoods 69–70; origins 2, 11; professionalization of 13, 18, 19; as prototype of sharing economy 11, 138; and quality of life, amenities 5, 37–38, 40, 63–69, 73, 88, 89, 95, 97, 141; and real estate investors 136; rhetoric 11, 12–14, 92; and short-term rental sector 136, 137–139; synergy between residential and tourism markets 1, 137; trajectory of 11–12, 137; and underutilized space 3, 12–13; as urban phenomenon 3–4, 141–142; and venture capital 2, 10; *see also individual cities, countries*

AirDNA 24–25, 30, 48n2, 44
Alexander, Jacqui 87
Alizadeh, Tooran et al. 88, 91, 95
Alliance of Downtown Civic Organizations (ADCO) *see* Boston
American Hotel and Lodging Association (AHLA) 71
Australia 4, 5, 17, 19n1, 69, 81–97, 104, 105, 106, 111, 136, 142; Airbnb reception 81, 85; amenity issues 89; apartment oversupply 96; commercialization of Airbnb 90; commodification of housing 84–85; concentration effects of Airbnb 89, 90–91; displacement and gentrification 95–96, 98n17; emergence of high-rise cities 86–88; financialization of housing 81, 82–84; homeownership and social equity 84–85, 95; house prices and affordability 84–85, 87, 95, 96; housing haves and have-nots 83, 84; housing sector and home finance 82–84; housing stock 83, 86–87, 90, 97n6; housing tenure 82, 84, 95; impact of Airbnb on disadvantaged neighborhoods 91–92; impact of Airbnb on housing 90–91, 92, 95; impact of Global Financial Crisis (GFC) on housing markets 83–84, 97; investor driven apartment boom 85, 87–88, 96, 97n1, 97n8; nation of homeowners 5, 81, 82, 84, 90; neoliberal policies 81, 82, 83; overview 5, 97; regulation 92–93, 97; renters and

rentiers 84–85; short-term lets (STL) 90; strata 69, 89, 93, 94, 95, 97n7; tax policy 83; vacant city apartments 83, 85, 87, 90–91, 97; *see also* Melbourne; Sydney

Barron, Kyle et al. 57, 58, 59
Berlin 5, 112–120; Airbnb activity 111; Airbnb protest 115, 127n15; Berlin *MieterGemeinschaft* (BMG) 115, 118; Berlin *MieterVerein* 110, 125; concentration in inner-city 118–119, 120; description 112–113, 127n11; Deutsche Wohnen 119, 127n20; displacement and gentrification 114, 115, 119–120, 126; enforcement 116–118; Expropriate Deutsche Wohnen 119; *Häusserkampf* 112, 114; housing crisis 112, 113, 114, 119–120; impact of Airbnb on housing 116–117, 118–119, 124–125; impact of Airbnb on neighborhoods 112, 114, 115, 117, 119, 124–125, 126, 127n15; *Mietendeckel* 113; overview 112, 120; post-reunification 106, 113–114; privatization of social housing 107, 113; real estate speculation 109, 116; regulation 115–117; tourism as development strategy 114–115; urban tourism 112, 114–115, 118, 120, 122; *Zweckentfremdungverbot-Gesetz* (ZwVbG) 115–116, 117–118
Bivens, Josh 71, 141; *see also* Economic Policy Institute (EPI)
BJH Advisors 29
black box effect 47, 70, 60
Boston 43–46, 47; Airbnb impact on housing 56, 57, 58; Airbnb impact on neighborhoods 62, 64, 69, 74n5; Alliance of Downtown Civic Organizations (ADCO) 44, 46; Boston Airbnb law 45–46; Chinese Progressive Association 64; commercial operators of Airbnb 60; Community Labor United 44; housing stock 43, 45; Inspectional Services Department (ISD) 43, 45, 46; overview 47
Brauckmann, Stefan 111
Brunner, Katharina and Christian Endt 111; *see also Süddeutsche Zeitung*
Bucks, Dan 70

Capital 111
Cavalleri, Ford 46; *see also* Boston
CBRE 60; *see also* Los Angeles; New York City

Chesky, Brian 6n3, 72
cities: access to data 141–142; Airbnb as an urban phenomenon 3–4, 141–142; as battlegrounds 5, 25–26, 46–48, 136; challenges to local authority 5, 26, 70–72, 141–142; competition between residents and visitors 141; data wars 23–48; governance and control 4, 25–26, 136; occupancy taxes 3, 29–30; zoning 23, 26, 71
city tourism *see* urban tourism, rise of
city wars *see* data wars
Communications Decency Act (Section 230) 5, 13, 24, 37
concentration effects *see also* Airbnb; displacement; gentrification; neighborhood effects; quality of life; *individual cities, countries*
Cox, Murray 24–25, 29–30, 34, 41, 92; and Tom Slee 28; *see also* data, data activists
Crommelin, Laura et al. 90, 91, 92; *see also* AHURI (Australian Housing and Urban Research Institute)

Daley, John et al. 84–85
data 23–26; access to 5, 23–27; Communications Decency Act (Section 230) 5, 13, 24, 37; data activists 24 (*see also* Cox, Murray, and Tom Slee); data wars 5, 9, 23–48, 140–141 (*see also* Airbnb; *individual cities, countries*); third-party data 6n1, 24
displacement 6, 9; *see also* concentration effects; gentrification; neighborhood effects
Displacement Research Action Network 64
disruptor 1, 11
Duso, Tomaso et al. 119

Economic Policy Institute (EPI) 67, 71, 141; *see also* Bivens, Josh
Economist, The 17, 143
Edelman, Benjamin et al. 29
Egner, Bjorn et al. 113, 114, 115
Ellen, Ingrid Gould and Brendan O'Flaherty 27, 38, 68
Ellis Act 32, 49n12; *see also* Los Angeles; San Francisco
Empirica 124, 125; *see also* Germany
European Commission 141–142

feedback cycle 3, 19, 143
Fields, Desiree 138–139; and Sabine Uffer 113

financialization of housing 2–3, 14–16; definition of 14; hyperfinancialization 14; *see also* Australia; Germany; United States housing sector
Frenken, Koen and Juliet Schor 13
Füller, Henning and Boris Michel 114, 118; *see also* Berlin

Gebbia, Joe 12
generation rent 17, 95; *see also* Ronald, Richard; Standing, Guy
gentrification 3, 5, 10, 29–30, 41–42, 63–65, 66–67, 95–96, 98n17, 109, 114–115, 119, 126; Airbnb-fueled gentrification 64, 67; racialized 5, 29–30, 63–64; *see also* concentration effects; displacement; neighborhood effects
Germany 4, 5, 104–128, 136, 142, 143; Airbnb reception 105, 110–111, 125; Deutscher Mieterbund 109, 110; Deutsche Wohnen (DW) 107, 113, 119, 127n20; displacement and gentrification 107–110, 112–113, 114–120, 122, 126; financialization of housing 104, 107; housing angst and housing crises 104, 107–110, 126; housing laws 105–106, 108, 110, 125–126; housing summit 109; housing tenure 104, 105–106, 107, 109–110, 127n6; impact of Global Financial Crisis (GFC) 104, 105, 106, 107, 113, 126; *Mietendeckel* 119; *Mietpreisbremse* 108–109; *Mietspiegel* 108–109; nation of renters 5, 16, 104, 105, 107, 126; overview 126; privatization and financialization of rental housing 107–109, 113, 126; regulation 125; sale of social housing 107–109, 121, 126; tax policy 109; urban tourism 110–111, 112, 114–115, 118, 120, 122, 125–126, 127n7; Vonovia 107, 121, 122; *Wohngemeinnützigkeit* 105, 106; *see also* Berlin; Munich
GEWOS 115, 116
Global Financial Crisis (GFC) 3–4, 5, 9, 14, 16; housing bubble 2, 4, 14–16, 96, 107; *see also* post crisis conditions; *individual cities, countries*
Goldman, Judy 68; *see also* Los Angeles, Keep Neighborhoods First
Grattan Institute *see* Daley, John et al.; Minifie, Jim
Great Recession 14, 19n2
Gurran, Nicole et al. 93, 97n4; and Peter Phibbs 83, 90, 91

Guy, Kevin 36; *see also* San Francisco, Office of Short-term Rentals (OSTR)

Henger, Ralph and Michael Voigtlander (Institut der Deutschen Wirtschaft) 108
Hoffman, Lily M., Susan S. Fainstein and Dennis R. Judd 3, 114
Holm, Andrej et al. (Hans Böckler Foundation) 108
home finance system *see individual cities, countries*
Horn, Keren and Mark Merante 44, 57, 58; *see also* Boston
Hotel Trades Council, AFL-CIO 30, 31, 72
housing 1, 4, 12–13; as financial asset 12–13; flexible nature of 13; haves and have-nots 84, 139; inequality and insecurity 6, 139–140, 141; and social stability 142–143; tenure modes 138, 139, 141, 142–143; as underutilized asset 12; *see also* Airbnb; financialization of housing; *individual cities, countries*
HR&A Advisors 24, 33
Hsi, Helen 116

InsideAirbnb *see* Cox, Murray

Jimenez, Sarah *see* Boston, Community Labor United
Joebges, Silke 120; *see also* Munich
Jordan, Evan and Jocelyn Moore 67; *see also* Oahu, Hawaii

Klossner, Christian 32
Kofner, Stefan 109, 106–107
Kritische Geographie Berlin 118; *see also* Berlin, Berlin *MieterGemeinschaft* (BMG); Füller, Henning and Boris Michel

Lee, Dayne 40–41, 56, 58, 60, 62, 63
Lehane, Chris 12, 36, 39, 71, 94
Leshinsky, Rebecca and Laura Schatz 92
Loftium 140–141
Los Angeles 37–42, 47; budgetary problems 39, 41, 42; commercial operators 60; enforcement 42; housing costs 37–38; housing stock 37, 38; impact on housing 56, 58; impact on neighborhoods 62, 64, 63, 65–66, 67, 69; Keep Neighborhoods First 49n16, 49n19, 65, 68; LA Short-Term Rental Ordinance 41–42; Los Angeles Alliance for a New Economy (LAANE) 38, 39, 40; overview 47; rent stabilization ordinance 38; Transient Occupancy Tax (TOT) and Voluntary

Collection Agreements (VCA) 39, 41, 42, 49n13, 49n17, 70; Venice Beach 38, 40, 49n19, 65–66

Massachusetts Airbnb law 46
Mazry, Omar 48; *see also* San Francisco, Office of Short-term Rentals (OSTR)
Melbourne: Airbnb hotspot 88; Airbnb impact on neighborhoods 90, 91, 96; amenity issues 88, 89, 94–95; code of conduct 94–95; commercial listings 90–91; concentration effects 89–91; description 86, 88; Owners Corporation Act 94–95; regulation 92, 94–95; strata 89, 94–95; vacant apartments 87, 88, 90, 91, 97; Victoria Independent Panel on Short-stay Accommodations 89; We Live Here 89, 94, 95
Merante, Mark and Keren Horn 44; *see also* Horn, Keren and Mark Merante
millennials 2, 11, 14, 16
Mindl, Felix 117, 118, 127n19
Minifie, Jim 89
Mobilization for Youth, Legal Services *see* BJH Advisors
Munich 5, 120–125; Airbnb impact on housing and neighborhoods 124–125; city policy 121; description 120–121, 122, 123, 128n24; enforcement 123; housing crisis 121–122, 127n5; housing protest 121–122; *Mieterstammtisch* 122; overview 120–121, 126; regulation 123, 124; rental housing stock 121, 122; tourism 120–121, 122; *Zweckentfremdungssatzung* (ZeS) 124
Murphy, Lawrence 83

Natiivo 12, 138
National Apartment Association (NAA) 138
National Association of Realtors (NAR) 72
National Multifamily Housing Council 138
neighborhood effects 61–68; Airbnb concentration 40, 56, 58, 61–63, 64, 65, 66, 67, 68, 69, 139; Airbnb marketing of 9–10, 69–70; displacement and gentrification 3, 5, 10, 29–30, 41–42, 63–65, 66–67, 95–96, 98n17, 109, 114–115, 119, 126; *see also* Airbnb, and quality of life, amenities; *individual cities, countries*
neoliberal *Zeitgeist* 3, 13, 18
New Orleans 66–67; *see also* Treme, New Orleans
New York City 26–32, 46–47; Airbnb disclosure law 31–32; commercial operators of Airbnb 60, 61, 62; housing stock 27; impact of Airbnb on housing 56, 57, 58, 59; impact of Airbnb on neighborhoods 62, 63, 64; New York City "advertising law" 29; New York State Multiple Dwelling Law (MDL) 27, 29, 31–32; New York State, Office of Attorney General Eric T. Schneiderman 27–30, 63; NYC Office of Comptroller Scott Stringer 30–31; NYC Office of Special Enforcement (OSE) 27, 29, 31; overview 46–47; rent regulation 27
New York Communities for Change and Real Affordability for All (NYCC and RAFA) 28, 31
Niido 12
Novy, Johannes 115

Oahu, Hawaii 67
overtourism 65, 111, 122, 127n8; *see also* touristification

Pasquale, Frank 23, 47
Peck, Emily and Charles Maldonado 67; *see also* New Orleans
platform capitalism 4, 10, 138; *see also* Srnicek, Nick
platform real estate 138, 142; *see also* Fields, Desiree; Shaw, Joe
post crisis conditions 4, 16–18, 84–85, 97; *see also individual cities, countries*
proptech (property technology) 138

quality of life issues 5, 37, 65, 73, 88, 89, 97, 141; Australia 88, 89, 97; transient visitors 65; Treme, New Orleans 66–67; Venice Beach, Los Angeles 38, 40, 49n18, 62, 64, 65, 66, 67; *see also* Airbnb, impact on neighborhoods; Airbnb, and quality of life, amenities; concentration effects; neighborhood effects

rentiers 4, 16–17, 84–85, 137; Australia 84–85; US 16–17
Ronald, Richard 95; *see also* generation rent

Said, Carolyn 33–34, 36
Samaan, Roy 39–40, 49n18, 56, 58, 60, 65; *see also* Los Angeles, Los Angeles Alliance for a New Economy (LAANE)
San Francisco 32–37, 47–48; Airbnb Law 34, 36; Budget and Legislative Analyst 34–35; commercial operators of Airbnb

60, 61, 62, 64, 69; enforcement 36–37; housing crisis 33; housing stock 32–33; impact of Airbnb on housing 56, 58; impact of Airbnb on neighborhoods 62, 64, 69, 74n5; Office of Short Term Rentals (OSTR) 34, 36; overview 47–48; Proposition F 35; Voluntary Collection Agreement (VCA) 70
Savills 107, 121
Schäfer, Philipp and Nicole Braun 118
Schiwy, Dorothee 125
Schor, Juliet 10
ShareBetter 30, 72
sharing economy: Airbnb as prototype 11, 138; criticism of 10–11; history of 9–10; homesharing 11–12; and real estate 138–139
Shaw, Joe 138, 142
short-term lets (STL) in Australia 90
short-term rentals (STRs) 1–6; and cities 3–4; commercialization 2, 4, 13, 19n4, 23, 60–61, 90–91, 115–117, 124, 136, 143; and hotels 19, 137–138; institutionalization of 12, 18, 136; legitimation of 11; professionalization 13, 18, 19; and real estate investors and developers 12, 19, 138, 143; and real estate sector 12, 19, 136–137; *see also* Airbnb, impact on housing; Airbnb, impact on neighborhoods; *individual cities, countries*
short-term rental sector 2, 18–19, 137–139; and Airbnb 19, 136–137; buy-to-rent 137, 139; convergence with real estate 137; digital technology 138, 139; and hotels 19, 137; impact on housing inequality and insecurity 139–141; new models (flexible/hybrid tenure) 137–138, 139, 140–141; new players 137, 138; and real estate 12, 137–139, 140–141; rent-to-rent 137, 140; residential and tourism market synergy 1, 137; size and growth 19, 139
Skift 27–28, 139
Slee, Tom 24, 44; *see also* data, data activists
Srnicek, Nick 10, 12; *see also* platform capitalism
Standing, Guy 17; *see also* generation rent; rentiers
Stors, Natalie and Andreas Kagermeier 120
strata 89; *see also* Melbourne; Sydney
Süddeutsche Zeitung 111; *see also* Brunner, Katharina and Christian Endt
Sydney: Airbnb impact on neighborhoods 89–91, 96; amenity issues 88; code of conduct 93, 98n16; concentration effects 89–91; description 86; Neighbors Not Strangers 89, 94; New Short-term Holiday Letting Regulations 93; New South Wales Parliamentary Inquiry 88; Owners Corporation Network 89, 98n14; regulation 88, 92, 93–94; strata 89, 93; vacant units 87, 90, 91, 97

Der Tagesspiegel 112, 117; *see also* Berlin, *Häusserkampf*
Tooze, Adam 15, 16; *see also* Global Financial Crisis (GFC)
touristification 5, 111, 115; *see also* overtourism
transient occupancy tax (TOT) 39, 41, 42; *see also* Voluntary Collection Agreement (VCA)
Treme, New Orleans 66, 67

Uffer, Sabine 113
unicorns 2, 10
United States housing sector: changes in housing tenure 16–18; changes in rental sector 17–18, 140; demographic composition of renters 16–17; financialization of housing 14–16, 140; Great Financial Crisis (GFC) 14, 16; Great Recession 16, 18; post-crisis housing 16–18; precarity of renters 17, 66, 139–140, 141; renters and rentiers 16–18; tenants' rights movement 141; *see also individual cities*
urban tourism, rise of 3–4

venture capital 2, 4, 6, 10, 138, 140
vertical communities 5, 68–69; *see also* Australia; strata
Voluntary Collection Agreement (VCA) 39, 49n13, 49n17, 70–71, 94

Wachsmuth, David 42, 59: and Wachsmuth et al. 30, 31, 57, 59, 61, 62, 63, 73n2; and Alexander Weisler 59, 64
Wijburg, Gertjan and Manuel Aalbers 104, 106, 107

Yates, Judith 96

zoning 5, 23, 26, 71, 73

For Product Safety Concerns and Information please contact our EU
representative GPSR@taylorandfrancis.com
Taylor & Francis Verlag GmbH, Kaufingerstraße 24, 80331 München, Germany

www.ingramcontent.com/pod-product-compliance
Lightning Source LLC
Chambersburg PA
CBHW061842300426
44115CB00013B/2475